T0360524

Angel
Investing
in China $

Angel Investing in China 💲

Manhong Mannie LIU
Research Center on Fictitious Economy and Data Science,
Chinese Academy of Sciences, China

Jiani WANG
Capital University of Economics and Business, China

Su CHEN
Renmin University of China, China

World Scientific

EW JERSEY · LONDON · SINGAPORE · BEIJING · SHANGHAI · HONG KONG · TAIPEI · CHENNAI · TOKYO

Published by

World Scientific Publishing Co. Pte. Ltd.

5 Toh Tuck Link, Singapore 596224

USA office: 27 Warren Street, Suite 401-402, Hackensack, NJ 07601

UK office: 57 Shelton Street, Covent Garden, London WC2H 9HE

Library of Congress Cataloging-in-Publication Data

Names: Liu, Manhong Mannie, author. | Wang, Jiani, author.

Title: Angel investing in China / Manhong Mannie Liu (Chinese Academy of
    Sciences, China), Jiani Wang (Capital University of Economics and
    Business, China), Su Chen (Renmin University of China, China).

Description: New Jersey : World Scientific, 2016. | Includes index.

Identifiers: LCCN 2016009432| ISBN 9789813108677 (hardcover : alk. paper) |
    ISBN 9789813108684 (pbk. : alk. paper)

Subjects: LCSH: Angels (Investors)--China. | Venture capital. |
    Investments--Government policy--China.

Classification: LCC HG5788 .L578 2016 | DDC 332/.041540951--dc23

LC record available at http://lccn.loc.gov/2016009432

British Library Cataloguing-in-Publication Data

A catalogue record for this book is available from the British Library.

中国天使投资：理论、方法与实践

Originally published in Chinese by China Development Press.

Copyright © China Development Press, 2015

Desk Editor: Qi Xiao

Typeset by Stallion Press

Email: enquiries@stallionpress.com

Printed in Singapore

What they say about the book ...

This book gives a detailed and systematic analysis of China's angel investing industry through surveys, case studies and interviews. It is a recommended reading.

Anthony Clarke, Co-Founder and CEO of Angel Capital Group,
President Emeritus of European Business Angels Network

Angel Investing in China will drive more people to join angel investing, and promote the development of innovation and entrepreneurship in China.

Mai Gang, Founder of Ventures Lab and President of China Young
Angel Investor Leader Association

This book is the first detailed and systematic examination of angel investing in China. It is a valuable resource for researchers interested in economic development in China, for policy makers and politicians seeking to enhance entrepreneurship, and for all who wish to gain a deeper understanding of the entrepreneurship process in one of the world's most important economies.

Professor Richard T. Harrison, University
of Edinburgh Business School

This book will be of great value to entrepreneurs, angel investors and policy-makers. If you want to try your hand at angel investing, you need to read it and learn from successes and failures at home and abroad.

Pei Xiasheng, Vice Chairman and Secretary-General
of China Association of Technology Entrepreneurship

Angel Investing in China gives us a panoramic view of China's angel investing industry; it has important theoretical and practical value.

John May, Founder and Honorary Chairman of the Angel Capital
Association and Co–Chairman of the Global Business Angel Network

I have learned a lot from the book, and I recommend it to anyone who aspires to be an angel investor, and also those who have already engaged in angel investing or its theoretical research.

Wang Shaojie, Chairman of Zhongguancun Private Equity & Venture Capital Association

Prof. Liu and Dr. Wang have given us a comprehensive and systematic analysis of China's angel investing market. Their book is a worthwhile reading.

Francisco Banha, Founder and President Emeritus of National Federation of Business Angels Associations in Portugal

Through documenting the scale and nature of angel investing in China and by showing the ways in which angel investing is similar to, and different from, its counterparts in Western Europe and North America, this new book makes a valuable contribution.

Professor Colin Mason, Adam Smith Business School, University of Glasgow

This book not only introduces theory and practice of angel investing, but also discusses the relevant methods, especially the practical experience of international angel investors. It is a must read.

Professor Zhang Luyang, Department of International Finance, Fudan University

By systematically introducing ways of raising angel investment funds, this book truly opens a window of opportunities to those who are interested in becoming angel investors.

Ven Yeung, CIO of Hong Kong Government, Former Chairman of Hong Kong Business Angel Network

This book has not only shed academic light on angel investment, it has also explored the practice of angel investment in China. Scholars, entrepreneurs and angel investors will benefit a lot from it.

Professor He Zhiyi, New Huadu Business School

Opening Address from Cheng Siwei (Director of Research Center on Fictitious Economy and Data Science CAS)

Opening Address from Jingan Zhang (Chairman of China Association of Science and Technology Industry Parks)

Opening Address from Zhiyi He (Chairman of New Huadu Business School)

Seminar on Angel Investing in China (Beijing, April 17, 2014)

Opening Ceremony of China Business Angel Association (Ningbo, June 14, 2013)

In May 2014, Asian Business Angel Forum was held in Hong Kong. The panel, "Angel investing in China", was hosted by Dr. Wang Jiani, and Prof. Liu Manhong. Mr. Mai Gang (Chairman of China Youth Angel Investor Leader Association) and Mr. David Chen (Co-founder of Angelvest) were invited for discussion.

In September 2014, Dr. Wang Jiani visited Business School of the University of Edinburgh and made a speech at the Center of Entrepreneurship

Book Launch for *China Angel Investment* (Beijing, March, 2015)

Angel Capital Association Summit 2015 (San Diego, US, April 2015)

2015 Global Angel Investment Forum (Beijing, November 2015)

Foreword

Over the past thirty years, the Chinese venture capital (VC) industry has undergone rapid development and now China is ranked number two in the world stage in terms of total capital raised and the number of deals invested, second only to the United States. VC participants in China include both local institutions and foreign institutions. However, compared with developed countries, China's VC still has a huge gap to fill. There are noticeable weaknesses in the Chinese venture capital industry. In addition, some new developments also need to be analyzed. The Third Plenary Session of the 18th Communist Party of China (CPC) Central Committee proposed to improve VC mechanism. This is an important message and I think there are many issues worth thinking about.

Three issues are on the top of my research priority list in recent years, one of which is "angle investment". The significance of promoting angel investment is mainly reflected in two aspects. First, as angel investment focuses on the early stage of a start-up, promoting angel investment not only can directly support the entrepreneurs, but also lays a solid foundation for the development of VC investment and private equity fund. Since the outbreak of the global financial crisis in 2008, the VC industry as a whole has shifted its strategy to focus on the late stage investment and paid less attention to the early-stage, especially seed-stage, projects, and this trend becomes obvious in particular with the rapid development of private equity fund. This problem is common in both the international and domestic markets and merits our attention. Second, angel investment helps discover and nurture innovative talents and support the entrepreneurs at the early-stage projects, providing them with an opportunity to show their ability, realize their dream and test the market response of innovative project through business operation. It is not talents that China lacks, but an ecosystem which can bring out the abilities of these talents. Many talented people have great ideas but lack proper support, which is really a pity. As a result, angel investment is critical to start-up founders. Meanwhile, angel investment is highly risky. According to my understanding of angel investment outside China, from proposing business plan by the entrepreneur to obtaining financial support from angel investors, and to final success, the success rate is only eight in ten thousand, while that of VC is about 30%; the success rate of tVC is much higher than that of angel investment. This indicates that compared with VC, angel investment faces greater challenge on project judgment and is more risky. But it is still much needed. Because of the high risk, angel investment abroad is generally supported by rich people or institutions. At present, group-based financing and crowd-funding operating models also begin to make their appearance in China but are in their experimental stage.

I currently serve as the Director of the Center for Fictitious Economy and Data Research at the Chinese Academy of Sciences. Considering that there are still some issues in Chinese VC field, which need further research, the Center established the Venture Capital Research Group in the summer of 2012 and invited Professor Liu Manhong (Mannie) from Renmin University of China as its head. Since the establishment of the group, we have carried out the research project on angel investment by cooperating with New Huadu Business School. Lately, in the China Angel Investment Seminar held in Beijing, we jointly issued the *Research Report on the Development of Angel Investment in China (2013–2014)*, a comprehensive overview of the development of and relevant polices on angel investment in China, which also forms the basis of this book.

The key to the development of angel investment is to discover innovative talents and help transform their innovative ideas into product or technology, so that they can contribute to the making of an innovative country. Moreover, angel investment as a new field has yet to attract enough scholars. We hope that this book can bring more experts and scholars into angel investment research and explore the inner laws and optimal development model of angel investment in China, so that they can provide technological guidance for practitioners, serve as the decision-making basis for policy makers and promote the development of China's angel investment in an orderly and healthy manner.

Cheng Siwei

Note:

Known as the "father of Chinese Venture Capital", Mr. Cheng Siwei was a famous economist and social activist. He was the former Vice Chairman of China's National People's Congress Standing Committee, former Chairman of the China Democratic and National Construction Association Central Committee, and former President of National Association of Vocational Education of China. Since 2001, Cheng Siwei had worked as the Dean of School of Management, University of Chinese Academy of Sciences. He died of illness in Beijing at the age of 80 on July 12, 2015.

Preface

Unlike angels in Western countries, China's angel investment started in a rather slow pace, but has seen unprecedented growth since the year of 2013. According to statistics from Zero2IPO, in 2015, the total amount of angel investment (by Chinese angel funds only) in China was RMB 3.35 billion into 766 deals in 2014. In comparison, in 2015, the total amount of angel investment reached RMB 10.188 billion (about US$1.5 billion), which was invested into 2,075 deals (averaging RMB 4.9 million or US$757.200 per deal) — a 304% increase in total investment amount and a 271% increase in total deals.

The statistics above only partially reflect the magnitude of China's total angel investing, because of the lack of statistics from individual angels and angel groups. Under this circumstance, the real scale of China's angel investing should be a lot bigger. In addition, China's angel funds by definition are different from those of the Western world. China's angel funds are primarily small-scaled venture capital funds where investors act like limited partnerships and put their money into a fund pool, and fund managers, most of them are successful angel investors or super angels, act like general partnerships to invest money into deals.

China's angel investment has come in such a big wave that the whole country has been growing into a vibrant innovative entrepreneurism. It happens just as an old Chinese saying goes: "at the right time, at the right place and with the right people" — at a time of the country's rapid economic growth; in a land full of entrepreneurial spirit; and with a large number of middle class people who have the capability and willingness to invest and innovative entrepreneurs who demand funding from angels.

A beautiful summer season of 2016 has witnessed China's angel investment being unleashed and fast developing. Our book *Angel Investing in China* is going to meet the readers worldwide. We believe many people are interested in learning the Chinese angel investment: its characteristics and its development.

The richness and completeness of the current book came from a young Chinese angel: Dr. Wang Jiani (Jenny Wang). She invested not money into this book, but her hard-work, her intelligence and her persistence to pursue her dream in the research of angel investing. In the past few years, she has interviewed many angel investors and angel groups throughout China, and collected firsthand materials investigating China's angel investing. She is an excellent researcher and a true collaborator of mine. Angel investment in China is rapidly growing, and, with its colorful development, countless new stories and lots of happenings, needs to be further studied and explored. I hope from the bottom of my heart that more young researchers and scholars will be interested in this area, to follow Dr. Wang's lead.

The research output in this book is part of the efforts of the Venture Capital Research Group, the Center for Fictitious Economy and Data Research at the Chinese Academy of Science. The Research Group was established in August 2012 and is focused on studying venture capital and angel investment in China and its related public policies and other measures. At the same time, the group is trying to promote venture capital research in the academic area throughout China. Moreover, this book also benefited from the sponsorship of National Natural Science Foundation of China (project numbers 71303224, 71573174) and is 2016 Research Project of Capital University of Economics and Business.

We appreciate all the help we have received from researchers, scholars and practitioners in the area, including Ph.D. students from Renmin University of China, in particular Ms. Chen Su, who is a co-author of this book, and Mr. Li Yang, Mr. Wang Jiepei, Mr. Zhao Changhai as well as Mr. Yin Ruizhe, who participated in organizing raw materials, analyzing cases, etc.

Lastly, but not the least, we would like to thank Professor He Zhiyi from New Huadu Business School. Our book cannot become a reality without their support.

Manhong Mannie Liu

Contents

About the Authors

Prof. Liu Manhong (Mannie) is the Director of Venture Capital Research Group at the Research Center on Fictitious Economy and Data Science, Chinese Academy of Sciences, and Director of National Venture Capital Research Committee, Chinese Academy of Management. Prof. Liu got her PhD from Cornell University in 1994 and used to work as a research faculty at Harvard University. Apart from academic positions, Prof. Liu also serves as a board member in a number of angel investment associations, including China Business Angel Association, and World Business Angel Association. Prof. Liu's main academic interests are private equity and venture capital, business angel investing, green investment (clean-tech ventures) and green economy.

Prof. Liu published *Venture Capital: Innovation and Finance* in 1998, one of earliest Chinese books on venture capital. Her latest English books, *Renewable Energy in China: Towards a Green Economy and Angels without Boarders*, were published in 2013 and 2015 respectively.

Dr. Wang Jiani (Jenny) is a lecturer at the School of Finance, Capital University of Economics and Business, China. She also serves as the executive Secretary of National Venture Capital Research Committee, Chinese Academy of Management. Dr. Wang began her study on SMEs financing and venture capital at Shanghai University of Finance and Economics in 2009.

In 2013, she began to work at the Research Center on Fictitious Economy and Data Science, Chinese Academy of Sciences as a postdoctoral fellow. She focuses on angel investment in China, and among her research collaborators are Mr. Cheng Siwei (the "Father of Venture Capital" in China) and Prof. Liu Manhong (one of the leading researchers on venture capital in China). Her latest Chinese books, *China Angel*

Investment (co-authored with Prof. Liu) and *Angels without Borders* (translated from English), were both published in 2015.

Ms. Chen Su (Susan) is a PhD candidate in finance, Renmin University of China, and her main research areas are angel investing, cross-border venture capital, among others. She contributed in the research for and translation of the two books, *Angel Investing in China* and *Angels without Borders*.

From 2011 to 2014, she worked as a researcher in China Venture Capital Research Institute. She was a member of the research team for *China Venture Capital Yearbook* (2012, 2013 and 2014). Ms. Chen graduated from the University of New South Wales, Australia, with a Bachelor's degree in Actuarial Studies and Accounting and a Master's degree in Finance.

Part I

Overview of Angel Investment

Chapter 1

The Origin and Development of Angel Investment

The Charitable Origins of Angel Investment

Angels are the messengers of God. In white robes, they fly to the earth with beautiful wings. They have great wisdom and strength and to help people in their time of need. Angels connote spring and hope. Entrepreneurs regard investors as angels to show their endless reverence. In religious beliefs, angels are God's messengers who pass on his messages to humans and are the saviors of mankind. In the reality of business, angels also play a similar role.

Although the history of angel investment as a career in finance is not a long one, the behavior has existed in economic life for a long time. In early 1874, the young Alexander Bell established the first telephone company in the world with the help of two angel investors. Bell initially wanted to obtain start-up capital from banks, but they believed that his ideas were too bold and risky and did not give him the loan. It was a successful lawyer and a furrier, both from Boston, who funded Bell and made his dream come true. In 1903, five angel investors invested $40,000, which helped Henry Ford realize his automobile dream to eventually establish the economic giant, Ford Motor Company. Amazon, which was listed in 1997, was funded by $1.2 million of angel capital from several investors. Later on, Amazon obtained a venture capital (VC) investment of $8 million (also referred to as start-up investment). Other major technology companies such as Apple and Google also received funds from angel investors at their early stage. People always say that the angel investor[1] has nerves of steel and a heart of gold. Without angel investors, there would be no Apple. Without the sharp market sensitivity and decisive judgment of angel investors, there would be no Google, too.

The concept of angel investment first appeared in the Broadway theater in New York at the beginning of the 20th century. Directors and actors had to invest dedication and hard work to rehearse a new play. During directing and rehearsing, they not only had to work hard, but also had to prepare costumes and props, which required a large sum of money. If the show was a big success, their input would bring fame and fortune. However, if it was a flop, all their dedication and hard work would be all for naught. Moreover, all money they had input previously, including their own money and loans from family and friends would come to nothing. It was quite risky to invest in new plays.

This concept was of great significance to one particular play. After substantial amounts of efforts, materials and money were invested in this play, the cast found themselves short of funds and there was a possibility that the play had to be abandoned. Everyone was filled with anxiety. On the one hand, they did not want to give up what they had input, but on the other hand, there were many uncertain factors deciding the success of a future play and it was hard to find external funding sources. People were desperate for help. In time of need, a wealthy man, who had made a successful show on Broadway, eventually reached out with a helping hand. This investor, with his bold and timely decision to invest, was like an angel sent by God to those desperate directors and actors. They called him an investment angel in honor. The term "angel investment" thus came into being.

Angel Investment Introduced to Business Transactions

The initial angel investment in Broadway had the nature of a charity fund. But later, angel investment became associated and used purely for business purposes. Individual equity capital invested in ideas or start-ups at the seed stage/early stage is called angel capital, and an individual who undertakes the high risk in the hope of possible high gains is called an angel investor. Like VC investors, angel investors not only offer start-ups with funding, but they also offer their valuable specialized knowledge, experience and well-connected social network.

Some say angel investing involves a clever combination of gambling and dedication. Like VC investment, angel investment also entails high-risk investment behavior. Before making the investment, angel investors are clearly aware that no matter how much prudential investigation has been conducted to the potential project, no matter how good the project looks like and how great the potential profit is, their future is unpredictable and their inherent risk is very high. Once an investment mistake occurs, it is highly possible that the angel investor's hard earned money will vanish without a trace. Even with such great risk, angel investors still engage in this type of investment, so on the surface, it does look like gambling. However, in reality, each step of investment decision made by the angel investor is prudential in order to avoid risk to the greatest extent. An experienced angel investor is more likely to be successful and will input substantial efforts to make pre-investment preparations, including an overall audit of the project.[2] This exercise in prudence is entirely different from gambling. Angel investors are also passionate, romantic and optimistic like an entrepreneur. They expect success and are eager to achieve it. And like an entrepreneur, they devote to it. We cannot understand why angel inverstors are so passionate about angel investment, let alone learn their secrets to success, if we are passionate about do not know their thought-process.

The Global Spread of Angel Investment

In the era of rapid development of the Internet and high technology, some successful and high-profile entrepreneurs have become "angel investors" and brought the little-known market of angel investment to the public's attention. Over the last five years, the number of individual angels across the world — including active regions such as the Europe and the United States — has increased rapidly. Angel investment through syndicates, groups and network organizations has also experienced a growth.

The World Bank issued a research report in 2014 on angel groups, giving an overview of angel investment, cases of global angel groups, establishment frameworks and operation processes of angel groups.[3] It could be seen from the report that global angel investors have become much more organized and institutionalized. It made seven key observations:

(1) There were approximately 350 active angel investment organizations and on average each organization had over 60 angels. These organizations were scattered across the country, particularly in the Silicon Valley and Boston. There was an active association of 30 angel organizations in Canada — most of which were established after 2008 in Ontario and British Columbia and their surrounding areas.

(2) The number of angel groups in Europe has grown rapidly over the past decade, with England and France becoming the most active markets in Europe. European governments have also encouraged public support to angel investment group and networks and the European Commission supported the establishment of the European Business Angel Network (EBAN) in 1999. According to the latest report of EBAN (published in 2014): business angel networks have been growing in number at an average of 17% for the past 10 years. In 2013, the number of active networks in Europe increased to 468.[4] The 2011 OECD research report pointed out that the number of angel groups and network organizations in the Europe and the United States increased rapidly during 1999 and 2009 (see Figure 1.1).

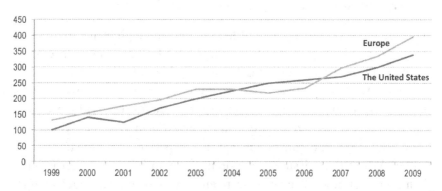

Fig. 1.1   Number of Angel Groups/Networks in the Europe and the United States (1999–2009).
Source: Adapted from the 2011 OECD research report, "Financing High-Growth Firms: The Role of Angel Investors".

(3) China's formal angel market has been on the rise, attracting both domestic and foreign investors. With this rise in angel groups, the government has begun providing policies to support such investments.

(4) The angel investment market in Australia has had a history of over a decade, but it was only in 2007 that the angel investment market became more formalized and standardized when the Australian Association of Angel Investors (AAAI) was established. In New Zealand, the public sector has established a powerful joint investment fund system to promote the development of an angel investment market.

(5) There were only 21 active angel networks in Latin America in 2013. Argentina, Brazil, Chile and Mexico were taking the lead in the development of angel groups, most of which were established after 2005. While angel investing is growing, the region as a whole struggles to develop a culture of equity investing.

(6) Israel has developed a mature angel investment market while the angel investment markets in Jordan and Bahrain remain underdeveloped. For other smaller markets, nation-wide levels of entrepreneurship have not reached their full potential and hence also remain underdeveloped.

(7) South Africa has the most developed angel investment market in Sub-Saharan Africa. Angel Hub is the first formalized group in the region. Angel groups have also emerged in Nigeria, Kenya and Burkina Faso in recent years. Generally speaking, the entrepreneurial ecosystem in the region is not mature and angel investors face challenges in finding high-quality investment projects.

It is worth noting that the flourishing of equity-based crowd funding and accelerators across the world has led to new changes in project sources, investment modes and management strategies of angel investors.

Notes

1. Considering the various forms of the subject of angel investment, the term "angel investor" is used to refer to an individual angel while "angel investment

fund", "angel group(s)" and "business angel network" are terms that are used to refer to institutional angels.

2. Robert Wiltbank and Warren Boeker, 'Returns to Angel Investors in Groups,' Working Paper, SSRN, November 1, 2007, available at http://papers.ssrn. com/sol3/papers.cfm?abstract_id=1028592.

3. The World Bank, 'Creating Angel Investor Groups: A Guide for Emerging and Frontier Markets,' Working Paper, December 9, 2014, available online at http://www-wds.worldbank.org/external/default/WDSContentServer/ WDSP/IB/2014/12/09/000442464_20141209131256/Rendered/PDF/93037 0WP0Box380ups0guidbook0final00.pdf.

4. EBAN, 'Statistics Compendium 2014,' available online at http://www.eban. org/wp-content/uploads/2014/09/13.-Statistics-Compendium-2014.pdf.

Chapter 2

Concepts and Financial Connotations of Angel Investments

Concepts of Angel Investment

I. Definition of Angel Investment

The Center for Venture Research, based at the University of New Hampshire, is a well-known angel investment research institution. Led by Professor Jeffery Sohl, the Center proposes that angel investment is a behavior of an individual with certain idle capital for equity capital investment in high-growth enterprise (project) in seed stage.

Angel investment is also called "informal VC investment." Similar to VC investment, angel investment also targets non-listed enterprises, in particular start-ups in seed/early stage for non-controlling investment. The difference between angel investment and VC investment is that the latter is institutional behavior while the former is individual behavior. In addition, VC investors invest with other people's money (mainly the capital of institutional investors) while angel investors invest with their own money, which is the visible difference between these two types of investment.

Strictly speaking, not all informal VC investments are angel investment. According to the research done by Professor Martin Haemmig, family members of the founders of start-ups usually constitute the main source of funding (43.7%), followed by friends or neighbors (29.2%), strangers (9.3%), and other relatives and colleagues (8.9%).[1]

Thus, the relationship between the investor and the invested is an important distinct feature of angel investment, in two ways.

In a broad sense, angel investment means that the investor uses his own money to provide fund support for enterprises at seed stage or start-up stage, including borrowing from family members as well as from friends and relatives. In a narrow sense angel investment only refers to an investment behavior where the investor uses his own money, regards investing as his/her profession (or vocation or avocation), and makes investments based on the profit prospect of the project or the ability, character, experience, responsibility or devotion of the project executor with the hope of obtaining high investment returns.

Strictly speaking, the subject of investment of an angel investor is usually that of a stranger. Strangers are defined to be individuals who are not related to founders by blood or social connections; the investment made by strangers is driven by purely business behavior.[2] They are willing to undertake the investment risk in order to obtain potential investment revenue by betting on the founder, the project and market. It can be seen that the angel investment in its true sense only takes up about 9.3% of capital source for informal VC investment. However, Professor Scott Shane believes that the figure is only about 8%.[3] The concept of angel investment therefore remains narrowly contested given these slight differences in figures.

There is a second implication of the concept of angel investment in narrow and broad senses: angel investment in the narrow sense only refers to those capital operational modes investing equity capital in start-ups for in seed/early stage — thereby making angel investment a subcategory of private equity. Angel investment in the broad sense however, includes other investment modes: for example, short-term borrowing, deferred payment, trade credit and other forms of capital loans. In China, some scholars have expanded the definition of angel investment beyond seed or early-stage investment, to include equity capital investment in middle and late stages. This definition is different from the current generally accepted definition of angel investment in the world, which is that angel investment is generally related to the financing in seed stage or early period of a project/enterprise.

John May (2008), the founder and former president of the Angel Capital Association (ACA), believed that angel investment is an individual and private equity investment.[4] Angel investors invest their after-tax fund in the early stage enterprise of a stranger to obtain non-controlling equity. They will then have to wait patiently for many years after investing, and during this period, the invested capital cannot circulate in the long run. Angel investors generally undertake a higher risk than general investment in order to obtain high returns.

This book proposes the adoption of two definitions: angel investment in the broad sense refers to all equity investment behaviors which engage in early stage first round external investment in the hope of profits, and the subjects of investment include individuals and institutions. It will also adopt the definition of angel investment in the narrow sense, which refers to equity investment behavior where individual investors invest his/her own fund in the seed or early stage enterprise with huge growth potential; these investors will not have any family relation with the entrepreneurs, and provide resource support to the enterprise other than financial support (see Table 2.1).

II. *Characteristics of Angel Investment*

Compared to VC investment, angel investment is scattered, individual, small-sized and informal. Angel investment has the following characteristics.

1. Small investment amount

It is seen as a "small-scale" investment given its individual and informal nature. For example, angel investment in the United States totaled US$ 25.6 billion in 2006; an amount that was almost equivalent to the total venture capital investment in the United States in that year. Angel investors invested 51,000 projects while VC investors only 3,146 projects. The average investment in each project of the former was about US$500,000 while the figure was US$7.5 million, about 15 times that of the former. Due to the small sum of each investment, the same amount of capital can support more start-ups. For enterprises at the seed stage, angel investment is not icing on the cake but is timely help.

2. Early investment stage

Since the beginning of the 21st century, it has become increasingly obvious that VC investment tends to invest in the late stage start-ups. This "private

Table 2.1   Concepts and Definition of Angel Investment.

Item	Angel Investment in (Strict) Narrow Sense	Angel Investment in (Loose) Broad Sense
Form of Subject	Individual investor	Group, institution, incubator, crowd funding, etc.
Capital Source	Self-owned capital	Self-owned capital, capital from other partners/ institutions
Capital Equity	Equity or debt-equity swap	Equity, debt-equity swap
Decision-making Mechanism	Individual decision-making	Lead investor, group or decision-making committee
Relationship between the Investor and Founder	Stranger	Not restricted (family angel, angel investor)
Share Holding	No	Not restricted
Investment Stage	Early stage (seed stage, start-up stage)	Early stage (seed stage, start-up stage)
Agreement Signing	Formal agreement	Formal agreement, oral-to-written
Post-investment Management	Offer some help to the start-up	Not restricted (give little or no attention)

Source: Authors' own compilation.

Table 2.2   VC Investment in China and US: Shifting to the Late Stage.

Stage of Development		VC Investment Distribution in the US	VC Investment Distribution in China
Early stage	Start-up stage	1%	1%
	Growth stage	39%	3%
Late stage	Pre-profit stage	50%	67%
	Post-profit stage	10%	29%

Source: Liu Manhong, *Theory and Practice of Angel Investment* (First edition), Economy & Management Publishing House, 2009.

equity" tendency of VC investment is not only seen in the circle of VC investment in China, but in other countries as well, including the United States. It can be seen from Table 2.2 that VC investment tends to be directed to middle and late-stage projects. Investment in enterprises during the growth period is generally considered a characteristic of VC investments — but that is changing. In 2007, the capital of VC investment invested in start-up stage and growth stage in the United States accounted for 40% of total VC investment and the remaining 60% was invested in the mid- and late stages of business development. However in China, this condition is on the rise albeit early investment only accounts for 1% in VC investment. The growth stage, which is the "investment window," is the major investment stage of VC investment. In this stage VC investment in China only accounts for 3% of total VC investment and the remaining 96% VC capital is invested in middle and late-stage projects.

Beyond the US and China, VC investment across the world more or less follows this "private equity" trend. According to the 2007 report issued by Ernst & Young, VC investment in all countries tended to be channeled to projects in late stages. Take the mean value of the "second round" of global VC investment as an example: between 2002 and 2006, VC investment in the United States grew by 12.5% for each round and the figure was 100% in Europe and Israel, and 233% in China. These figures show that VC investment tends to transfer to late-stage investment, i.e. the larger the investment amount, the more difficult for start-ups to obtain early financing. The fund supply for projects at seed and start-up stages is unable to cope with the capital demand, forming an obvious capital gap, which in turn deepens the contradiction of early-stage investment and financing for start-ups. The formation of this capital gap on the one hand causes great capital difficulty for start-ups, but on the other hand creates an unprecedented opportunity for early-stage financing for enterprises. Angel investment is an important source of funds for closing this gap. Because of this nature of angel investment, all central governments and local governments tend to issue preferential policies, including tax preferential policies to encourage angel investment in the country or region, thus further promoting the development of local start-ups, in particular high-tech start-ups.

3. High investment risk

This characteristic of angel investment is closely related to the early investment stage of angel investing. Generally speaking, the earlier the investment period, the higher the investment risk is. In the early stage start-up, particularly in the seed stage when the technology is not fully mature because the product has yet to receive recognition from the market; the operating mode has not been tested by business competition and the start-up's management has not been subject to real-world business environment conditions. All things are in the trial period and many unpredictable variables and uncertainties will create new problems and contradictions. One can only imagine how high the risk the investor has to take by making an investment at this stage.

However, "high risk and high potential return" is one of the basic elements of the financial world. Because of the high risk of angel investment, once it succeeds, the investment return will be quite considerable. Angel investors thus tend to have strong risk tolerance as they invest with their own money. Angel investors are awarded heavily for their risk-taking spirit and their contribution to help start-ups financially and for providing guidance based on personal experiences.

Theoretically, the potential risk and expected future revenue will be higher for early investment in start-ups. If this were not the case, no one would invest in early projects, in particular seed stage projects. Of course, high risk does not guarantee high revenue. There will be no "high risk" if the expected future revenue is certain.

In sum, compared to VC investment, angel investment has an early investment stage, high potential risk and high expected future revenue. Compared with private equity, VC investment is characterized by high risk and high expected future revenue. For individuals, investing in government bonds has the lowest risk and low expected future revenue while investing in real estate is a more complicated process. Between the late 1990s and the early 21st century, real estate prices increased significantly in almost all countries, forming real estate bubbles. In China, the real estate bubble came later than other countries — nevertheless, investment in real estate at the late stage at the peak of the formation of real estate bubble does not guarantee expected high revenue.

4. Low investment cost

Compared with VC investment, the cost of angel investment is lower. The biggest difference between angel investment and VC investment is that VC investors manage other people's money while angel investors use their own money for investment. In China, angel investment has become more institutionalized: some VC investors began to focus on early stage start-ups with small amount of investment; some newly placed "angel investment fund" specially engages in equity investment in start-ups. The operation mode of this type of fund is similar to VC institutions and the difference is that their fund is of small size. Limited partnership is generally individualized and the investment stage is at the seed stage and start-up stage. A single investment is generally less than RMB 5 million, which is the combination of traditional angel investment and VC investment.

Limited partnership is generally adopted for typical operation of VC investment. Under limited partnership, the fund investors are the limited partners while a VC investor is usually the fund manager i.e. the general partner. As an angel investor is not the investment manager, management and supervision costs will be incurred and this type of cost can be explained by principal–agent relationship. For VC investments, VC investors manage other people's money, and a principal–agent relationship is formed between the VC investors and investors, thus giving rise to principal-agent cost. In contrast, angel investors invest with their own money, and therefore, no principal–agent cost will be incurred at this level. From this point of view, the investment cost of angel investment is relatively low.

5. Quick investment decision-making

This characteristic of angel investment is related to its other characteristics: as angel investors invest with their own money, and make their own decisions without intermediately links, the decision to invest can be made quickly. On the contrary, VC investors are institutional investors and they will not rush into any project without detailed investigation and due diligence. Sometimes, negotiation, discussion and final decision-making might have to be carried out among general partners within a VC investment company. Unlike VC investors, angel investors can make quick investment decisions if they feel certain about the potential project. Decisions made by angel investors, based on their investment experience or even their instincts, can thus be made within a short time.

Angel Investment vs. VC Investment

I. *Similarities between Angel Investment and VC Investment*

In this section, we will reiterate and further discuss the differences between angel investment (individual investment) and VC investment (institutional investment). In actual operations, there is "institutional angel investment" which has the characteristics of angel investment and VC investment, i.e. angel investment fund.

Strictly speaking, angel investment and VC investment belong to "private equity." In terms of enterprise life cycle, angel investors generally invests in the seed and start-up stages of an enterprise. Angel investment is at a stage between 3Fs (family, friend, founder) and VC investment. The mission of angel investment is to fill in the gap (see Figure 2.1).

In recent years, VC investment has increasingly focused on the middle and late stage start-ups and financing the needs of start-ups has been neglected. This makes angel investment more popular and attractive for start-ups.

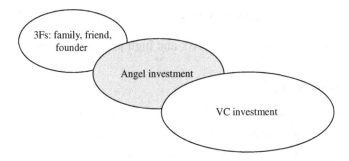

Fig. 2.1 Angel Investment: Between 3Fs and VC Investment.

The development of VC investment can be traced back to the Second World War. From the Second World War until the 1980s, VC investment was considered to be investments of relatively small scale, and in projects at an early investment stage with low value assessment.

In 1990, the first VC investment fund of US$100 million appeared. This was big news in international VC investment circles and came to be known as the "Mega Fund." Two years later, the first US$500 million fund appeared; and in 1998, the first fund to be valued at US$1 billion appeared. In 2007, there were 741 VC investment companies in the US that controlled US$257 billion worth of VC capital — which averaged US$166 million per fund.

VC investment mega funds can be found everywhere. The amount that makes up a single investment can also grow in tandem with the size of the fund. In 2007, US$30 billion was invested in 3,226 projects in the US, averaging at US$9.3 million per project. The investment amount increased with the size of VC investment. This phenomenon continued until the outbreak of global financial crisis at the end of 2008. The decline in VC investment then thus explains the emergence of angel investment.

The similarities between angel investment and VC investment are summarized as below.

1. Equity form

Both are equity investment in start-ups. Angel investment is dominated by equity investment although it also makes debt investment or credit guarantee related to equity investment.

2. Risk-revenue characteristics

Both are characterized by "high risk and high potential revenue."

3. Focus on growth

Both involve investing in start-ups with rapid growth and development potential. "High growth" is the main criterion for selecting investment object. In addition, factors such as management team, market, product/ service, patent and other intellectual property rights are also important factors for making investment.

4. Participation in post-investment management

Both participate in the management and construction of the invested enterprise to a certain extent.

5. Investment strategy

Both prefer joint investment modes of a certain form with the hope of reducing investment risk.

6. Investment cycle

Both focus on long-term capital to a certain extent, although currently, VC investment tends to focus on the late stage start-ups.

II. *Differences between Angel Investment and VC Investment*

Angel investment as an informal VC investment is different from formal VC investment. Some differences have been described in the discussion of the characteristics of angel investment. Here we summarize the differences of these two from basic concepts (see Table 2.3).

1. Capital source

Angel investors invest with their own money while VC investors invest with other people's money. This is the most fundamental difference

Table 2.3   Differences between Angel Investor and VC Investor.

Procedure	Angel Investor	VC Investor
Financing	Invest with their own money and basically does not need funds from others	Invest with other people's money and need to finance from rich individuals, families and mainly institutional investors
Investment	Investment stage: seed stage, start-up stage and post-start-up stage, dominated by seed stage and start-up stage	Investment stage: seed stage, start-up stage, growth stage, mature stage and dominated by the growth stage
	One-time investment, and generally lack subsequent fund input	Multi-round investment, and generally has subsequent fund input
	Investment instrument is dominated by common stock and preferred stock	Investment instrument is dominated by convertible preferred stock
	Rarely attaches risk control provisions to the investment instrument	Generally attaches risk control provisions to the investment instrument
	Rarely uses investment by installment to reduce agency cost	Generally uses investment by installment to reduce agency cost
	Rarely uses additional provisions to protect the interests at liquidation.	Generally uses additional provisions to protect the interests at liquidation.
	Rarely enters into anti-dilution provisions at investment	Generally adds anti-dilution provisions in the investment provisions

(*Continued*)

Table 2.3 *(Continued)*

Procedure	Angel Investor	VC Investor
Post-investment management	Actively participates in management	Actively participates in management
	Rarely serves as a director and do not believe that participation in the board of directors is the main means for participating in the management of the invested enterprise	Generally serves as a director and believe that participation in the board of directors is one of the main means for participating in the management of the invested enterprise
	After investment, the founder still holds the absolute control of the enterprise	After investment, the founder may lose the absolute control of the enterprise
Exit	Equity redemption, transfer, sell, merger, IPO, liquidation, but rarely participate in IPO	Equity redemption, transfer, sell, merger, IPO, liquidation, and generally IPO is the preferred exit strategy of investors.

Source: Authors' own compilation.

between these two and many other distinctions are based on this point. As angel investors invest with their own money, its operation process lacks one link compared with VC investment. VC investment has four links to projects and these are: financing, investment, post-investment management and exit. Angel investments on the other hand only involve: investment, post-investment management and exit.

2. Operation process

The process of VC investment can be divided into financing, investment, post-investment management and exit. The "investment stage" here is the stage where VC investors make an investment in the enterprise, but they will not become shareholders. They are financiers who make money with capital and they will exit from the enterprise with huge investment profits if the project realizes its full potential. After exiting, they will distribute the profits (capital gain) between the fund investors (limited partners) and VC investors (general partners), and then begin a new round of investment cycle. These four stages of VC investment form a fund recycle process. Unlike VC investment, the investment cycle of angel investment only has three stages, i.e. investment, post-investment management and exit. Financing from investors is not necessary as angel investors invest with their own money, and thus the financing stage can be omitted. In addition, profit distribution among angel investors is also not necessary (see Figures 2.2 and 2.3).

3. Investment management

Although angel investment is sometimes viewed as informal VC investment, its status of being seen as such is gradually changing with the emergence of professional angel investment institutions and organizations. VC investment as formal investment stresses more on organizational structure, which in turn emphasizes on review procedures, investment management and is a means of risk mitigation. For founders, VC investor is "institutional investor" while angel investor in narrow sense is scattered, individualized and more approachable "individual investor."

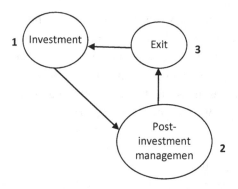

Fig. 2.2   Three Stages of Angel Investment.

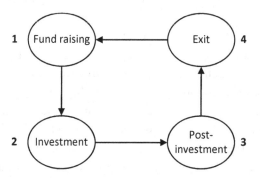

Fig. 2.3   Four Stages of VC Investment.

4. Principal–agent relationship

VC investment has two layers of principal–agent structure, thus giving rise to dual agency costs, which angel investment can avoid by only having one layer of it. The first layer of principal–agent relationship of VC investment is generated in the stage of VC fund raising. During fund raising, the investor (also called limited partner) is the principal and VC investor is the agent (general partner). As the fund manager, VC investor should represent the interests of principal–investors and execute their will. The second layer of VC investment is generated in the investment stage and post-investment management stage. During investment, the active participation of the VC investor in the management of the invested enterprise leads to the VC investor changing roles and becoming the principal while the entrepreneur of the invested enterprise becomes the agent. As the fund user, the founder should represent the interests of principal-fund manager and execute their will. VC investor plays different roles in the two layers of principal–agent relationship.

In contrast, the whole process of angel investment involves only one layer of principal–agent relationship and the angel investor is always the principal. From this perspective, the principal–agent relationship of angel investment is simpler and the principal–agency cost of angel investment is accordingly lower (see Figures 2.4 and 2.5).

5. Investment stage

Compared with VC investment, the investment stage of angel investment occurs much earlier. According to research done by Andrew Wong,[5] the average angel investment is made about 10 months after a start-up idea is launched and is invested at the seed and start-up stages of a project. The investment period of VC investment in contrast, is spread over a long period of time: at the seed stage, start-up stage and growth stage but mainly focused on growth stage. In recent years, many countries have witnessed a growing trend of late stage investment by VC investors. This trend therefore enables angel investment to play an increasingly important role in the early financing process of start-ups.

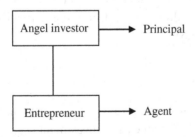

Fig. 2.4   Angel Investment: Single Principal–Agent Management.

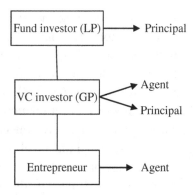

Fig. 2.5   VC Investment: Dual Principal–Agent Management.

6. Investment size

Compared with VC investment, angel investment is done on a smaller scale. VC investment is an institutionalized capital operation mode while angel investment generally is non-institutionalized, individual, scattered equity investment form. Because it is an institutionalized operatiom, VC investment will grow larger.

7. Number of projects

Angel investment can be spread across more projects. It can be said that only one project out of a hundred is chosen by VC investors. For example, if a VC investor browses through 100 business proposals within one month, only three to five proposals will be read carefully, only two to three projects will be subject to due diligence and only one enterprise will receive VC funding (see Figure 2.6).

8. Investment risk

Compared with VC investment, angel investment involves higher risks since angel investment has an earlier investment stage compared with VC investment; the earlier the investment, the more uncertain factors there are with regards to the invested project. These uncertainties are born with the enterprise and will weaken as the enterprise grows. The more mature the enterprise is, the less uncertain these factors will be. These uncertainties come from technology, market, management team, production process, macroeconomy, laws and regulations, political system and other aspects, all of which contain risks. In addition to these uncertainties, information asymmetry will also bring investment risk. Information asymmetry is more obvious in the early stage start-ups and the potential risk grows with it. It is worth noting that uncertainty will exist in the whole life cycle of the enterprise and can only be reduced without being eliminated.

9. Investment cost

Compared with VC investment, angel investment costs less. The reasons for high cost of VC investment are as follows: firstly, VC investment is institutionalized investment management and this formal investment form brings efficiency as well as higher management costs to the operation of VC investment. Angel investment however is informal VC investment and costs less in management. Secondly, VC investment contains two layers of principal–agent relationship, thus

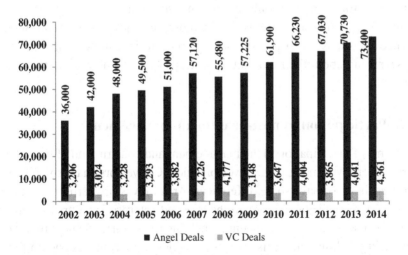

Fig. 2.6   The Number of Deals by Angels and VCs in the US during 2002–2014.
Source: Research Report by the VC Investment Research Center of New Hampshire University (2002–2014), NVCA Yearbook 2015.

the principal–agency cost is higher than angel investment, which only has one layer of it. Thirdly, VC investors are trained professional fund managers with rich experience. Their salaries and profit shares are also generally high. Angel investors on the other hand, tend to not make angel investing their chief profession; they tend to be experienced entrepreneurs, bankers, investors or other financially successful individuals. Having achieved a lot in their respective careers, they enjoy the process of investment, are more inclined to help entrepreneurs build their enterprises and are more involved in the growth of these enterprises. From this point of view, monetary gain is not their only purpose. Thus, angel investors spend less in management because of self-participation.

10. Decision-making cycle

Compared with VC investment, the fast decision-making process of angel investors is possible as they invest with their own money. On the one hand, they do not need to obtain the license or permission from others, pass certain bureaucratic processes, consult its partners, or discuss or communicate with them — all of this thus saves both start-ups and investors a substantial amount of time. On the other hand, they tend to also invest in fields or technologies they are familiar with, hence the decision to invest does not require investors to spend time researching about the field that the enterprise is in; thereby saving time as well.

11. Participation in post-investment management

In terms of participation in the management and construction of the enterprise after investment, angel investors and VC investors share some similarities, but also have some differences. Angel investors participate in the management and construction of the invested enterprise and provide other help besides fund to it, for example, helping to organize the next round of financing, helping enterprises to find business opportunities and correcting or revising existing growth strategies. However, institutionalized investors tend to have more social and business connections, which can faciliate refinancing (see Table 2.3).

Financial Connotation of Angel Investment

I. *Traditional Financial Theories and Angel Investment*

According to Marxist theory of political economy, the functions of finance, or to be more specific, the functions of money are as follows:

(1) Measure of value
Money acts as a common denomination and standard measure of trade. Measure of value is the most basic and important function of money. As a measure of value, money renders the value of all goods and services the same in unit but comparable in quantity. Marx believed that the reason why money can function as a measure of value is that money itself is a commodity and has its own value.

(2) Medium of exchange
When money is used to intermediate the exchange of goods and services, it functions as a medium of exchange. Money has two characteristics when it is performing this function: (a) the money must be a real currency; (b) it can be replaced with currency symbol. For example, paper money.

(3) Store of value
A store of value is the function of money that can be saved. Once saved, the money then independently represents a form of value and the social wealth of its owner.

(4) Standard of deferred payment
A standard of deferred payment is an accepted way to settle a debt, to pay tax, rent or salary, etc. It is a one-way transfer of value.

(5) World currency
With the development of international trade, money can play the role of a universal equivalent in the world market. However, Marx pointed out "once money is out of domestic circulation field, it will lose its local forms such as value criteria, token, fractional currency and value symbol obtained in this field and restore its original form as a precious metal." According to Marx, the function of world currency is based on precious metal while paper money and electronic money cannot play the role of world currency, as they do not have inherent value. However, in real life, money appears as a universal equivalent in the world market, playing the role of world currency.

In modern Western finance, there are different views on the function of finance. Liu Manhong and Zvi Bodie believe that the financial connotation can be explained by its functions.[6] They argue that finance has six functions which are as follows: (a) as a payment, it facilitates trade of goods and services; (b) it diversifies, transfers and manages risks; (c) it realizes resource transfer in time and in space; (d) it provides a mechanism for capital concentration and share divisions; (e) it provides price information; and (f) it solves the issue of incentive mechanism. In sum, most of the functions — except the function of payment — can also be found in VC investment and angel investment.

1. Angel investment provides the investor and invested with the channel to diversify, transfer and manage risks

Firstly, when angel investors invest in a start-up, he/she provides a channel of risk diversification for the invested. At the seed or start-up stage, the project tends to have low levels of technology, untapped markets, an untrained team and untested business model — all of which impose high investment risk on the enterprise. Entry at this time means that angel investors assume part of the risks from the founder and from this point angel investors are also founders. Angel investors and VC investors who make investment in the seed stage are honored as "the founder behind founders." Based on one single investment made by angel investors, early investment increases the investment risks of investors. But if that enterprise is merely one out of a package of projects, it can diversify risk. This is because angel investors also invest in other fields besides start-ups, which make up a larger investment package or portfolio for the angel investor, for example, they will invest in the stock market, real estate market, etc.

Secondly, risk is transferred the moment angel capital flows into the enterprise. It transfers the risk from the early stages of start-ups to the middle and late stages, and transfers part of start-up risks from the enterprise to the angel investor or group. Active participation of angel investors in the establishment of enterprise not only provides funds that are necessary for growth, but also offers start-ups their time, experience and connections. And in most cases, their concepts, expectations and emotional investment are also of help.

2. Angel investment realizes resource transfer in time and in space between the invested and angel investor

Angel capital is transferred from angel investor to the founder, thus realizing the transfer of resources in physical spaces. Angel investment can also convert idle capital into practical capital, thus realizing the transfer of resources over time. The input of angel investment therefore provides timely resources for seed/early stage start-ups: with angel capital, the start-ups can buy raw materials, pay salaries and rent in order to engage in production or re-production. For angel investors, the output of angel capital is a starting point for obtaining potential revenues.

3. Angel investors are often regarded as "saviors"

Angel capital also provides a feasible way for founders to realize their dream at a quicker rate. When injecting into the start-up, angel investors provides urgent funds for production and development. Without this funding, the start-up can only be "potential resource" instead of an actual resource even if it has the best business model, start-up team and the most excellent technological know-how. The input of angel investment also becomes part of equity that the founder shares with the angel investor. Under certain circumstances, with the input of angel investment, angel investor requires the founding team to achieve a more reasonable distribution of internal equity, thus promoting capital concentration and acting as an equity division mechanism.

4. Value assessment is an important part of the angel investment process

The process of angel investment includes initial screening, participation in roadshows, due diligence, assessment negotiation and investment. The selection process of angel investment is a complex process to select objects for investment from applicants. In order to obtain angel investment, the applicant must have qualified business plans to formally submit financial application. Followed by initial screenings and roadshows, due diligence is carried out. Investment is not secured for the applicant even if he passes the due diligence because the value assessment of angel investor on the enterprise may not be accepted by the applicant, and both parties should communicate and negotiate on this matter. Once agreement is reached, angel capital can be injected to the enterprise. The assessment of enterprise value by the angel investor provides enterprise with price information. The acceptance or refusal of value assessment by the founder is based on their value judgment on the enterprise. It can be seen that both angel investor and applicant provide price information for the enterprise during value assessment.

5. Angel investment tackles the "incentive mechanism" problem in two aspects

Firstly, before investing their capital, angel investors generally require the founders of the enterprise to have a reasonable management team structure, including matching the performance with the projected revenue each member of the management team might bring, thus incentivizing the corporate management team from the beginning. The founder, when applying for financial backing, will often streamline the management team, improve the integrity of enterprise management team and establish this, or other incentive mechanisms as this would be of great importance to the angel investors.

Secondly, the sharing of risk and eventual results/achievements, after the injection of capital, between the angel investor and the invested is also an incentive mechanism. Generally speaking, the angel investor will not control the shares of the invested as the capital they input is limited and thus does not warrant them control of the shares. They might also not wish to control the shares of the invested. The equity structure of the invested will be overturned if the angel investor controls the equity, and the founder will lose their initiatives and drive behind their initial project of entrepreneurship. If the angel investor was to be a primary shareholder, the driver of the project will be the investor and not the founder — this will destroy the original incentive mechanism and might result in stagnancy or failure. Therefore, like VC investment, angel investment is not simply a finance discipline, but is a combination of the finance, management and entrepreneurial theories. In fact, angel investment is closely related to leadership skills, strategies, marketing and human resources in the management.

II. *Alternative Financial System and Angel Investment: The Case of China*

Each country chooses their own financial management system based on their economic system, cultural traditions and management concepts. The regulation system of three carriages is adopted in China: the China Banking Regulatory Commission is in charge of the banking system, the China Insurance Regulatory Commission in charge of the insurance system and the China Securities Regulatory Commission in charge of the securities system. Under these three systems, banking, insurance and securities industries operate separately. These three carriages are interconnected and independent from each other. A comprehensive financial system, in addition to banking, insurance and securities, should also add another category, which is "Alternative Finance." This category of financial system covers private equity as well as VC investment and angel investment. They do not belong to the bank, insurance or some financial business of the securities industry. In addition to private equity, operational finance would also cover hedge funds, financial leasing, and account receivable management and factoring.

In recent years, hedge funds have increasingly made an appearance in the field of private equity. Based on this new concept, we believe that the financial system can be divided into four sub-categories: banking, insurance, securities and optional finance (alternative finance). We can see that private equity is an important part of optional finance and it includes (but is not limited to) angel investment, VC investment, merger and acquisitions (M&A) fund and hedge fund (see Figure 2.7).

Unlike banking, insurance and securities industries, alternative finance (optional finance) lacks clear boundaries and it is this very nature that makes it difficult to define and analyze. However, a field with unclear boundaries is not an impractical field. In fact, we can see that in real economic life, many financial businesses fall into the scope of alternative finance (see Figure 2.8). Although the boundaries of alternative finance are undefined, experts and scholars can further discuss and study its

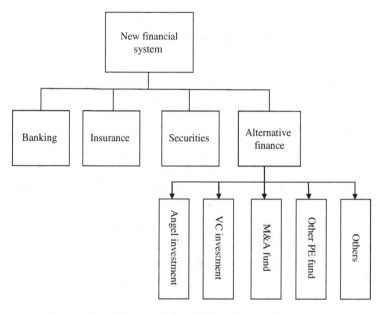

Fig. 2.7   The Financial System in China.

Source: Liu Manhong, 'VC Investment and VC Investment Management,' Course Notes, Renmin University of China, 2007.

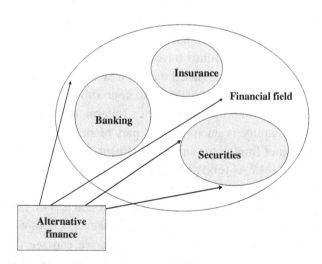

Fig. 2.8   Definition of Alternative Finance.

Source: Liu Manhong, 'VC Investment and VC Investment Management,' Course Notes, Renmin University of China, 2007.

nature from the perspective of capital operation. The proposal of this concept of "alternative finance" is based on the theoretical exposition of angel investment and it is not coined by us. We merely propose that alternative finance be treated on a level-playing field together with the fields of banking, insurance and securities. Hence, we believe there is potential in widening up the discussion, opening the topic up for debate, and, eventually, promoting in-depth development of "alternative finance" amongst experts and practitioners alike.

III. *Private Equity Market and Angel Investment*

Private equity is a powerful tool of financial strength in the financial market and angel investment is only a subcategory of private equity. To further understand the characteristics of angel investment, we will discuss the characteristics of private equity.

1. The connotation of private equity

Private equity is the opposite of public equity.

As previously mentioned, from the perspective of a capital market, the two basic instruments of finance are equity and debt. In fact, all financial derivatives in the financial market are only the combination, variation and derivative of equity and debt.

Equity has two definitions. Equity in the narrow sense only refers to general equity while equity in the broad sense refers to financial securities of any equity nature, including common stock, convertible preferred stock, convertible bond, subordinated debt with convertible provision, warrant and other financial securities which can be converted into equity.[7] Therefore, equity in broad sense is the extension of equity in narrow sense and as a result is called equity-linked securities.[8]

Figure 2.9 covers basic types of capital, equity and debt, pure equity, equity linked, private equity and public equity. We should note here that the content of this section is the research results of Liu's earlier work in the early 21st century. In these studies, the author did not analyze hedge fund and other new derivative financial instruments, for example, subordinated debt or centralized debt obligation in detail. These derivative

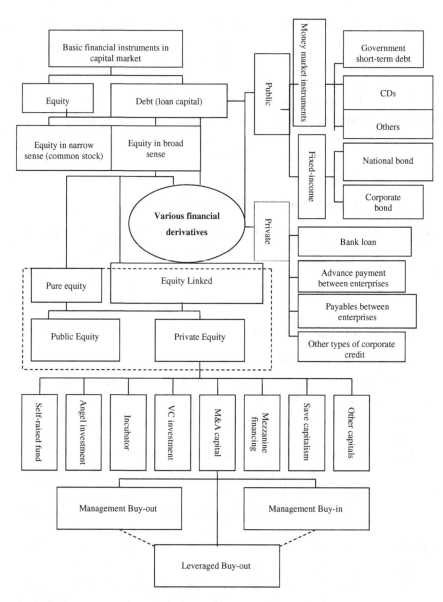

Fig. 2.9   Basic Capital Types and Angel Investment.

Source: Liu Manhong, 'Issues on the Concept of Private Equity,' Working Paper, Center for Venture Research, Renmin University of China, 2004.

financial instruments are critical to real economic life. For example, the financial storm that spread across the globe in 2008 proved the misuse of these derivative instruments would be detrimental for the financial field and global economy. These problems require further study by the academic circle.

Debt can be divided into public debt and private debt by its financial connotation. The former can be further divided into money market instruments and fixed income securities. Money market instruments include short-term debts, for example, short-term government debt (government bond), certificates of deposit and others. Fixed income securities consist mainly of two types: national bond and corporate bond. On the contrary, private debt refers to debt which cannot circulate on the market, for example, general bank loans (short-term, medium-term and long-term loans), advances, accounts receivable and other types of corporate credit. It is worth noticing that public debt can be issued and circulated on the market. This circulation is the factor, which distinguishes public long-term debt, for example, corporate bonds and government bonds with high liquidity, from private debt. Some forms of private equity have good liquidity, i.e. short-term working capital loans. Some private equity have poor liquidity, i.e. long-term loan, accounts receivable, etc. Debt can be further divided into senior debt, subprime debt and subordinated debt by repayment priority.

Similar to private debt and public debt, we can also define the public equity and private equity scopes for equity. The difference is the circulation in public equity market. Unlike debt, our definition of public equity and private equity is based on the equity in broad sense, i.e. equity-linked securities. Our analysis covers all financial securities of equity nature: public and private securities.

Strictly speaking, only equity listed in financial market can be called public equity, and all kinds of equity other than public equity are called private equity. Any individual or enterprise, if they have certain amounts of funds, can be a shareholder of a listed company. However, it is not easy to become the shareholder of a non-listed company. Assuming Company A is a non-listed company, it will not disclose whether it needs new investment under certain conditions, when investors should be introduced, how much capital needed and at what price for exchange. Generally,

Company A only discloses this information to carefully selected potential investors (company, investment fund or individual). This is the most essential distinction between private equity and public equity.

In terms of total amount of listed companies there are in the world today, the number of non-listed company outnumbers that of listed companies. There are only about 2,000 listed companies in China. Even in such a developed country as the United States, the number of listed companies is less than 10,000 listed companies.[9] Therefore, the total amount of private equity is far larger than public equity. Shares issued inside the numerous non-listed companies also belong to private equity. This not only includes the equity of founding members, but also the equity of new shareholders during enterprise development. This not only includes equity invested by individuals in the enterprise, but also includes those invested by enterprises. As long as the invested enterprise is not listed, the equity of sole proprietorship, controlling and participation is private equity. The equity invested by a non-listed enterprise in a non-listed enterprise is private equity but can hardly be understood as individual equity.

2. Private equity

Private equity features a large aggregate amount but limited trading volume because of many factors, such as the condition of economic development, implementation of relevant laws, capital supply and demand scale, the quantity and quality of employees, and etc. In perspective of trading activity, the trading volume of public equity capital is far greater than that of private equity. Therefore, the amount of private equity in trading is generally far smaller than the potential amount of private equity for trading. Typical private equity takes, without limitation to, the following forms: self-raised capital, angel capital, technology incubators, accelerators, venture capital, other early equity capital investment, acquisition capital (including management acquisition[10] and leveraged buy-out), mezzanine investment, venture leasing, distressed finance and other late-stage equity capital.[11] Among these forms, mezzanine investment, technology incubators and venture leasing are not pure equity capital, but connected with equity capital.

(1) *Self-raised capital*

Self-raised capital refers to capital raised by founders on their own, including personal savings, borrowing based on personal credit and so on. Self-raised capital is sometimes called "bootstrapping," indicating that founders use very limited resources to start businesses frugally and diligently through hardship; it is the oldest and most primitive source of funds. "Bootstrap" originally means a shoestring. "Bootstrapping" was preliminarily used in an electronic computer program. In economics, "bootstrapping" means to get out of difficult situations using existing resources, including establishment of short-term goals for payables, capital shortage (tightening the belt) and cash flow prior to profit. Most founders rely on self-raised capital at the very beginning. Self-raised capital and capital from the 3Fs are the most essential capital sources for start-up enterprises. Some people consider 3Fs' capital as the basic component of self-raised capital, as described above. The 3Fs refers to friends, family and founders, or 'fools' — as some may name those who make venture capital investment.

Prior to incoming of external funds, owning self-raised capital is critical to success of a founder. According to Inc. 500 statistics, for the top 500 enterprises with the fastest growth, self-raised capital comprised nearly 80% of the capital source upon their start-up (see Table 2.4).

Table 2.4   Capital Sources of Start-ups.

Capital Sources of Start-ups	Proportion in the Overall Capital Source
Savings of founders	74%
Friends and families	5%
Angel investors	7%
Venture capital	5%
Non-financial companies	6%
Commercial banks	0%
Public market (stock market)	3%

Source: Liu Manhong, *Angel Investing: Principles and Practice*, Economy & Management Publishing House, 2009. (in Chinese)

(2) *Angel investors*

Angel investors are sources of informal venture capital or informal risk capital,[12] while angel investment is an early form of equity investment. Contrary to venture capital that develops gradually in a mode of fundraising from large professional institutional investors, angel investors prefer private, small, hidden and informal financing and investment. If we say venture capitalists use others' capital (commonly institutional investors), then angel investors use their own capital.

Compared with other forms of investment, angel investment is advantageous in the following aspects: there is an earlier time horizon, higher investment efficiency, lower investment cost and a faster rate of investment decision-making. As private, spontaneous, individual and scattered as it is, angel investment is independent of venture capital and other forms of investment, and it has become an individual investment form of great vitality. In the perspective of the number of investment projects, angel investment has many more projects than venture capital; and with economic developments, the advantages of angel investment will grow more prominent.

(3) *Technology incubators/accelerators*

Technology incubators, incubators for short, are an organizational form supported by governments, universities or other scientific research institutions that help innovative enterprises convert their goals into technological achievements. In China, technology incubators are present in the form of various science and technology parks or start-up parks. Incubators supported by governments, universities or scientific research institutes are often non-profitable, while private or corporate incubators are sometimes profitable.

Technology incubators often have office buildings or factories provided by governments or universities to attract innovative enterprises with development potential to settle in at relatively low rents. Generally, innovative enterprises shall submit applications to technology incubators for approval before settling in the parks. In addition to favorable rents, technology incubators also provide other service facilities for settled enterprises, for example, common conference rooms, telex machines and photocopiers etc. Furthermore, some incubators even offer lectures for settled enterprises on how one can manage, finance and develop an enterprise. Local governments recognize that technology incubators have long-term influence on the development of local economy and hence, they tend to implement some preferential policies, i.e. a policy of tax exemption in the first three years of business, and tax reduction in the subsequent two years.

In China, most technology incubators at the very beginning were institutional organizations. Now, more and more incubators are adopting the corporate operation mode. For example, recently many "innovative incubators" have emerged to attract funds and support the development of small-scale start-ups in the form of investment and services, having made great contributions. While collecting rents from enterprises settled in them, the incubators often hold a small proportion of shares of the enterprises. Such a mode of operation is somewhat connected with equity capital, and makes the incubators members of the private equity family.

Accelerators are a variety of incubators and were innovations in the early years of the 21st century. In recent years, the number of accelerators has been constantly rising, and they have been developing quickly in China, for example the emerging "innovative incubator" in Beijing Zhongguancun Science Park (see the case study below). Similar to incubators, accelerators also assist start-ups by providing services such as strategic instructions, market consultation, product development and refinancing services. However, the two are different in the following aspects: incubators provide more assistance to start-ups in aspects of logistics and hardware, i.e. cheap offices and production factories, while accelerators often focus on assistance in software by providing regular training courses and consultation services to established start-ups. Accelerators also have their own angel investment funds, which can help enterprises solve their early financing problems.

(4) *Venture capital*

Venture capital (also known as risk capital)[13] is a special kind of private equity. According to the definition provided by the American National

Venture Capital Association, venture capital is a kind of equity capital investment in emerging enterprises that develops fast with great potential competitiveness. In principle, venture capital is not restricted to high-tech enterprises, but are applicable to all enterprises with aggressive growth. In fact, it is practically demonstrated in different countries that venture capital is closely related to the development of high technology. Martin Haemmig found that the proportions of venture capital in high technology reached up to 97%, 84% and 84% in Israel, America and Sweden respectively, and the innovative connotation of venture capital coincided well with the internal factors of high-tech development.[14]

In the United States, scholars found that the contribution of venture capital to technological innovations was about three to four times of that of R & D. From the late 1970s to the early 1990s, though the total amount of venture capital only accounted for 3% of enterprises' R & D, it supported 10–12% technological innovations of the enterprises.[15] Due to the great promoting effect of venture capital on technological innovations and high-tech industries, governments in all countries have implemented various policies to greatly support venture capital in aspects of funds and taxes.

(5) *Acquisition capital*

In the process of combining venture capital and private equity, acquisition capital is commonly in the mode of leveraged buy-out (LBO), i.e. the buyer realizes acquisition mainly by obtaining the equity of the targeted company through the financial leverage (borrowings). Leveraged acquisition generally refers to an instance when the investor leverages a large amount of borrowing with a small portion of equity capital to buy an enterprise. The buyer mortgages the assets of the enterprise to be acquired to obtain a bank loan and then repays the loan gradually by using earnings and cash flow. Sometimes, leveraged acquisition can absolutely change the mode of a company: Through leveraged acquisition, an acquired listed company may be turned into a non-listed company for overall reform of the corporate governance structure. In most cases, as the buyers try to repurchase all listed stocks of the acquired companies, the public shareholders of the acquired companies can get share discounts higher than the market prices. When a company, having been delisted due to leveraged acquisition, goes public again, it is known as reverse leveraged acquisition. According to Steve Kaplan, the average asset-liability ratio of companies acquired through leverage was 88%, and that figure was only 19% before acquisition.[16]

Sometimes, acquisition is performed by managers who use leveraged capital (capital financed by borrowing) to acquire a targeted company, so as to radically change its ownership structure and lead to the identification of the operation of the enterprise with new ownership. In China, it is hard to realize leveraged acquisition because of its financial system and economic environment, among other factors. For acquisition, a company is commonly registered to act as the subject of acquisition by various means of financing (such as temporary borrowings from friends and relatives); it is common for people to adopt installment plans to avoid one-time cash payments. Such acquisition can be seen as a form of leveraged acquisition, but with funds from various informal channels other than from banks and other formal channels.

Management acquisition may be either management buy-out (MBO) or management buy-in (MBI). For a listed company, managers may buy the stocks it has issued for the purpose of making the company exit the stock market and become delisted. Commonly, the management is required to pay a premium higher than the market price, so as to acquire all the stocks the company has issued to the whole market. Sometimes, the management needs to rely on large amounts of bank loans to accomplish such acquisition; in such a situation, leveraged buy-out (LBO) is adopted in management buy-out (MBO).

Management buy-out may occur for many reasons:

- To avoid a hostile takeover by a buyer who attempts to replace the management;
- To avoid various pressures of a listed company: for example, short-term returns, maintaining a rising trend of the stock price, levels of inspection by supervisory departments, requirement for information disclosure, etc.
- To facilitate reform of the company and to promote the productivity by letting management owning more shares.

An MBI refers to the situation where an external investor attempts to buy most shares of a company (generally to the extent of controlling the company) and claims to retain the existing management of the company. The external investor is commonly a risk investor who looks to a promising future of the company's products or services and hopes to promote the company's productivity and explore its potential by controlling it. An MBI is different from an MBO. For the former, acquisition is dominated by external investors; for the latter, it is dominated by company management, i.e. acquisition is facilitated by the management of the company to be acquired. Both MBI and MBO can be realized by leveraged acquisition. International MBOs generally adopt leveraged acquisition, which is realized with bank loans obtained by mortgaging the assets of the companies to be acquired.

Leveraged acquisition needs a large amount of loan capital, and thus loan capital is a feature of leveraged acquisition. However, leveraged acquisition is commonly considered to be associated with equity capital because risk capital or other private equity is involved. Private equity investors will provide a portion of capital to the management as sweat capital. Generally, the management will hold around 30% of shares, while the investors participating in acquisition will require a seat on the board of directors, so as to generally monitor the operation of the company. The company to be acquired is commonly a listed company with large assets, and thus acquisition of the company requires a large amount of capital; meanwhile, the management of the company hopes to hold a certain proportion of shares. For this purpose, acquisition of such a huge capital company with limited funds can only be realized by using a large amount of loans.[17] This is "leveraged buyout."

Suppose a listed company with assets worth RMB500 million is to acquired. If no leverage is used, the manager needs RMB150 million to purchase only 30% of shares. Such a large amount is almost impossible to afford (even though senior officers in some large foreign companies have high income, they are salaried employees other than capitalists), and thus it only works through leveraged acquisition. Based on practices carried out in foreign countries, it is common that acquiring investors combine funds with the managements of the companies to be acquired to realize management buy-outs by using large amount of loans. In China, management buy-outs are largely different from international practices — the managements of companies to be acquired commonly join hands with private equity investors (or acquisition investors) to realize acquisition by other financing means.

(6) *Mezzanine investment*

The term "mezzanine" is used to describe an intermediate floor between the first and the second floors of a library, warehouse or large factory. It was originally created for making full use of space. Mezzanine in financial and investment theories refers to a kind of investment between two investment periods. Some also consider it as a kind of investment between equities and bonds. Mezzanine investment is commonly short-term bridge-type investment, which uses loans and has features of equity capital, such as convertible securities or equity warrants. In principle, mezzanine investment is connected with equity capital.

When a company has completed preliminary equity financing and is ready for public listing, i.e. during the process of initial public offering (IPO), it may have temporary capital demand. In such case, it is common that the company will seek financing through mezzanine investment. Compared with other means of private equity financing, mezzanine investment features relatively short terms, simple formalities and fast investment-related decision-making. Mezzanine investment is also favored by investors due to its equity capital features.

(7) *Distressed finance*

Distressed finance can be divided into distressed securities and private distressed capital. The former, also known as "cheap securities," refers to the stocks or debentures of companies in financial trouble. As financial troubles of the companies may be temporary and the prices of their stocks or debentures are commonly lower during such a period, the stocks or debentures are attractive investment instruments and the name of "cheap securities" is derived. Low prices attract external investors, while inflow of the investors' capital may bring the companies out of trouble and turn them around.

Distressed capital in private equity refers to capital needed by some large companies that are confronted with temporary financial troubles during operation to get out of financial difficulty and achieve rejuvenation through internal reform. However, not all companies in financial difficulty are the objects of distressed finance. Only those temporarily troubled companies with promising market prospects, productivity and development potential can attract distressed finance. These companies can be renewed to improve their poor management or structure-caused low productivity through control and restructuring.

All in all, if we include the concept of angel investment in the system of private equity, then angel investment is only a category of private equity, and characterized by the features of private equity.

3. Private equity, corporate life cycle and risk analysis

(1) *Private equity and corporate life cycle*

It is an organic process for the start-up to grow and eventually mature into an enterprise. During the process, whether the enterprise can survive, develop and expand largely depends on whether it can be financed successfully. Capital is blood, sufficient circulation of which is vital to an enterprise.

Private equity is active at stages throughout the life cycle of an enterprise, particularly at the seed stage, the start-up stage and the development stage. Capital invested at the above three stages is commonly called early-stage investment, while that invested in the mature and stable stages is commonly known as late-stage investment. Based on the different features of equity capital and loan capital, early-stage investment commonly adopts equity capital, while late-stage investment can adopt equity capital in combination with loan capital.

(2) *Corporate life cycle and risk analysis*

Private equity can be invested at any stage throughout the life cycle of an enterprise. However, the earlier the investment is made, the higher risk there will be. Investment at the seed stage is of the highest level of risk, followed by that at the start-up stage, the expansion stage, and so on so forth. At the seed stage, investment is of a rather high level of risk, as the enterprise is still in the bud and its core technology or patent has not been tested by practical production, while the backbone team has not been formed yet and production, sales, finance and other aspects have not been standardized. As the enterprise grows from the start-up to maturity, the risk suffered by investors is gradually alleviated; correspondingly, the expected investment returns of the investors are also gradually reduced.

Due to various uncertainties, an enterprise may experience many unexpected changes and risks arising from the changes during the process from birth to maturity. Even for the most promising start-up enterprises, risk is inevitable. In the best circumstance where the possibility of failure is 20% at each development stage of an enterprise, i.e. the average success rate of the enterprise is up to 80%, as angel investment at the seed stage will experience the seed stage, the start-up stage, the expansion stage, the mature stage and the stable stage, its final success rate is only $(1-20\%) \times (1-20\%) \times (1-20\%) \times (1-20\%) \times (1-20\%) = 32.78\%$. This is the approximate success rate of angel investment in the best circumstances (see Figure 2.13). Similarly, if the average success rate at each development stage is supposed to be 70%, then the success rate of angel investment is only 16.8%: $(1-30\%) \times (1-30\%) \times (1-30\%) \times (1-30\%) \times (1-30\%) = 16.8\%$. That is why venture capitalists, particularly angel investors, are prudent at every step of investment, but they are still confronted with very high investment risk at the end.

Figure 2.10 shows the success rate of an enterprise is 80% at the seed stage where if it fails, it will disappear in history; and if not, it will enter the start-up stage where if it fails, it will disappear in history; and if not, it will enter the growth stage where if it fails, it will disappear in history; and if not, it will enter the expansion stage where if it fails, it will disappear in history; and if not, it will enter the stable stage. If angel investment is made at the seed stage, then upon completion of the corporate life cycle, the success rate of the angel investment is 32.78%.

Yet this is an absolutely abstract example in theory, and does not commonly occur in real life. First, angel investors often quit successfully before enterprises enter the next cycle, and few constantly hold on to the end of the enterprises' life cycles. Many angel investors quit upon entry of venture capitalists. Second, the level of risk differs at different stages

Success Rate of Investment

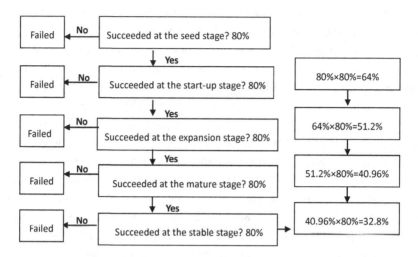

Fig. 2.10   **The Success Rate of Angel Investment is Inversely Proportional to Risk.**
Source: Liu Manhong, 'Venture Capital and Venture Capital Management.' Lecture Notes, Renmin University of China, 2005.

throughout the life cycle of an enterprise, and thus the possibility of failure also differs at different stages: obviously, the weaker an enterprise, the higher the possibility of failure. Therefore, our assumption is greatly limited. The assumption of the same possibility of failure at different stages throughout the life cycle of an enterprise lacks real-life support. Third, the assumption of success rate of 80% at each stage in the life cycle of an enterprise is too ideal for an enterprise at the seed stage. The assumption is so made to simplify narration and for better and more direct recognition by the readers. As described above, even the most promising enterprises will have to take unpredictable risk. In reality, many start-up enterprises just end up in the "valley of death."

4. Features of private equity and angel investment

The collection of private equity is called private equity market. Compared with the four major features of public equity market (fairness, efficiency, liquidity and transparency), the private equity market has the following features which are also reflected in angel investments: They have a high degree of privacy; relatively low trading efficiency; poor liquidity; long-term investments; high participation and value-added investments; and have weak transparency.

(1) *High degree of privacy*

Private equity commonly adopts a non-public or private equity investment mode. As the investment is directed to non-listed companies, investors and investees are not obliged to or necessarily disclose any investment-related information to other people. Private equity transactions are made between investors and the investees; the scale and price of such transactions are completely decided by the transaction parties and no one else. The major difference between the private market and the public market lies in that: the latter features low information asymmetry due to public disclosure of information, while the former features high information asymmetry. The degree of privacy and asymmetry of information can make the effect of financial operations in the private market differ greatly: some investment might end up as great successes, while other might reap in less-than-ideal results. If the operation mode of equity capital is a result of high risk relating to private equity investment, then angel investors who are capable of acquiring information will have the possibility of success largely promoted, while those who have no channel to obtain abundant and relatively accurate information are inevitable to fail.

(2) *Low efficiency*

The low efficiency of private equity corresponds to the efficiency of public equity. The public equity market can be explained by using the "efficient market" theory. Efficient markets are divided into highly efficient markets, relatively efficient markets and poorly efficient markets. In a highly efficient market, prices will reflect all relevant information; in a relatively efficient market, prices will reflect all publicly disclosed information; while in a lowly efficient market, it is assumed that the provided prices reflect all history information. Compared with the different degrees in the efficiency of the public equity market, private equity market has the poorest efficiency and lowest benefits. That is to say the final price reached by the parties (the buyer and the seller) during the process of investment does not necessarily reflect true information behind the transaction.

Due to illiquidity of information and low market efficiency, investment results in the private equity market may differ greatly: investors may succeed and yield 10, 20, 50 times or higher investment returns, or suffer heavy losses. This situation may occur for angel investors. Experienced angel investors and green angel investors may have largely different investment returns. However, highly experienced angel investors may also make investment mistakes that lead to large losses.

The low efficiency of the private equity market constitutes one reason for its high risk. Private equity, especially early-stage investment such as angel investment, features high risk and high-expected returns. The dialectical relationship between high risk and high expected returns lies in that high risk is a necessary cost for obtaining high returns, while high returns are just a possible result of high risk. The investment decision-making process of private equity capitalists is a process of weighing returns against risk, i.e. to predict expected returns that are to be obtained in future and to estimate and determine potential risk. In fact, in the process of investing private equity, measures against risk are taken at each procedure, including primary and further selection of projects, prudent investigation (due diligence), organization of joint investment, constant supervision and management after investment and design of quitting channels etc. For example, to avoid high risk, private equity investors often adopt combined investment, while the investors are investment partners and not seen as competitors. Through combined investment, a cooperative relationship of "lead-investment" and "follow-investment" is generally formed. "Lead-investors" will complete primary and further selection of projects, prudent investigation (due diligence), evaluation and negotiation and final pricing, while other investors will follow to invest based on the evaluated pricing.

Currently, combined investment between private equity investors has been gradually formed in China, and the relationship between "lead-investment" and "follow-investment" is constantly being practiced and explored. For example, at the Beijing International Finance Exposition on October 31, 2013, the Rules on Angel Capital Lead Investors in China launched by the Angel Crunch of Zhongguancun Science Park was jointly released by multiple frontier investors and financial institutions. These rules clarified the responsibility and liability of founders and investors during the process of crowd funding, investment and financing, as well as basic procedures, and further promoted normalization and standardization of angel investment in China.

(3) *Poor liquidity*

It is generally known that public equity investors can convert the stocks or other securities they hold to realize liquidity timely. Though they may have gains or losses during the trading process, the investment is strongly liquid. Compared with public equity, private equity is illiquid, because once it is invested in an enterprise, it is integrated into its original assets or becomes an integral part of the corporate capital utilized to purchase equipment, instruments or to pay salaries, rent and other expenses. Private equity investors cannot easily withdraw their investment (commonly cash with liquidity) in the short term, unless they sell the shares of the invested enterprises to initiate the process of exiting the investment project.

Private equity is commonly known as "buy-side financing," which is a special financial operation mode that is different from traditional financial services. The capital investment by private equity investors in enterprises is actually to buy assets of the enterprises. For example, an investor A invests an amount of RMB1 million in a start-up enterprise B in exchange for 30% shares of B. In this case, it can be considered that the investor A pays RMB1 million for acquiring 30% assets of the start-up enterprise B. In the transaction process, the buyer has to be cautious due to information asymmetry. In fact, the buy-side financing position of private equity investors is also a major reason for various measures taken during the process of investment project selection against risk. However, it shall be noted that private equity is not simply financial operation, but an emerging investment mode to support start-up enterprises.[18]

Due to its illiquidity and buy-side financing position, private equity has corresponding features of long term and participation. These features are particularly reflected in practices of angel investment.

(4) *Long-term feature*

Due to its illiquidity, private equity has a long-term feature, particularly for early-stage private equity, which is also called "patient capital." The long-term feature of private equity also has a different operation mode from traditional financial mode.

Private equity capitalists commonly construct "money pools" first and then use capital in the pools to purchase assets. Form the perspective of angel investment, the money pools are not obtained through financing from other investors but through individual wealth accumulation. Investment with private equity, the buy-side financing, is a process of acquiring assets with equity capital. After acquisition, the private equity capitalists will actively participate in operation to increase the value of the assets, finally turn the assets into cash and realize investment withdrawal. It can be seen that private equity investment has a rather long operation process, with long term and weak liquidity. As a form of private equity, angel capital is commonly invested at the early stage of start-up enterprises, while the earlier it is invested, the more obvious the long term will be.

In China, many private equity investors focus on late-stage investment, so as to reduce the potential risk arising from the long term and illiquidity of private equity. This occurs due to corporate systems on the one hand and the macro-environment on the other hand. However, it is just because of the late-stage investment tendency of private equity that angel investment is playing an increasingly important role.

(5) *High participation-value added investment*

Private equity investment also features high participation, which is associated with its illiquidity and long terms. Participation is usually extremely obvious in early-stage investment, such as angel investment and venture capital investment. Investors are commonly active in participation in management of invested enterprises and helping the enterprises to increase value. They will help the enterprises find resources, or seek for markets, or coordinate the relationship between the enterprises and the enterprises' customers and suppliers, or associate the enterprises with financing banks and financial institutions, so as to facilitate listing or acquisition of the enterprises. Therefore, private equity investment, particularly angel capital and venture capital investment at the early stage, is also called value added investment, while angel investors/venture capitalists are glorified as "founders behind founders."

According to statistics of the American National Venture Capital Association, the average time that American venture capitalists spend after investment accounts for 75% of the total duration of the investment period (including participation in strategic decision-making and strategic design of the invested enterprises, provision of consultation services to the invested enterprises, helping the invested enterprises recruit management personnel, aiding the maintenance of public relations, design of quitting channels and organizing of enterprises to quit, but excluding financing and quitting), while the time they spend in the investment accounts for only 25% (including seeking target enterprises, investigation and evaluation, meetings and negotiations, pricing, organizing combined investment etc.). As a matter of fact, post-investment management is closely related to another discipline: that of enterprise management. In this aspect, China needs a large number of venture capitalists and angel investors who are masters of management, technology and finance, while the shortage of them has become one of the bottlenecks inhibiting the development of the Chinese private equity market. We lack no "hard capital" (i.e. cash investment), but "soft capital" (i.e. investors who are well-experienced in and capable of establishing start-ups, management, technology and finance).

(6) *Weak transparency*

Due to the privacy and illiquidity, the private equity market has low transparency, which is reflected in aspects of both investors and the invested. As private equity investment is a private investment behavior, it is not necessary or obligatory for investors or the invested to disclose their business modes and financial information to the public, nor is the China Securities Regulatory Commission or other supervisory departments responsible for auditing the financial conditions of the investors and the invested. Nevertheless, in the private equity market, investors and the invested mutually require each other to fully disclose information as far as possible. On the one hand, investors can make investment decisions only after investigation of the technology, market, team, products, financial conditions and other information of the invested. On the other hand, the invested needs to generally know the background, credit and capability of the investors to cement further cooperation.

Because of low transparency in the market, parties involved in the investment project (i.e. the investors and the invested) are usually very cautious and prudent. This often results in a relatively long process of decision making before a deal is struck.

Notes

1. Martin Haemmig, 'Venture Capital,' Lecture Notes, Renmin University of China, 2008.
2. This definition is in dispute in both academic and industrial circles. Some believe that a "stranger" can sometimes become friends, and therefore, it is hard to distinguish a stranger from a friend. The distinction of angel investor in a broad and narrow sense depends on whether the investor is a family member or relative of the invested (Global Entrepreneurship Monitor Report, 2003).
3. Scott Shane, *Fool's Gold? The Truth Behind Angel Investing in America* (First Edition), Oxford University Press, 2008.
4. Liu Manhong, *Angel Investing: Principles and Practice*, Economy & Management Publishing House, 2009. (in Chinese)
5. Andrew Wong, 'Angel Finance: The Other Venture Capital,' Working Paper, University of Chicago, 2002.
6. Liu Manhong and Zvi Bodie, *Venture Capital and Financial System Reform*, China Finance Publishing House, 2002. (in Chinese)
7. George W. Fenn, Nellie Liang and Stephen D. Prowse, 'The Economics of the Private Equity Market,' Board of Governors of the Federal Reserve System (US), Staff Studies No.168, 1995.
8. Paul Gompers and Josh Lerner, 'An Analysis of Compensation in the U.S. Venture Capital Partnership,' *Journal of Financial Economics*, 1999, 51(1): 3–44; and William A. Sahlman. 'The Structure and Governance of Venture-Capital Organizations,' *Journal of Financial Economics*, 1990, 27(2): 473–521.
9. As of April 25, 2016, there were 1,764 listed companies in Shenzhen Stock Exchange and 953 listed companies in Shanghai Stock Exchange. As of June 2016, there were 3,695 and 3,149 issues in New York Stock Exchange and NASDAQ respectively, totaling 4,974 listed companies.

10. Management acquisitions consist of management buy-outs (MBO) and management buy-ins (MBI).

11. George W. Fenn and Nellie Liang, Stephen Prowse, 'The Economics of the Private Equity Market,' Board of Governors of the Federal Reserve System (US), Staff Studies No.168, 1995.

12. John D. Aram, 'Informal Risk Capital in the Eastern Great Lakes Region,' Final Report, US Small Business Administration, ARAM Research Associates, Inc., Cleveland. 1987.

13. John Downes and Jordan Elliot Goodman, *Dictionary of Finance and Investment Terms* (Barron's Financial Guides, Sixth Edition), Barron's Educational Series, Inc., 2003, David W. Pearce, *The MIT Dictionary Of Modern Economics* (Fourth Edition), The MIT Press, 1992; and Cary Lucius, *The Venture Capital Report Guide to Venture Capital in Europe: How and Where to Raise Risk Capital* (Fifth Edition), Oxon: Venture Capital Report, 1991.

14. Martin Haemmig, *The Globalization of Venture Capital*, Swiss Private Equity & Corporate Finance Association, 2003. Also available online at http://www. martinhaemmig.com/downloadable/2003-03%20--%20Globalization %20of%20VC%20(14-p%20Summary).pdf.

15. Paul Gompers and Josh Lerner. 'Short Term America Revisited? Boom and Bust in the Venture Capital Industry and the Impact on Innovation,' in Adam B. Jaffe, Josh Lerner and Scott Stern (eds.), *Innovation Policy and the Economy, Volume 3* (MIT Press, 2003), pp. 1–28; Samuel Kortum and Josh Lerner, 'Assessing the Contribution of Venture Capital on Innovation,' *RAND Journal of Economics*, 2000, 31(4): 674–692; and Gordon Baty *et al.*, 'Roundtable on U.S. Risk Capital and Innovation (with a Look at Eastern Europe),' *Journal of Applied Corporate Finance*, 1992, 4(4): 48–78.

16. Liu Manhong, *Angel Investing: Principles and Practice*, Economy & Management Publishing House, 2009. (in Chinese)

17. According to Steve Kaplan, after a leveraged acquisition is realized, the average debt ratio of the company is up to 98%, while that of the reference company is only 44%.

18. In the traditional planned economy, investment and finance are two concepts, one from the financial system and the other from the banking system. However, in the market economy, investment is only a subcategory of finance. See Liu Manhong, 'Financial Connotation of Venture Capital,' Venture Capital Investment Development and Research Center of, the Renmin University of China, Working Paper, 2002.

Chapter 3

The Necessity and Feasibility
of Developing Angel Investment

The Valley of Death of Enterprises and Angel Investment

An enterprise will experience many hardships in the process from birth to growth, and later, maturity. For start-up enterprises, the least desirable, but inevitable, stage to be at is that of the "valley of death." Just as the name implies, the valley of death is mostly present for small and medium-sized start-up enterprises; it is the hardest time of an enterprise during development and a stage where an enterprise is most likely to die out (see Figure 3.1).

Figure 3.1 clearly states where the "valley of death" is situated through the life cycle of an enterprise. In the figure, the horizontal axis represents the time, i.e. the development process of an enterprise from the seed stage to the start-up stage, the growing (expansion) stage, the mature stage and the stable stage; the vertical axis represents the business income of the enterprise.

At the seed stage during the development of enterprises, the 3Fs (family, friends and founders) are commonly the main source of capital. Upon entry into the start-up stage, angel investment, government-backed funds, technology incubators and other sources of capital may become available, in addition to the 3Fs. Upon entry into the growing stage, also known as the expansion stage, the enterprises may seek for venture capital (high-growth enterprises with great development potential may become the objects of venture capital investment). Upon reaching a mature stage of growth, private equity (also known as non-public equity) or commercial banks will be involved. Enterprises entering into this stage of stability may also get financed through the capital market.

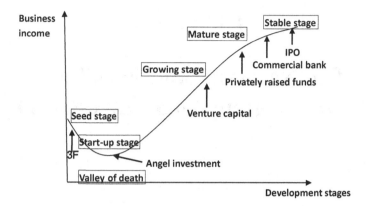

Fig. 3.1   Enterprise's Growth and the Valley of Death.
Source: Liu Manhong, 'Venture Capital,' Lecture Notes, Renmin University of China, 2009.

The valley of death is mostly present for small and medium-sized start-up enterprises. Upon the start-up of an enterprise, the financial condition of the enterprise is theoretically zero as there is no income or expenditure. However, once an enterprise starts operating, expenditure is incurred — whether or not any income is made. When the enterprise enters the start-up stage after the seed stage, it has no income, or even if it does, its income would still be insufficient to cover its expenditure, and might still be in a difficult financial position. In a scenario where the enterprise has income that is far too short to cover its expenditure — despite developing business connections and gaining some income — it will still be situated in the valley of death, i.e. in a belt or at a time where/ when the enterprise is liable to die off. Enterprises situated in the valley of death do not have sufficient income to pay employees, as they have no income but have incurred expenditure, or low income and a disproportionately higher expenditure than income. Enterprises may be confronted with many hardships but financing is commonly listed as the toughest. In the valley of death, many enterprises may have exhausted self-owned capital sourced from the 3Fs, and have to resort to borrowing money due to the lack of other capital sources. Enterprises that have exhausted financing channels however, will end up being swallowed up by debt. This is why angel investment could potentially play an important role as an alternative to hard money loans, in the development process of enterprises.

The concept of the "valley of death" can be analyzed in terms of an enterprise's financial conditions (see Figure 3.2). The vertical axis shows the income line of the enterprise: the part above zero represents positive income and that below zero represents negative income. The horizontal axis shows the development stages of the enterprise, starting from establishment at the zero point; as the enterprise develops, it will go through the seed stage, the start-up stage, the growth (expansion) stage, the mature stage and the stable stage. In the figure, the line represents the enterprise's income-expenditure curve. When the curve goes downwards (from the zero point to the first break-even point), the enterprise has less income than expenditure; when the curve goes upwards (after the first break-even point), the enterprise has more income than expenditure. It must be noted that the curve shown in the figure only applies to enterprises subject to normal development. Many enterprises may die off in the valley of death, and some might continue to struggle in the valley of death for a rather long time.

Under normal circumstances, an enterprise has no income or expenditure (negative income) at the beginning of development. After established, it needs workers, offices/production workshops, raw materials, equipment and instruments; given such cash flow requirements, it is faced

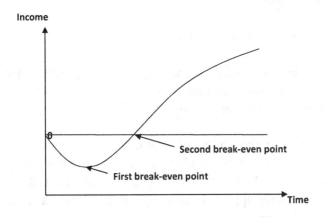

Fig. 3.2   Break-Even Point and The Valley of Death.
Source: Liu Manhong, 'Venture Capital,' Lecture Notes, Renmin University of China, 2009.

with a financial situation where there is less income than expenditure and might hence enter the valley of death. As production/services of the enterprise are carried out, its cash flow turns around, while its income gradually increases and net loss gradually reduces to realize cash flow balance, i.e. the enterprise comes to its first break-even point. At this time, the enterprise has basically balanced income and expenditure (negative income), but it has not recovered capital invested at the very beginning, and the total income is still negative.

The first break-even point is also the bottom of the valley of death. From this point on, if the enterprise continues to develop positively, it will increase its income, gradually improve its cash flow, maintain greater income than expenditure and gradually bring itself out of the valley of death. When the enterprise comes to the second break-even point, its total income and total expenditure are balanced, i.e. the total investment upon start-up of the enterprise is finally recovered by income. From the second break-even point on, the enterprise starts to gain profit. Therefore, the second break-even point is also a turning point where the enterprise turns losses into gains.

Compared to Figure 3.1, Figure 3.2 describes the valley of death during the development process of an enterprise from another angle, where the valley of death exists because of insufficient capital (i.e. a problem of cash flow and temporary income less than expenditure). The solution is to reduce the application of capital by the enterprise, or to increase capital sources that include:

- 3Fs (family, friends and founders or fools)
- Angel investment
- National funds that support technological development projects
- Technology incubators/accelerators
- Guaranteed loans for enterprises

Upon falling into the valley of death, many enterprises may have exhausted their 3F sources. In addition, the third and fourth items above may only apply to high-tech enterprises, while guaranteed loans from banks are commonly applicable to enterprises that have walked out of the valley of death. Angel investments may hence play a critical role in helping enterprises walk out of the valley of death.

Bottlenecks at the Early Development Stage of Enterprises

No enterprise can survive without capital during the process of development from an embryo to a start-up, and in its subsequent growth and expansion. Capital to an enterprise is just like blood to a human body. Blood flows to organs in the body as the heart beats to maintain the vitality of the body. Similar to a human being, an enterprise, as a "legal person" with a life cycle, has capital for "blood" which flows in and out of different departments of the enterprise. Capital brings great vitality to the enterprise during its growth and expansion.

Capital is therefore the lifeline of an enterprise. For start-up enterprises, capital plays an even more important role. As mentioned above, capital sources of small and medium-sized start-up enterprises include the 3Fs, angel investment, technology incubators, government-backed funds and venture capital. In the past, venture capital played a significant role in financing small and medium-sized start-up enterprises with great development potential. However, this role seems to have gradually weakened with the entry of angel investment.

Since the end of the 20th century, venture capital has been more widely present at the middle and late stages in the biological chain of enterprises, with focus gradually transferred from start-up to growth enterprises of small and medium sizes, and from the start-up to the expansion stage of enterprises. In recent years, some venture capital funds seemed to have transferred focus further from the expansion to the post expansion stage, or even to the mature stage of enterprises. For example, in 2001–2003, the growth rate of venture capital investment throughout America slowed down, with returns reaching the lowest level in 30 years. In addition, the financial crisis during 2008–2009 in America led to venture capital facing negative growth. As American market along with global economy recovers from the financial crisis, venture capital gradually grows again (see Figure 3.3).

Based on the figure, one can see that as the scale of venture capital funds grows, the average sum of venture capital invested in enterprises also increases proportionately. This situation is inevitable as the number of management personnel venture capital funds does not increase proportionately to the enlarged scale of venture capital, and each venture

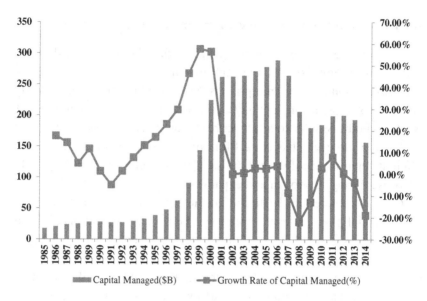

Fig. 3.3   Scale of Venture Capital in America (1985–2014).
Source: Collation of data presented in the NVCA Yearbook, 2015.

capitalist can only participate in the management of a limited number of invested enterprises within a period of time. Suppose each venture capital fund invested in 10 enterprises, then the average scale of funds in 2002 was US$22 million and the average investment in each project was US$2.2 million. In 2007, the average scale of funds was US$147 million, and the average investment in each project was US$14.7 million dollars, marking an increase of 568% within five years. As such, the increase of venture capital funds inevitably facilitated an overall increase in the average sum of venture capital investment invested in each project, which hence, resulted in overall transfer of venture capital from late-stage investment to early-stage enterprises with larger capital gaps.

According to Professor Sohl, in 1997, the amount of venture capital investment at the early stage (including the seed stage and the start-up stage) accounted for 6% of the total investment; in 2000, the proportion decreased by half to 3%. In 2001, it decreased further to 2%; in 2002, it decreased to 1.4%; and in 2007, it was 1%.[1] Capital shortage is a common problem for enterprises in their early stages. Against such a background, angel investment emerges as an alternative form of finance. Between 1997 and 2003, the number of angel investors in America increased at an annual rate of 12–14% — making angel investment an important force among various financing channels for enterprises. According to a recent investigation done by Scott Shane on founders in America, 15.1% entrepreneurs expressed their need for external investment, and the amount of investment ranged from 250,000 dollars to 500,000 dollars.[2]

In China, capital shortage for small and medium-sized enterprises is more common. This contradicts the important theoretical role of small and medium-sized enterprises in China's fast-growing national economy. The number of small and medium-sized enterprises accounts for 99.3% of the total number of enterprises in China; they also account for 55.6% of China's gross domestic product (GDP); the amount of corporate tax they pay accounts for 46.2%; and they account for 75% of China's overall workforce. However, for the small and medium-sized enterprises, hard money financing has become a major bottleneck that inhibits their development.

Angel investors undertake the mission to help bridge the financing gap that enterprises in their early-stages might face. In Europe, the financing gap is around 200 thousand to 2 million euros; in China, it is around RMB1–10 million. It shall be noted that when angel investors in different countries were asked about their investment motives, none of them answered "for the purpose of entrepreneurship," but gave near-identical answers that echoed this sentiment: "We are looking for innovation." Not all start-up enterprises with a financing gap can get angel investment. Only those with innovations — which refers, but is not limited, to technological innovations, but also innovative management, innovative business modes and market innovations — might attract angel investments.

Necessity of Developing Angel Investment

For small and medium-sized enterprises, it is hard to obtain bank loans, let alone short-term loans or even mid-term and long-term loans. According to a survey, 81% of small and medium-sized enterprises in China held that their working capital for one year could only satisfy partial needs; 60.5%

of enterprises did not have access to 1–3 years' mid-term and long-term loans. Among the failed small and medium-sized enterprises in China, 47% closed down due to capital shortage.[3]

Capital shortage for small and medium-sized enterprises due to hard financing has limited and affected the survival and development of the enterprises, and hence does not match the contributions that these enterprises have made to the economic and social development of China. The increasing demands for financing by small and medium-sized enterprises have not been met as the promotion of providing capital to these enterprises has not been active on the part of the government. Furthermore, venture capital, as one source of capital for small and medium-sized enterprises, tends to be of a larger scale with later investment stages as described above. This phenomenon is not just present in America or in China, but generally present around the world (see Table 3.1).

Table 3.1   Comparison of Investment Amount in Each Round of VC Investment (Mean Value) in Different Countries.

	America	**Europe**	**China**	**India**	**Israel**
Total Venture Capital ($)	30.3bn	6.6bn	2.5bn	862m	1.5bn
Investment Rounds	2695	991	249	77	218
Amount of Each Investment Round (Mean Value) ($)	7.6m	4.9m	8.0m	9.0m	5.0m
IPO of Invested Enterprises ($)	6.7bn	1.0bn	3.6bn	—	533m
IPO of Invested Enterprises, (Quantity)	74	39	30	—	4
Time of IPO (Mean Value)	6.8yrs	6.3yrs	1.9yrs	—	5.2yrs
Acquisition of Invested Enterprises ($)	93m	28m	—	—	31m
Acquisition of Invested Enterprises (Quantity)	435	271	6	—	31
Time of Acquisition (Mean Value)	6.1yrs	6.6yrs	4.5yrs	—	6.5yrs

Source: Martin Haemmig, 'Venture Capital,' Lecture Notes, Renmin University of China, 2008.
Note: Data as of 2007.

Based on the data presented, in 2007, the total amount of venture capital investment in America, was US$30.3 billion and US$2.5 billion (equivalent to around RMB 17.1 billion) in China; the amount of each round of capital investment (mean value) in America was US$7.6 million and over RMB 50 million in China. Such a large amount would not have been invested in small and medium-sized start-up enterprises. Similar situations were also reflected to different degrees in India, Israel and European countries. Besides, the tendency for venture capital investment to only be inputted at the middle and late stages increases the financing difficulties of small and medium-sized enterprises. This gap in financing allows demand and supply of angel investment for enterprises, and hence helps to objectively promote the development of angel investment.

Angel investment is necessary due to the capital sources of small and medium-sized start-up enterprises being limited, as well as the risk of investment in such enterprises. From a seed stage to establishment, growth, maturity and death, an enterprise needs different amounts of capital and is subject to different levels of risk at different stages of its life cycle. Generally, an enterprise needs the least amount of capital when it is at the youngest stage, but faces the highest risk; correspondingly, the capital investor that gives it financial support will face higher risk. As the enterprise grows and develops, it needs more and more capital, while the risk faced by the investor will gradually reduce. The length of a life cycle of an enterprise is proportional to its demand for capital and it has an inversely proportional rate of risk. For investors, they will determine their investment stages based on their tolerance to risk and expectations for returns. For example, short-term deposits are key sources of capital for commercial banks; their tolerance to risk and expectations for high returns are low. Commercial banks therefore commonly invest in late-stage development of enterprises (i.e. the mature stage and "stable stage"), when the enterprises just need working capital to solve the problem of temporary capital shortage. Enterprises at these stages are relatively mature with great demand for capital and their risk is relatively reduced. The development process of an enterprise, the demand of the enterprise for capital and the level of risk it faces can be seen in Figure 3.4.

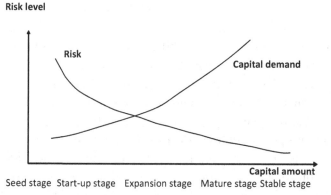

Fig. 3.4   Risk Level and Capital Demand.
Source: Liu Manhong, 'Venture Capital,' Lecture Notes, Renmin University of China, 2007.

Based on the figure above, an enterprise will face less risk as it grows, but it will need more capital. At the seed stage, it only needs a small amount of capital to put through, but such a small amount of capital is hard to be acquired due to high investment risk. Though it is a small amount, it is hard for an inexperienced investor to make an investment decision due to difficulties in knowing the real evaluation of the project to be invested. Meanwhile, such an investment decision cannot be made without an innate passion to support the enterprise or a desire to achieve high returns. On the contrary, it is relatively easier for an enterprise to get financed at the late stage when it needs more capital, because it has developed into its mature or stable stage after its product has been shaped, its technology has been tested by the market, its business model has been validated in practice, its team has become more experienced, resulting in the anticipated risk for an investor being relatively lower.

From the perspective of investors, enterprises at the early stages of their life cycles are confronted with financing risks arising from technology, market and management. These high risks are present mainly due to the following five reasons:

1) *Information asymmetry.* Real conditions of start-up enterprises regarding capital, market potential, material supply, sales channels

etc. are well-known by themselves, but can hardly be fully known by investors. If the enterprises have developed into the growing or mature stage, the above-mentioned financial conditions can be reflected by the market operation. Due to difficult identification of the above information of enterprises at the seed or start-up stage, investors are often very cautious.

2) *Intangible assets.* Valuable assets of start-up enterprises are often intangible, such as patents, trademarks, innovative ideas, unpatented technological inventions or innovations, or new information. These intangible assets may be of great value in the future, though their value is hard to be reflected at the time. Therefore, it is almost impossible for investors to mortgage these intangible assets for bank loans. In addition, investors are also concerned about protection of these intangible assets. If there are not applicable laws and regulations that enforce the protection of intellectual property rights, investors will be confronted with great risk.

3) *Untested business model.* Innovative projects or ideas of start-up enterprises have not been recognized by the market. These new projects or ideas may encounter unexpected barriers imposed by national policies, macroeconomic conditions or management regulations, which seem uncertain or risky to investors.

4) *Technological risk.* Investors may face technological risk when they undertake a decision to finance high-tech start-up enterprises. They may worry about whether the technological products of these enterprises can fully realize market-based transfer, whether the technological contents can stand the test of time, and whether these technological innovations would be substituted by new technological achievements before entering into the market. All these may impose great technological risks.

5) *Inexperienced management teams.* Management teams of start-up enterprises have not been tested by the market. Many founders are technical professionals who are enthusiastic about entrepreneurship but lack management experience. Even if there are some experienced management personnel within a team, it would still need to be tested by time as a collective unity — for example, testing whether the team members can collaborate, trust, complement and understand each

other needs to be observed over a period of time. After all, there have been only a few founders who eventually become members of the top management, and the founder of Microsoft, Bill Gates, is one of them.

Due to the above-mentioned reasons, enterprises at the early stages of their life cycle will face high risk and many other challenges. However, just as with human life, if there is no infancy, there will be no childhood, adolescence or post-adolescence. An enterprise might be weak before becoming strong, and if there is no seed stage, there will be no maturity stage. In fact, enterprises are in the most urgent need of capital at the early stages of their development, i.e. the seed stage and the start-up stage. Among the top 500 small enterprises in America according to Inc. 500, 60% have less than US$20,000 upon their start-up.[4]

The international competitiveness of a country is not only contributed by strong large enterprises, but also by a sizeable number of start-up enterprises with development potential. Such start-up enterprises are reserve forces of large enterprises and are the future of the country. To support small and medium-sized start-up enterprises, angel investment is an important capital source. Angel investment, just like an angel that helps start-up enterprises at their weakest time, plays an irreplaceable role in the development chain of enterprises, and it fills the financing gap between the 3Fs and venture capital (see Figure 3.5).

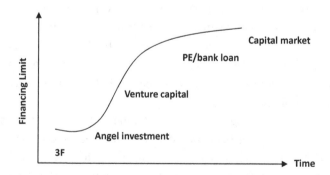

Fig. 3.5 Angel Investment: Bridge Between 3Fs and VC.
Source: Liu Manhong, 'Venture Capital,' Lecture Notes, Renmin University of China, 2006.

In Figure 3.5, the vertical axis represents the financing limit, and the horizontal axis represents the development stages of an enterprise. Generally, the enterprise will have greater demand for capital as it develops further. The figure shows how the capital demand of the enterprise changes with time. At the initial development stages, particularly the seed stage, the enterprise has low demand for capital and its capital is mainly sourced from the 3Fs. At the growth stage (expansion stage), venture capital is one example of available capital sources. Following this stage, the enterprise may select bank loans as debt financing, or private equity and equity financing. When the enterprise arrives at a more stable stage, it can be financed through listing with the stock exchange. Angel investment is an important financing mode connecting the 3Fs and venture capital. As described above, angel investment fills the financing gap at the early stages of enterprises if the gap needs about RMB 1 million to 10 million to be filled. For amounts less than RMB 1 million, founders may commonly raise the funds from the 3Fs; for amounts over RMB 10 million, founders may seek the assistance of venture capitalists; angel investment is therefore a bridge between the 3Fs and venture capital. According to an April 2014 report by Professor Jeffery Sohl, the amount of angel investment at the seed stage and start-up stage of enterprises accounted for 45% of the total investment in 2013, with an obvious increase based on that (35%) in 2012.[5]

It shall be noted that:

- Such development of enterprises only applies to partial but not all small and medium-sized start-up enterprises. Only those start-up enterprises with development potential are objects of angel investment.
- In terms of investment period, angel investment is a common bridge between the 3Fs and venture capital, but this is not always the case. Sometimes, angel investment is attracted at the seed stage as an alternative source to capital provided by the 3Fs, or at the growing stage when the start-ups might look toward venture capitalists for assistance. Similarly, angel investment may sometimes be present at the seed stage, the start-up stage or even the mature stage of enterprises.

Feasibility of Developing Angel Investment

Since the opening-up of China that initiated its reform era in the 1980s, China's national economy has developed rapidly. The country's GDP increased extraordinarily from RMB 903.99 billion in 1985 to RMB 63,613.87 in 2014. In 2014, China's GDP reached RMB 63,613.87 billion, and the per capita income reached RMB 46,629 (see Figure 3.6). Though the speed of economic development in China was affected by the global financial crisis of 2007–2008, the economic growth trend in China remained second to none in the world. Under such circumstances, more and more people within China had surplus capital and could still make investments. Commonly, investment of residents is limited in the capital market, valuable metals, real estate and works of art subject to appreciation etc. Few people invest in industries. On the one hand, investment in start-up enterprises requires relatively large amounts of capital; on the other hand, investors need to know more industry and market information and have some experience. Therefore, not everyone can make investments in

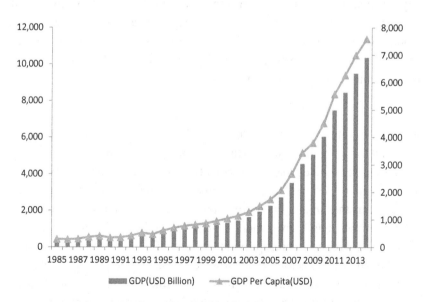

Fig. 3.6 China's GDP Growth (1985–2014).
Source: National Bureau of Statistics of China; available online at http://data.stats.gov.cn/workspace/index?m=hgnd.

industries, particularly angel investment — with its high-risk features and relatively strict requirements for investors. However, it can be observed that more and more wealthy people are becoming the basis for expansion of the angel investor group.

As described above, angel investment features small amounts, early investment stages, low investment costs, high risks and fast investment decision-making. Due to these features, angel investment is suitable for those who are capable of financing and experienced in investment, including entrepreneurs, well-experienced capital managers, bankers, educators, scholars, celebrities of entertainment and sports. There are plenty of such professionals in an economically developed society like that of China, which paves the way for the formation of a potential group of angel investors.

In sum, angel investment plays an irreplaceable role in the development of small and medium-sized enterprises in a country. It makes a great contribution to the development of start-up enterprises, particularly high-tech start-up enterprises, at their seed/early stages. Angel investment also fills the gap between capital supply and demand at the early stages of enterprises. Due to its flexibility, spontaneity, dispersed nature and diversity, angel investment can do what other types of financing modes cannot do: provide timely help by being an alternative mode of financing to entrepreneurs.

Notes

1. Liu Manhong, *Angel Investing: Principles and Practice*, Economy & Management Publishing House, 2009. (in Chinese)
2. Scott Shane, 'The Importance of Angel Investing in Financing the Growth of Entrepreneurial Ventures,' Working Paper, Report for Small Business Administration, Office of Advocacy, 2008.
3. Guo Zujun. 'New Thinking Required for Financial Demands of Small and Medium-sized Enterprises — Construction of an Angel Capital Market in China,' *Monthly Journal of Technology Entrepreneurship*, No. 4, 2006. (in Chinese)
4. Liu Manhong, *Angel Investing: Principles and Practice*, Economy & Management Publishing House, 2009. (in Chinese)
5. Jeffery Sohl, 'U.S. Angel Investor Market Recovery Continues on an Upward Trend in 2013,' UNH Center for Venture Research, April 30, 2014.

Part II
Angel Investment Practice

Chapter 4

The Study of Angel Investment in China

Current Studies of Angel Investment in China

It is generally known that business angels are individuals who provide venture capital to small private start-up enterprises and they are the second round of capital providers to start-up enterprises, and angel investment occurs after the enterprise's founders have spent all money sourced from their families, friends and before the founders contact venture capitalists.[1] In many documents, "informal investor," "private venture capitalist," "informal risk capital investor" and "business angel" are often used inter changeably.[2]

Systematic study on angel investment can be traced back to a paper by Wetzel on angel investment in New England, in which he pointed out the significant role of business angels in financially supporting hi-tech small enterprises.[3] Subsequently, studies on angel investment in other regions of America followed and updated Wetzel's early work. In the late 1980s and early 1990s, Harrison, Mason started their study on angel investment in Britain.[4] Afterwards, studies on angel investment began to develop across countries, involving such countries as Canada,[5] Norway,[6] Japan,[7] Argentina,[8] Singapore,[9] Sweden[10], Chile[11] and Italy.[12]

At present, there are only a few studies on angel investment that are set against China's economic background. In some earlier studies, simple descriptions were given.[13] In more recent research, some data were presented in the investigations of angel investment features[14] and analyses of decision-making behaviors of angel investors[15] were provided. Compared with the developed markets in Europe and America, local academic study

73

on angel investment in China is still at the preliminary stage. There are a very few domestic scholars who conduct systematic studies on the angel investment market in China. When "angel investment" is used as key words of retrieval at the CNKI.net (one of China's top academic databases), fewer than 300 academic papers are retrieved, and even fewer papers are published in core journals. These papers lack quantitative approaches to studying this field, as the papers mainly focus on several topics based on qualitative analysis and normative study, including "environmental development," "market features" and "operating mode."

I. *Operating Mode of Angel Investment in China*

Li Yaokuang, Yao Qian and Jiang Zhuqing summarized the development models of angel investment in China and put them into three categories: angel investor clubs and angel investor networks; Kai-Fu Lee's "Innovative Works"; and a combination of angel investment with social-undertaking-type enterprises incubators.[16] Shao Kun, on the other hand, came up with five models based on different ways and features of angel investment: (a) angel investors as the subjects; (b) angel investment groups with angel investor clubs and angel investment federations as the subjects; (c) angel investment funds with professional institutions as the subjects; (d) angel investment connection incubators; and (e) angel investment platforms based on the Internet and information technology.[17] However, these operating modes are also problematic. For example, "clubs and network organizations" do not have specific targets, "Innovative Works" lacks entrepreneurial momentum, and many angels and incubators have different objectives when it comes to investing.

II. *Policy Suggestions for Angel Investment in China*

There are factors that have inhibited the development of angel investment in China. As pointed out by Xu Hao,[18] the study of angel investment does not receive much attention; there is a lack of communication between angel investors and founders; and most start-up enterprises face credit deficiency and legal imperfection. He proposed some specific policy suggestions, including increasing publicity through media coverage, credit construction, optimization of the legal environment, theoretical guidance and talent cultivation. Yu Lin (2012) studied the current situation of angel investment in China and discovered that it was small scale, relatively concentrated on industries, and China's investment environment was insufficiently internationalized and had to be improved.[19] In his opinion, the government should establish guiding funds; perfect the legal system; and issue tax incentive policies and other financial policies to facilitate the development of angel investment.

III. *Regional Analysis of Angel Investment in China*

In addition to general descriptions of the development of angel investment in the whole country,[20] some scholars also introduced comparative experiences in regional development. Gu Zange and Bu Qingjun took Zhejiang as an example to empirically analyze the role of angel investment in financing high-tech start-up enterprises and proposed suggestions on cultivating angel investment markets.[21] Ma Fengling analyzed practical integration of incubators and angel investment in perspective of hi-tech enterprise incubators.[22] Qin Yi pointed out the presence of multiple types of angel investment — including individual investors, institutional investors and incubators — at the very beginning of angel investment in Wuhan, as well as great government support to angel investment and other market features, contributed to the angel investment field in Wuhan being more developed compared to other cities.[23]

Investigations and Secondary Data of Angel Investment in China

I. *Angel Investment Research in China*

The role of raw data in studies cannot be replaced by secondary data. Upon collection of raw data, researchers will design their own investigation tools, methods and channels based on the purposes of their research. In the process of angel investment, questionnaires and interviews are common methods used to collect raw data. However, both methods are limited to some extent. For example, for questionnaires, the reason "investors are busy, cannot be reached, or will not disclose relevant information," among other reasons, is used to explain a low response rate; making on-site visits to enterprises on the other hand has shortcomings: they cost time, energy and might incur high travelling expenses.

1. Studies on individual angel investors

Angel investors are the primary subjects for the research on angel investment. Questionnaires for angel investors mainly include the following information: basic information about their investment history and background, behavioral characteristics of angel investment, and comments on public policies for angel investment. Specific investigation items and options are given below:

(1) Basic information of an angel investor: pertains, but is not limited to the gender, age, academic degree, major, working years, profession and position of the investor.

(2) Behavioral features of angel investment include, but are not limited to, the investor's angel investment experience, the number of projects he/she has invested in, the number of projects he/she has withdrawn from, the total amount of projects that have been invested in, the proportion of investment in total assets, the average shareholding level of projects, the average returns from projects, capital sources, project sources, investment motives, industries of projects, locations of projects and other features of projects invested; investment strategies, such as main indexes for selecting projects and due diligence, project investigation means, contents of project investigation, investment decision-making period, whether an agreement is signed, whether there is joint capital, participation in post-investment management, and industrial prospect.

(3) Angel investors' opinions on public policies for angel investment are also useful in providing insights into its current state. Some examples of public policies include the establishment of angel investment industrial certification standard, setup of an angel investment industrial information platform, provision of places for incubation of angel investment projects, perfection of an angel investment withdrawing channel mechanism, implementation of angel investment-related preferential tax policies, setup of special risk subsidies for angel

investment, provision of support to angel investment intermediary organizations, establishment of a credit system for the angel investment industry and organizations that have been set up to educate and train angel investors.

2. Studies on angel investment organization

At present, the global angel investment market is developing a trend of including more institutional angel investors, and the subject of angel investment has also become more diversified in China.

(1) Questionnaire investigation. Questionnaires on angel investment organization generally contain information such as basic information, behavioral features of angel investment, and other open questions as mentioned above. Specific investigation items and options are sometimes also explored: investors filling up the questionnaire might have to provide information about, the time and place of the establishment of their organization, its organization type (profitable or non-profitable), its nature (service platform, association, fund company, incubator etc.), its organizational system (membership system or corporate system), capital source, management mode, types of members, angel scale, and what the organization's "regular" activities are.

(2) Open questions. These might contain, firstly, general questions, such as the investor's basic knowledge of angel investment, barriers to development of angel investment in China, operation models of angel investment in China, expectations for the prospect of the angel investment industry, public policy suggestions to facilitate greater levels of angel investment, and international comparisons of angel investment. They might also pertain to professional questions, including the communication mechanism between angel investors and start-up enterprises, organization, operation mode and development of angel investment, the relationship between angel investment and VC/PE, demand of enterprises for value-added angel investment services, strategies for controlling risk of angel investment, bottlenecks in research on the angel investment industry and countermeasures.

3. Studies on start-up enterprises

Start-up enterprises are another subject that studies on angel investment can be focused on. Questionnaires for small and medium-sized enterprises in need of financing at their early stages generally contain basic information about the enterprises, early-stage financing features of the enterprises and their comments on public policies relating to financing at the early stage. Specific investigation items and options include the corporate name, the industry which the enterprise belongs to, gender of the founder, location of the enterprise, date of foundation, current development stage of the enterprise, the number of employees, business income, registered capital and other basic information; source of early-stage capital, whether it has support from angels, the way and content of angel investment, the financing decision-making period, whether and how an agreement is signed, financing behaviors of the enterprise at its early stages and comments on public policies.

II. *Secondary Data of Angel Investment in China*

In current reports, most data are sourced from Zero2IPO Research Center, China Venture Research Institute and other general market investigations. These reports can be used to analyze the profile of the angel investment market, but it is hard to obtain data of individual behaviors, and thus it is impossible to carry out more microscopic studies.

1. Existing study reports

(1) *Commercial organizations*

- *Beijing Software and Information Services Promotion Center.* At the angel investment summit held in China at the end of 2006, Beijing Software and Information Services Promotion Center, Internet Laboratory and New Economy Weekly jointly introduced the first angel investment research report in China. The report gave a comprehensive introduction to the angel investment industry in China on aspects such as its definition, features, operating mode and examples of investment opportunities for angel investors. Quantitative data in this report were mainly derived from investment and financing cases of Internet-based enterprises.

- *Zero2IPO Research Center.* At the end of 2011, Zero2IPO Research Center introduced a Special Research Report on China's angel investment sector. It had relevant definitions and features of angel investors, presented the sector's development history and current conditions for foreign and domestic angel investment, discussed the operating process and development of angel investment, the problems angel investors have encountered, and proposed suggestions to improve the sector. In this report, there was not much quantitative data about China, but more qualitative descriptions and analyses. In November 2012, Zero2IPO Research Center and STEP jointly released a research report titled "China's Angel Investment and Angel Incubation" which described the operating features of China's angel investment based on the statistical data and relevant studies of Zero2IPO Research Center.

- *China Venture Capital Research Institute.* In 2011, China Venture Capital Research Institute carried out an investigation of angel investment over three months, which investigated the characteristics of angel investment and the mechanisms behind the characteristics from the perspective of angel investors, the projects they invested in, their operation processes, and the applicable laws regulations and policies they were subject to.

- *Entrepreneur.* At the annual meeting of entrepreneurs held at the end of 2012, the Entrepreneur Research Center released a report titled, "China's Angel Investment" in 2012. In the report, the Entrepreneur Research Center gave an in-depth analysis of China's angel investment on aspects of investment fields, scale and regions based on in-depth industrial interviews and investigations, collated and summarized well-known angel investment and incubators in both the US and China.

- *China Venture Research Institute.* In November 2013, China Venture Research Institute and STEP jointly released a research report on China's Angel Investment in 2013, in which multiple structures of angel investment subjects were analyzed and practices of angel investment were discussed in combination with data obtained through their study. In July 2014, China Venture Research Institute released the latest data for the first half of 2014.

(2) *Political and academic institutions*

*   *Hefei University of Technology.* From July 2011 to February 2012, Professor Li Yaokuang from the School of Management of Hefei University of Technology led a research team to give out 2,547 copies of questionnaires to financial employees, EMBA and MBA students in higher education institutes. They received 677 completed questionnaires and identified 88 angel investors from these replies. Among the copies received, 78 effective questionnaires were used for statistical information of investors and analysis of investment behaviors and preferences.
*   *CAS Research Center on Fictitious Economy & Data Science.* The research center, where the co-author of this book Prof. Liu Manhong works, established a venture capital research office in August 2012. Investigation of angel investment is a main research subject of the office. In April 2014, the Research Center, jointly with New Huadu Business School, released a Research Report on the Development of China's Angel Investment (2013–2014). In this report, behaviors, organization and policies relating to angel investment were fully collated based on data obtained through questionnaires and interviews.

2. Databases available

Through various investigations, it has been noted that current databases have accumulated partial data relating to angel investment; however, due to lack of scientific concept definition and unison in voice, the databases are independent of each other. Since most angel investment cases are also private, there is a great shortage of relevant data, and history information can only be collected from news media.

(1) *Zero2IPO Research Center.* Zero2IPO Research Center is the most comprehensive, accurate and timely professional database that provides professional and convenient data for many limited partners, VC/PE investors, strategic investors, government organizations, law firms, accounting firms, investment banks, research institutes, listed companies, growth and start-up enterprises, etc.

If we retrieve "angel investment" as the key words,[24] we can obtain the following information:

- 19 entries relate to institutional investors, including information on amounts and types of capital, registration places, and introductions to investment fields.
- 8 entries relate to funds, including information on the raising status, targeted scales, currencies of the funds, registration places, dates of foundation, introduction to fund investment fields and investment strategies.
- 427 entries relate to investors, including introduction to, careers and investment cases of the investors.
- 183 entries relate to investment cases, including information on the investees, investment times, equities, investment amounts, estimated values of enterprises, case introduction and investors.
- Three entries relate to the withdrawal cases, including information on the investors, time and ways of withdrawal, involved enterprises and industries, invested amounts, case introduction.

Generally, the information is scattered and incomplete, and it is still far from satisfaction for scholars to use for academic research.

(2) *CVSource.* In CVSource, information on China's equity investment market, equity transactions, corporate finance and relevant research achievements, analytic data relating to fund raising, fund returns and investment performance, statistic data relating to LP information and investment preference, history investment records, research and analysis of investment strategies and investment trend of active VC/PE organizations are available.

There are two search ways for financing cases: by financing round, i.e. whether it is an angel, or VC-A, VC-B, VC-C, and by enterprise stage, i.e. whether it is in the seed stage, the early stage, the growth stage and other stages.

According to a search based on the financing round of "Angel"[25] and development of the invested enterprises at the "early stage,"[26] the authors of this book found some interesting results. First, enterprises with the company in Angel round are not necessarily at the early stage of development, but may be at the growing stage or the expansion stage (see Figure 4.1). Second, the funding resource of enterprises at the early stage is not necessarily angel capital, but may be A, B, C, D rounds of VC or PE investment (see Figure 4.2). Based on information obtained from the database, it can be preliminarily determined that "angel investment" is considered an investment round in CVSource, generally before VC-A round.

CVSource

资本市场-VC/PE融资 数据导出：

筛选条件：

融资性质：Angel

导出数据如下：

企业	国标行业分类	地区	融资时间	投资机构	投资人	融资性质	发展阶段	金额	
九尾科技	应用软件服务	广东>广州市	2014-04-22	N/A	N/A	Angel	早期	N/A	
梦想邦	互联网信息服务	北京>朝阳区	2014-04-09	N/A	N/A	Angel	早期	N/A	
热气球	互联网信息服务	广东>深圳市	2014-04-01	N/A	N/A	Angel	早期	800.00	万元
海淘贝	互联网信息服务	山东>济南市	2014-03-12	N/A	N/A	Angel	早期	100.00	万元
泡否科技	邮购及电子销售	北京>朝阳区	2014-03-03	N/A	N/A	Angel	早期	6,000.00	万元
钱程网	互联网信息服务	N/A	2014-03-01	N/A	N/A	Angel	早期	N/A	
G友	其他软件服务	广东>深圳市	2014-02-26	N/A	N/A	Angel	早期	136.00	万元
行动派	互联网信息服务	四川>成都市	2014-02-01	N/A	N/A	Angel	发展期	80.00	万元
轻ing	邮购及电子销售	上海>静安区	2014-02-01	华光资本	N/A	Angel	早期	N/A	
孝贤堂	邮购及电子销售	北京>西城区	2014-02-01	真格基金	N/A	Angel	早期	N/A	
Knewbi	互联网信息服务	广东>深圳市	2014-02-01	锴资本/真格基	N/A	Angel	早期	N/A	
钱小二	互联网信息服务	四川>成都市	2014-02-01	N/A	N/A	Angel	早期	N/A	
椰壳网络电台	应用软件服务	上海>徐汇区	2014-01-27	N/A	N/A	Angel	早期	N/A	
领团科技	基础软件服务	北京>海淀区	2014-01-15	N/A	N/A	Angel	早期	N/A	
Bintels	其他软件服务	北京>朝阳区	2014-01-08	N/A	N/A	Angel	早期	20.00	万元
顺付卡	移动电信服务	北京>东城区	2014-01-07	N/A	N/A	Angel	早期	150.00	万元
简单BIZ	其他软件服务	广东>深圳市	2014-01-05	N/A	N/A	Angel	早期	N/A	
百思科技	应用软件服务	北京>海淀区	2014-01-01	N/A	N/A	Angel	扩张期	N/A	
环城洗	互联网信息服务	上海>闵行区	2014-01-01	N/A	N/A	Angel	早期	N/A	

Fig. 4.1 Screenshot of Data Obtained by Searching for Enterprises with Financial Backing of an "Angel."

CVSource

资本市场-VC/PE融资 数据导出：

筛选条件：

发展阶段：早期

导出数据如下：

企业	国标行业分类	地区	融资时间	投资机构	投资人	融资性质	发展阶段	金额	
票巢网	互联网信息服务	广东>广州市	2013-09-28	N/A	N/A	Angel	早期	N/A	
乐视新媒体	电视	天津>滨海新区	2013-09-26	江苏红土	N/A	VC-Series A	早期	1.38	亿元
中粮鸿云置业	房地产开发经营	江苏>南京市	2013-09-26	中城赋比兴天	N/A	PE-Growth	早期	3.67	亿元
Moxtra	互联网信息服务	美国	2013-09-25	创新工场/思科	N/A	VC-Series A	早期	1,000.00	万美元
Hotel Quickly	应用软件服务	中国香港	2013-09-25	N/A	N/A	VC-Series A	早期	116.00	万美元
极路由	通信传输设备制造	北京>海淀区	2013-09-24	N/A	N/A	VC-Series A	早期	N/A	
Distill	其他软件服务	美国	2013-09-18	创新工场/DN	N/A	VC-Series A	早期	130.00	万美元
微步	应用软件服务	浙江>杭州市	2013-09-14	真格基金	N/A	VC-Series A	早期	N/A	
法斗士	互联网信息服务	北京>海淀区	2013-09-11	N/A	N/A	VC-Series A	早期	100.00	万美元
穿衣助手	应用软件服务	上海>杨浦区	2013-09-10	华映资本	N/A	VC-Series A	早期	N/A	
映趣科技	钟表与计时仪器制造	广东>深圳市	2013-09-06	N/A	N/A	VC-Series A	早期	2,000.00	万元
拉勾网	互联网信息服务	北京>朝阳区	2013-09-03	N/A	N/A	Angel	早期	N/A	
基金豆	互联网信息服务	北京>朝阳区	2013-09-01	华创资本	N/A	VC-Series A	早期	N/A	
佳付乐	应用软件服务	上海>浦东新区	2013-09-01	乐搏资本	N/A	VC-Series A	早期	N/A	
发信息啦	其他软件服务	北京>朝阳区	2013-09-01	险峰华兴创投	N/A	VC-Series A	早期	N/A	
鹏比宝科技	应用软件服务	广东>深圳市	2013-09-01	荷多投资	N/A	VC-Series A	早期	N/A	
世界邦	互联网信息服务	北京>朝阳区	2013-09-01	N/A	N/A	Angel	早期	N/A	
追光动画	音像制作	北京>石景山区	2013-09-01	N/A	N/A	VC-Series A	早期	500.00	万美元
淘当铺	互联网信息服务	上海>闵行区	2013-09-01	蓝驰创投	N/A	VC-Series A	早期	N/A	
康康血压	应用软件服务	北京>朝阳区	2013-09-01	N/A	N/A	Angel	早期	400.00	万元
敏想	互联网信息服务	上海>杨浦区	2013-09-01	华岩资本	N/A	VC-Series A	早期	N/A	
阿姨帮	应用软件服务	北京>海淀区	2013-09-01	N/A	N/A	Angel	早期	N/A	
隐私卫士	应用软件服务	福建>福州市	2013-09-01	N/A	N/A	Angel	早期	N/A	
流量超人	应用软件服务	北京>海淀区	2013-09-01	亚信联创	N/A	VC-Series A	早期	N/A	
阿姨厨房	应用软件服务	上海>杨浦区	2013-09-01	中路集团	N/A	VC-Series B	早期	N/A	

Fig. 4.2 Screenshot of Data Obtained by Searching for Enterprises at the "Early Stage."

The database has included nearly 600 entries of data relating to angel investment (1995–2014), which describe some basic features of the angel investment market based on industries. They reveal that angel investment can be found in multiple industries, including retail, manufacturing, finance, electronics and Internet, but mainly in the TMT (technology, media, telecommunication). These data entries also provides regional perspectives and reveal how angel investment is mainly concentrated in Beijing, Shanghai, Guangdong and Zhejiang regions; and they also show that the amount of angel investment ranges between RMB 100,000 to RMB 105 million, and the average financing amount is RMB 3.785 million.

(3) *Online platform for angel investment.* AngelCrunch (http://angel crunch.com/), founded in November 2011, is the first equity-based crowd funding website in China. By March 2014, the website had had 14,000 projects online and 1,000 certified investors. Investors that have been certified by AngelCrunch through evaluation will have their introduction, investment philosophy, value-added services, preferential investment (investment amount and stage, focused industries and investment regions) published on the website.

Methodology of Research on China's Angel Investment

I. *Construction of Theoretical Framework*

Angel investment is a research field involving economics and management science: when it is focused on financial objects, it is in the category of economics; if its research is focused on investment behavior, it is a category of management science. As an equity-financing channel for non-listed enterprises, angel investment can be placed in a category of private placement and a procedure in the financial industrial chain as it has characteristics of financial products. However, angel investment is different from common private equity investment funds. In addition to providing financial support, angel investors focus on early-stage start-up enterprises and help improve governance structure and development of the enterprises; on the other hand, angel investment individuals, organizations or funds have different operating modes, as well as different management styles and decision-making mechanisms. More importantly, the effect of government intervention on the angel investment market with current conditions of low market efficiency is also a part of the existing theoretical research framework (see Figure 4.3).

II. *Sample Selection and Data Collection*

Like many foreign countries, China has scarce empirical data related to angel investment and this has led to great difficulty in scholarly output on the field. From April 2013 to August 2014, the authors of this book carried out a comparative study in nine regions: Beijing, Shanghai, Suzhou, Guangzhou, Shenzhen, Ningbo, Wuhan, Chengdu and Hong Kong. During the investigation, the authors found angel investors who were involved in existing angel investment projects, and new contacts through questionnaires or one-to-one interviews. The questionnaire response rate was only 20% and the interviews proved to be efficient despite the high consumption of time, energy and incurrence of costs. Nevertheless, we think the research cycle will continue to actively explore new approaches to solve research problems that scholars face in this field. At present, bottlenecks are present in two aspects: how to identify angel investors and how to acquire effective data.[27] Some scholars prefer doing research on late-stage investment and secondary market to early-stage investment due to the pressure to publish more academic papers and the pursuit for short-term interests. We think China's research on angel investment is still at the "start-up" stage and the spirit of adventure and persistence is needed. On the other hand, as angel investment is developing fast in China, it is a golden and opportune period to study angel investment theories. Scholars should seize the opportunity to explore the unique "Chinese characteristics" in the area of angel investment and summarize the development patterns of angel investment in China. In our opinion, possible breakthroughs can be made from the following aspects.

1. Capital provider

Public databases can be used to collate a list of angel investors and angel investment organizations. Additional tools that can help in this collation

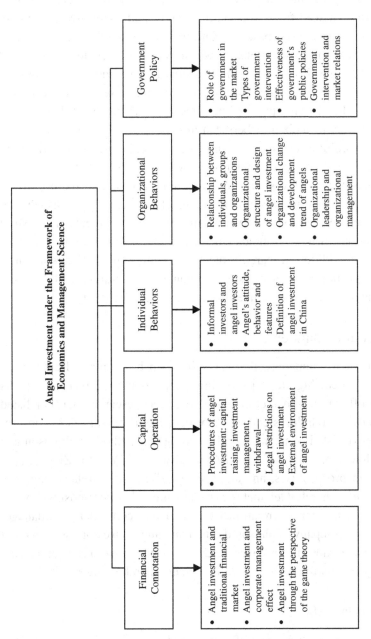

Fig. 4.3 Theoretical Framework of Angel Investment in China.

Source: Authors' own compilation.

include giving out questionnaires via email, postal mail, etc; collating lists of government seed funds and guiding funds, and angel investment case studies, through the databases of Zero2IPO Research Center and China-Venture; providing hyperlinks to websites of research institutions and relevant forum websites; collecting information on associations and investor clubs and other organizations relating to angel investment in different regions — thereby creating opportunities to collaborate with them so that questionnaires to their members can also be given; setting up a special investment column via mainstream financial media outlets and arranging researchers to have special interviews with well-known angel investors and angel investment organizations in China; and adding more in-depth questions to questionnaires, relating to angel investment (such as whether the invested enterprises have ever obtained angel investment) in industrial investigations of relevant fields (such as venture capital, innovative start-up, etc.). In addition, research projects involving senior officers in enterprises, high net-value customers of financial institutions, EMBA/MBA groups and other potential investors can also be carried out.

2. Capital demander

For non-listed companies, the research group has contacted enterprises located in local high-tech parks, high-tech zones and incubator parks through official and market channels to collect research data. For listed companies, shareholders can be identified, based on studies of the prospectuses of listed companies, and by using the methods of Johnson and Sohl,[28] Johnson,[29] and Li Yao and Zhang Ziwei.[30] Li Yao and Zhang Ziwei defined, in prospectuses, an "angel investor" as "an unrelated financial investor or a shareholder that has never undertaken any position in the company or had any correlation with the actual controller and management of the company." Johnson defined an "angel investor" as "a natural person that is not an employee or does not undertake any position and have any correlation with any senior officer (shareholding <=1%)."

3. Secondary data

Secondary data includes identifying special websites of the angel investment field (such as angelcrunch.com, vc.cn, and dajiatou.com) through search engines, collating and analyzing supply-demand information and intermediary service information relating to angel investment projects; obtaining information from angel investment research reports released by media, such as the Research Report on China's Angel Investment (2006), the first research report on the angel investment industry in China, jointly introduced by Beijing Software and Information Services Promotion Center and other organizations, and reports released by Zero2IPO Research Center (2011, 2012, 2014), China Venture Capital Research Institute (2011), Entrepreneur (2012), China Business Angel Association (2013) and China Venture Research Institute (2013), etc.

Case I: Angel Investment Data Service Agency — China Venture

Interview with YANG Xiaolei: "The study of angel investment should be 'practical'."

Time/site: August 1, 2014/Beijing, China

Yang serves as the vice president of ChinaVenture and executive member of Angel Development Camp. Yang is good at strategic planning, organization, operational performance and lean management. He has implemented consulting projects for many medium and large-sized public welfare enterprises in China and has an in-depth understanding of the Internet industry. In his current position, he is in charge of research consulting, financial data and website media. He previously worked in Accenture China and Baidu China and focuses on public welfare and Technology, Media & Telecommunications (**TMT**).

Founded in 2005, ChinaVenture (http://www.chinaventure.cn/) is a leading special service agency on the equity investment market in China and was one of the first news portals for the market in China. It provides professional and multi-level products and services to industries and customers through businesses such as financial data, research consulting, media information, transaction platform, meetings and activities and financial training. Its key product, CVSource data terminal, is an accurate, timely and comprehensive data product in China's equity investment field. It also has a professional research-consulting wing called CVInstitute. Another product called CVMarket provides efficient project matching services for enterprises, investment institutions and financial consultants. Another extension called CVConference is

(Continued)

Case I: (*Continued*)

committed to building a cooperation and communication platform for equity investment industry, and last but not least, CV School of Finance provides customized professional training support for the development of financial enterprises.

Incomplete Disclosure of Early Investment Information

In November 2013, the 2013 Angel and Early Investment Summit organized by Shanghai Technology Entrepreneurship Foundation for Graduates was held in Shanghai and an angel investment research report jointly written by STEPVC and CVInstitute was published. In January and July 2014, CVInstitute officially issued the 2013 Annual Report of Angel Investment in China and Report of Angel Investment in China for the First Half of 2014. These reports were mainly prepared by Yang and his research team.

In his reports, Yang and his team concluded that angel investment is a challenging research field and there are challenging demands and conditions to be met for research purposes. The lack of data has been a common problem in both the enterprise and the research fields. Yang said that he is quite interested in the angel investment field. The research process of angel investment will be smooth if the following are taking place: long-term tracking, conversation with the industry and research continue within ChinaVenture. However, in the process of communication with investors, incomplete disclosure of data for early projects is common. Although some undisclosed data can be obtained through interviews and private communication, these data cannot be easily recorded in the database if one considers confidentiality agreements. Data in angel investment reports are mainly processed based on existing information in the investment database and are properly expanded in fields where data can be relied upon but are still not closely related to actual market conditions.

ChinaVenture Studies: Market-Oriented, Trend-Grasping and Rule-Discovering

Currently, there are a number of institutions engaged in the study of angel investment. In addition to commercial institutions such as investment institutions and consulting companies, government authorities represented by the

(*Continued*)

Case I: (*Continued*)

technology department and local technology bureaus and scholars in universities focused on venture investment fields also study angel investment. Yang believes that each research institution or department more or less has its own data and materials. However, due to different statistical criteria and complicated data sources, the research results of the political circle and academic circle do not accurately describe market realities and are not applicable to market participants. With many years of cooperation with investment institutions, ChinaVenture has obtained some first-hand data through interactive communication and compared with academic institutions and government authorities. ChinaVenture's research results will thus be closer to market realities and therefore, it highly recommends others to learn from the experiences of investors and have more conversations with industry insiders.

In fact, no data from a single institution can reflect actual market conditions and even funds registered with the government may lack some information. Under such conditions where the general angel investment data is lacking, the research reports of ChinaVenture are market-oriented and are not restricted to the analysis of a certain point but focus on the horizontal comparability of data to reflect market trend. Yang highlights the research thinking of ChinaVenture, which is that it does not artificially amplify a certain point but uses some statistical calibers. For example, the number of active investors and investment institutions is crucial to understand their professional experience and market laws so as to avoid result differences caused by the change of sample size as possible.

Defining the Scope of "Angel Investment:" Public Information + Institution Accreditation + Amount Restriction

CVSource investment database has a classification label of "financing nature" when one searches investment cases, including "Angel," "VC" and "PE." Can "angel investment" be defined simply by the investment subject, investment round, and stage of the invested or investment amount? In the "Angel" cases in the database, the following was derived: the authors of this book find that the angle investors not only refer to individual investors, but also to institution investors; the investment amount of certain projects exceeded over RMB 10 million; and not all

(*Continued*)

Case I: (*Continued*)

invested projects are early enterprises. Yang pointed out that there are three aspects to be considered by ChinaVenture for defining the boundaries/scope of angel investment data, which are as follows: firstly, the initial description of first-hand data (i.e. through mainstream media); secondly, individual investment can be regarded as "angel investment." Some individual investors engage in special venture capital investment and there are several fund companies focusing on seed and initial stage start-ups, for example, Inno Angel Fund, LeBox Capital and Unity Ventures; and thirdly, venture investment with the investment amount of Round A investment under RMB 5 million is also considered "angel investment."

To explain the data source of angel investment, Yang also invited senior analyst of ChinaVenture Institute Ms. Li Ling to participate in the interview. Li has written many research reports on angel investment and has an in-depth understanding of angel investment industry. She highlighted that some VC data included institution-based data disclosed in the angel investment report published by ChinaVenture. There is a set of input specification on background operations in ChinaVenture's database. If angel investment appears in individual form, such investment will be input under "angel" item, and if in institution form, such institution will be regarded as "angel institution," and if some investment comes from "venture investment institutions," these cases will be generally input under "VC-SeriesA" item. If the financing amount for an enterprise is less than RMB 5 million, such investment will be regarded as "angel investment case" by ChinaVenture Institution. It can be seen from the above that part of the statistical criteria is from individual "angel" cases and the rest consists of "VC-Series A (VC-Round A)" cases with an investment amount less than RMB 5 million.

The Development of Angel Investment in China Should Stick to Market-Dominated and Government-Supported Principles

The 2013 Annual Report on Angel Investment in China issued by ChinaVenture Institution pointed out that the emergence of angel investment is closely related to the development of the venture capital investment market in China. There is a risk that venture investment has become more PE-like and focuses on late-stage investment, which results in more investment

Case I: (*Continued*)

space for early-stage investment. Angel investment also becomes more VC-like which is highly represented by the emergence of angel investment funds. During my research in the Silicon Valley, I have also discovered some special investment modes such as "Micro-VC" and "Super Angel" in the US. On this point, Yang couldn't agree more. He believes that the resource mismatch is common in China's private equity market. VC in the US supports early projects while the VC (in renminbi) in China is not so comprehensive. Much VC capital is invested in projects with quick returns ("VC PE-like") and pure VC is seen as an "angel investment fund." Currently, the placement size of angel investment funds is increasing rapidly and the operation mode and project selection methods are identical to VC (in US dollars). These funds focus on enterprise innovation, highlight value-added services and exit through the listing of start-ups in capital market.

The emergence of angel investment should be a market behavior and the judgment of ChinaVenture Institution shows that the government should pay more attention to this field to improve external environment and develop more preferential policies (i.e. tax incentives). ChinaVenture Institution issued a report on angel investment policies on July 31, 2014, which pointed out that angel investment is a long process, involves many legal matters and requires the protection of laws and regulations from many aspects at many levels. In China, there are no national laws and policies to regulate the behavior of angel investors beyond local policies on angel investment. The report also highlighted that angel investment is an important financial source of support for the development of start-ups and the government should increase their efforts in developing angel investment policies.

Notes

1. Stephen Prowse, 'Angel Investors and the Market for Angel Investments,' *Journal of Banking & Finance*, 1998, 22(6–8): 785–792.
2. László Szerb, Gábor Rappai, Zsolt Makra and Siri Terjesen, 'Informal Investment in Transition Economies: Individual Characteristics and Clusters,' *Small Business Economics*, 2007, 28(2): 257–271.
3. William E. Wetzel, Jr, 'Angels and Informal Risk Capital,' *Sloan Management Review*, 1983, 24(4): 23–34.

4. Richard T. Harrison and Colin M. Mason, 'International Perspectives on the Supply of Informal Venture Capital,' *Journal of Business Venturing*, 1992, 7(6): 459–475.

5. A. Ellen Farrell, 'Informal Venture Capital Investment in Atlantic Canada: A Representative View of Angels,' A Report Submitted to the Atlantic Canada Opportunities Agency, Moncton, 1998.

6. Patrick Coveney and Karl Moore, *Business Angels: Securing Start Up Finance*, John Wiley & Sons, 1998.

7. Yasuhisa Tashiro, 'Business Angel in Japan,' *Venture Capital: An International Journal of Entrepreneurial Finance*, 1999, 1(3): 259–273.

8. Lusi E. Pereiro, 'Tango and Cash: Entrepreneurial Finance and Venture Capital in Argentina,' *Venture Capital*, 2001, 3(4): 291–308.

9. Poh Kam Wong, and Yuen Ping Ho, 'Characteristics and Determinants of Informal Investment in Singapore,' *Venture Capital*, 2007, 9(1): 43–70.

10. Sofia Avdeitchikova, On the Structure of the Informal Venture Capital Market in Sweden: Developing Investment Roles,' *Venture Capital*, 2008, 10(1): 55–85.

11. Aruna Chandra and Magda Narczewska, 'Business Incubator Financing and Financial Services in Chile,' Working Paper, available at http://ssrn.com/abstract=1377802.

12. Vincenzo Capizzi and Giovanni Tirino, 'The Scale, Growth and Returns of Informal Venture Capitalists' Investments in Italy,' Working Paper, available at http://ssrn.com/abstract=1927878.

13. Liu Tingchi and Chen Po Chang, 'Business Angel Investment in China Market,' *Singapore Management Review*, 2007, 29(2): 89–101.

14. Yaokuang Lia, Shuoyuan Jiang, Dan Long, Huidao Tang and Juan Wu, 'An Exploratory Study of Business Angels in China: A Research Note,' *Venture Capital: An International Journal of Entrepreneurial Finance*, 2014, 16(1): 69–83.

15. Zhujun Ding, Sunny Li Sun, Kevin Au, 'Angel Investors' Selection Criteria: A Comparative Institutional Perspective,' *Asia Pacific Journal of Management*, 2014, 31(3): 705–731; Zhujun Dinga, Kevin Au and Flora Chiang, 'Social Trust and Angel Investors' Decisions: A Multilevel Analysis Across Nations,' *Journal of Business Venturing*, 2015, 30(2): 307–321.

16. Li Yaokuang, Yao Qian and Jiang Zhuqing, 'Exploration on Operation Models of Angel Investment in China,' *Journal of Hefei University of Technology* (*Social Science*), 2011, 2: 11–15. (In Chinese)

17. Shao Kun, 'Exploring Operation Models of Angel Investing in China,' *Capital Market*, 2012, 3: 104–105. (In Chinese)

18. Xu Hao, 'On the Factors Limiting Development of Angel Investing in China and the Solutions,' *Business Culture* (second semimonthly), 2011, 11: 138. (In Chinese)

19. Yu Lin, 'On the Current Status of Angel Investment in China and Measures for Further Development,' *Reformation & Strategy*, 2012, 10: 66–68. (In Chinese)

20. Chen Honghui and Zhao Zhengtang, 'Angel Investment: Status Quo, Problems and Solutions,' *Market Weekly*, 2004, 8: 34–35 (In Chinese); Li Yaokuang and Ang Zhaowen, 'Building Operation Models of Angel Investing in China,' *Review of Investment Studies*, 2009, 6: 42–44 (In Chinese); Yu Lin, 'On the Current Status of Angel Investment in China and Measures for Further Development,' *Reformation & Strategy*, 2012, 10: 66–68. (In Chinese)

21. Gu Zange and Bu Qingjun, 'Study on the Role of Angel Investment in High-tech Start-ups,' *Journal of Industrial Technological Economics*, 2005, 12: 136–139. (In Chinese)

22. Ma Fengling, 'Practice of Angel Investing of S&T Business Incubator in Tianjin,' *Perspectives of Science & Technology Achievement*, 2012, 6: 16–17. (In Chinese)

23. Qin Yi, 'On the Current Status of Angel Investment in Wuhan and Measures for Further Development,' *Pioneering with Science & Technology Monthly*, 2013, 11: 44–43. (In Chinese)

24. Accessed on July 15, 2014.

25. In CVSource, the financing nature of Angel refers to the event type of investment by an angel investor.

26. In CVSource, early-stage enterprises include enterprises at their seed and start-up stages. Enterprises at the seed stage are mainly engaged in initial research and development of products or services, when the enterprises are just established or under preparation, with no management team formed and no income from the market; enterprises at the start-up stage have primary products and services that have not been put into production or application, implement rough operation plans, have incomplete management teams, with almost no user or income from the market.

27 In November 2013, the research team had an exchange with Professor Li Yaokuang, a leading scholar of the angel investment field in China. The conclusions that arose from the discussion are that identification of angel investors and acquisition of data are the greatest bottlenecks restricting research on angel investment in China.

28. William Johnson and Jeffrey E. Sohl, 'Initial Public Offerings and Pre-IPO Shareholders: Angels Versus Venture Capitalists,' *Journal of Developmental Entrepreneurship*, 2012, 17(4): 1250022, 23 pages.

29. William C. Johnson, 'Private Firm Investors and Product Market Relationships: Certification and Networking,' *Journal of Economics and Business*, 2013, 65 (January–February): 55–85.
30. Li Yao and Zhang Ziwei, 'Private Equity, Angel Capital and the IPO Underpricing on ChiNext Stock Market,' *Journal of Finance and Economics*, 2011(8). (in Chinese)

Chapter 5

How Founders Can Win Over Investors

Pre-Financing Preparations

I. *Importance of Having a Business Plan*

A business plan is the declaration of entrepreneurship. It is the complete description of project development blueprint by the founders, is the first step to successfully attract funding and is the bridge for comprehensive communication between the start-up's founders and angel investors. Any enterprise that wishes to obtain angel investment should provide a detailed business plan to the angel investors as it provides the basis for angel investors to conduct a comprehensive evaluation on the start-up. For start-ups looking for funds, the business plan is like a business card. The quality of the business plan may determine the success of the enterprise's financing activity.

The importance of having a business plan is shown in two aspects. Firstly, it can help founders have a clear understanding of how they would want the project to develop. The founder should ask himself what is the rationale behind this project. By developing a business plan, the founder can clear their thinking and test their core concepts one by one. In this way, the founder can have a clearer understanding of the project so that their thought process is rational and aligned to real-world conditions. One angel investor said that if you want to sell the enterprise to others, you have first sell it to yourself. The process of writing a business plan will enable the founder to build confidence, passion and expectations for their prospective enterprise. Secondly, a business plan can also help the founder to sell the start-up to angel investors, VC investors or other investors and raise the required funds which can in turn, help attract more business partners.

Of course, an excellent business plan is the cornerstone of success but the real challenges begin when the founder meets with angel investors who are interested in investing in their projects. This is a major test on the personal charm and communication skills of the founder. Only the founder can persuade the angel investor the competitiveness of the project and assure the angel investor of the maximum return on investment (ROI) so that angel investors will invest and give the founder the opportunity and responsibility of managing the enterprise. When writing a business plan, some founders place too much stress on the future of the enterprise and neglect the potential return of the investors; thus failing to take into account the investors' perspective. The founder can only be recognized by the investor if he considers the interests of the latter and connects the enterprise's future with the future of the investors. Investors after all take great risks by investing money in start-ups; in this sense, the investors are the founder's business partners.

In sum, a detailed and well-proven business plan can play a key role on the successful financing of the founder and future development of the start-up. A rational business plan can attract the attention and favor of angel investors who may have interviews with the founders before making any investments. Therefore, an enterprise's business plan is key to obtaining angel investment and is integral to the success of the start-up's initial financial future.

A business plan is also important in the following aspects:

1. The angel investor is not a relative or friend of the founder

Angel investors are a group of "angels" who have led successful careers, have accumulated enough capital, and they are passionate about entrepreneurship. They are willing to help founders, who they believe have a bright future, with their capital, experience and intelligence. For them, the founder is also a stranger and the business plan is hence a bridge connecting two strangers.[1]

2. The important role played by the business plan

The business plan not only can help potential investors understand the general condition, development prospect, cash flow and other financial conditions of the start-up. More importantly, it can help the founder to streamline their entrepreneurship concepts, analyze their strengths and weakness, harvest the development potential of the start-up and identify the bottlenecks hampering its development.

For the above reasons, the business plan should be preferably written by the founder and not by external parties as a business plan which is copied or "purchased" might fail to convince angel investors the potential of the project. This is because firstly, only the founder knows the real entrepreneurship concept, core technology concept and key important market development potential well. Secondly, the investor might only be convinced about the potential of the project if the founder pitches his idea and business plan. Thirdly, the founder can streamline his ideas, the entrepreneurship concept and elaborate on its core competitiveness by writing the business plan. Many founders discover their weaknesses during the course of writing the business plan and might eventually see their development potential or competitive advantage that they did not know before. The founder should hence regard the writing of the business plan as a compulsory process for streamlining their thoughts.

3. The executive summary of a concise and comprehensive business plan is of critical importance

Angel investors generally do not have time to read through each business plan as they tend to receive many at any one point of time. During the initial selection process, angel investors tend to only read the executive summary on the first page. Therefore, the executive summary should be placed on the first page when the business plan is submitted to an angel investor or angel investment institutions. If the angel investors are interested, they will ask the founder for the entire business plan.

II. *Four Elements of a Business Plan*

According to the research of Professor William Sahlman from Harvard Business School, the four elements of a business plan are people, opportunity, environment and risk/return balance analysis.[2]

1. People

This element mainly covers who is the founder, the management personnel, the target consumer group, the suppliers, patent owner, etc. Angel investors care very much about the qualification, competence and determination of the management team. Most angel investors believe that the management team is the key to the success of each angel investment.

The résumé of the founder should also be attached to the business plan, whch will be examined by investors. They will look at the education background, experience, social connections, entrepreneurship experience, success or failure of entrepreneurship, past performance, related experience and complementary skill sets of the team. Of course, before making investment, the angel investors will conduct a field trip to the start-up's office site to ensure consistency with the description that has been laid out in the business plan. In some sense, the field visit by investors to the start-up is like the four diagnostic methods, which are look, listen, question and feel:

Look: Observations will be made about the founder — including the confidence, physical and mental health, patience and cooperative spirit of the founder.

Listen: Investors will listen to other people's opinion on the founder from other sources, for example, company employees, family members, friends, suppliers, etc.

Question: Investors will ask the founders some questions, for example, the current state of operation, financial condition, cash flow, production and sales, etc.

Feel: Investors will get a feel of what state the start-up is in by visiting the start-up's office/site to check if the reality matches with the written description of operations as laid out by the founder.

Angel investors care more about the founder's experience of failure. They believe that success comes from experience while experience comes from failure. A successful founder may attribute his success to many contingent factors while an unsuccessful founder will learn from his failure. Some angel investors tend to gravitate towards founders with experience of unsuccessful ventures as they believe that these founders have perseverance, are strong-willed and resilient. Over the course of their history, the Walt Disney Company announced seven bankruptcies and Ford also announced two bankruptcies. Failure is not a terrible thing and the most terrible thing occurs if one cannot recover after a setback.

With regards to failure, the Chinese should learn from the Westerners: to admit, tolerate and accept failure instead of blindly celebrating success. China's publicity of entrepreneurship should not only tell successful stories but also should tell unsuccessful stories, in particular the stories of founders who are resilient after failures. There are many failure cases among all common teaching cases of Harvard Business School. These unsuccessful stories are more thought-provoking than successful stories. People can learn the deep meaning from failures instead of surface success experienced by successful start-ups/enterprises. In sum, success is desirable, but failure is not a shameful thing. The traditional idea that "the winner takes it all" should be abandoned. Indeed, the fund manager Bill Unger of Mayfield VC Fund considers the failure experience of a founder as an important factor in his investment criteria.

2. Opportunity

Opportunities should be elaborated in long length in the business plan, covering four aspects: (A) Is the enterprise part of a rising industry? (B) Is the product/service competitive? (C) What is the business model (i.e. how will the enterprise make money)? If the enterprise comes from a flourishing industry or its product/service is competitive, which business model should the enterprise adopt to make profits? The description of business models is an important part of the discussion of "opportunity." The existence of business opportunity indicates that there are some issues to be solved in the market. For these to-be-solved issues, which specific solution should the entrepreneurs adopt to solve these issues? And last but not least: (D) Who is the enterprise's competitor? If there is no exiting competitor, will there be any potential rivals? What is the particularity of the enterprise? What makes the enterprise competitive?

3. Environment

Generally, the environment refers to the macroeconomic environment, political environment and legal environment. Since 2008, the impact of the financial crisis has spread from the US across nearly every corner in the world and the world economy has witnessed the severest economic setback since World War Two. The harsh macroeconomic environment inevitably exerts a huge impact on the entrepreneurs. Apart from the macroeconomic environment, the political environment and the legal environment also affect the entrepreneurs. Assuming that a country is undergoing political turmoil, the entrepreneurship and the investment will without a doubt be confronted with barriers. In addition, state laws and regulations, as well as tax policies in particular, will have a direct impact on the success or failure of the entrepreneurship; tax incentives are hence essential to the successful materialization of a business plan.

4. Risk–benefit analysis

Any kind of start-up will inevitably be confronted with certain risks and the angel investors who provide entrepreneurs with external funds will face the risks associated with these uncertainties. People often have a misunderstanding that the entrepreneurs are keen on taking risks. The entrepreneurs, however, only spot the opportunities and decide to pursue their plans when the opportunities outweigh the risks they may face. The entrepreneurs are therefore often optimists. They see the opportunities, the potential rewards are great, and that the financial future of their ideas are bright. But they often underestimate the risks, the difficulties and the financing gap. In their mind, the benefits play a larger part than the risks. In comparison, angel investors tend to be more prudent in terms of making investment in start-ups. As previously mentioned, the entrepreneurs should put themselves in the investors' shoes and think about not just how to make money for the enterprise but also how it can be developed. The entrepreneurs should figure out the answer to these questions: why should the investors have an interest in my enterprise? Why do they invest in projects? Under what circumstances will they invest or not invest? In the risk-benefit analysis made in the business plan, the entrepreneurs should elaborate on the exit strategy, the exit timing and the benefits of the exit. In sum, simply thinking from the perspective of an entrepreneur will not help the entrepreneur secure any angel investment and it is important for the entrepreneur to put himself in the investors' shoes.

III. *Principles that Apply to the Preparation of a Business Plan*

1. Be clear, objective and concise

It should be clear to the entrepreneurs that angel investors will read many business plans every day, among which, only a few can draw their attention. For this reason, a sound business plan should draw the angel investors' attention within a few minutes. A concise abstract or overview is important; it summarizes the business plan in terms of its content but its length is short (normally one to two pages) and it is not in-depth. An effective business plan often introduces the general situation as well as the features and the strengths of the company to the investor in a very short period of time.

A business plan is after all, not the end, but the start of the financing process for an enterprise. In consequence, every figure should be evidence-based as far as possible. Unrealistic exaggeration of potential income and underestimation of cost are considered taboo to the investors.

2. Get one's ideas into shape

As mentioned earlier, a business plan will help shape the entrepreneur's thought process, help the entrepreneur investigate thoroughly the external market conditions, and the internal advantages and disadvantages of the enterprise rationally. The most time-consuming part of the business plan preparation is the comprehensive investigation and survey of the market, and the collection of various kinds of information. The entrepreneur should analyze the industry and think about the development prospect carefully, figure out the mission he has undertaken as well as the challenge, the opportunity and the uncertainties confronted by the enterprise, and understand the development trend of the industry that the enterprise is part of.

3. Technology and market positioning

The technical and market details may be attached to the business plan in the form of an appendix. Many enterprises were once engaged in technical work, and they often elaborate on the innovativeness and the selectivity of their technology in the business plan and ignore the fundamental issue, i.e. how to transform the technology into commercial products. While technology, without a doubt, is important, knowing the market, product, industry and business model, is essential. Meanwhile, the entrepreneur should prepare a powerpoint presentation, which can not only help the audience be clear about the business plan but also enhance future road shows to attract more investors.

4. Put yourself into the investors' shoes

The entrepreneur should review the business plan from the perspective of the angel investors. He should assume that he is an angle investor who is going to invest with the capital that has been hard-earned, and figure out the risks associated with the investment and the factors requiring prudent consideration. Prospective earnings, risk prevention, business model and the entrepreneur's exit strategy are some of the factors that an investor would keep in mind when reading a business proposal.

5. Fewer visions and more details

Many entrepreneurs make the mistake of describing rosy prospects at length while overlooking the entrepreneurial process. However, detail should not be sacrificed as details are what attract interest from prospective angel investors.

IV. *Notes on Business Plan: "9 + 14"*

The business plan may vary according to the industry, product, region and consumer base. However, regardless of the content, the following specific questions should be answered. The questions below include 9 questions about the enterprise's business model and 14 questions about the entrepreneurs.[3]

The description about the business model should be able to answer the following nine questions:

1. Who is the target consumer?
2. What makes the consumer decide to use your product/service?
3. To what extent is your product/service a necessity to the consumer?
4. How to price your product/service?
5. How will your product/service reach your target consumer group?
6. What's the per capita cost (time and resources) of additional consumer?
7. How much will the production and the marketing of your product/service cost?
8. How much will it cost to provide one consumer with sales and after-sales service?
9. How much will it cost to retain existing consumers?

Apart from these nine business model-related questions, details about the entrepreneur as well as the entrepreneur's team should be stated in the business plan as people play a decisive role in entrepreneurial process.

The following are 14 people-related questions:

1. Where are they from?
2. What's their education background?
3. Where have they worked and whom have they worked for?
4. What achievement has they accomplished at work or in life?
5. How is their reputation in their business circles?
6. How many experiences do they have which are related to this entrepreneurship?
7. What skills, knowledge and capacities do they have?
8. Have they fully understood the probability of success and the potential risks they may face?
9. Does the team require reinforcement and what kind of talents do they need?
10. Are they willing to accept more experienced and capable talents?
11. How do they cope with the inevitable difficulties in the entrepreneurial process?

12. Do they have the courage to start a business?
13. Will they go all out for it?
14. What is your/their motive to start this business?

V. *Format and Content of Business Plan*

A complete business plan should comprise following contents: the abstract of business plan, the mission statement, the company profile, the product or service, the competition, the risk-benefit analysis, the management team, the financing needs, the financial plan and the appendix.

1. Abstract

The abstract is an overall introduction to the business plan. It briefs the reader on the overall content and is the essence of the business plan. Under general circumstances, the angel investors may read the abstract for information and decide whether he should read further. It is thus clear that the abstract is of great importance. The abstract should be clear, concise, objective, logical and plain.

2. Mission statement

The mission statement describes the mission of the entrepreneur in one sentence.

3. Company profile

The company profile mentioned here is not a summary of the company in a general sense, but a more comprehensive introduction covers aspects such as the development goal, the market competition strategy and the development strategy of the company. The company profile makes more comprehensive supplements to the previously mentioned brief introduction and details following information: (A) Basic information such as the company name, location, time of establishment, registered capital, major shareholders, equity ratio, main business, past business performance and brief introduction to the main management staff; (B) Scope of business; (C) Development target; (D) Organizational structure; (E) Human resources development plan, including recruitment plan, employee training plan, remuneration and bonus system and incentive system; (F) Introduction to the engaged financial consultant, accountants, lawyers and bankers, including associated expenses and business transactions.

4. Product or service

The description of the product or service should be succinct and accurate to avoid the overuse of terms and jargons. Do describe the use and benefits of the product or service and the patents and government approvals related to the product.

The core of a business plan is the product or service proposal and the value of the product or service to the end user. The market value of a product or service is mainly reflected by two features: (A) The uniqueness of the technology — the angel investors expect the product or service to be unique in terms of the technology and the means, which will increase the technical barriers to entry encountered by similar products or services. The higher the technical barriers to entry are, the higher the price may be charged for the product or service; (B) The profitability of the technology. These two features are two exact unique advantages which the enterprise should cultivate.

5. Marketing

Whether a technology is advanced or not is not an indication of market share and only those technologies that can satisfy the market demand are viable. The success and failure of an enterprise depends on the popularity of the products among the consumers. Technological achievements are not necessarily commercial products. The key is to transform scientific and technological achievements into real commercial products. In a sense, the success or failure of an enterprise depends on its marketing campaigns. People sometimes compare enterprise to a group with marketing at the center. There are only two divisions in an enterprise: the marketing division and the division supporting the marketing division. What can an enterprise offer and what the market needs determine what kind of product/service the enterprise will provide. The analysis of market covers the analysis of the industry to which the enterprise belongs. For instance, what's the development status of the enterprise in the industry? What's the development trend of the industry? How do innovation and technological advancement affect the industry? How do economic development and government policies affect the industry? An enterprise should be able to describe the complete picture of the target industry and point out the factor that will exert the core influence on the development of the industry.

6. Competition

The key to a successful business plan is to conduct a comprehensive analysis of the market competition. Opportunities indicate competition. No entrepreneurs can say that she/he has no rivals. Only under two circumstances an entrepreneur may think there are no competitors: the so-called market does not exist or you have not recognized existing and potential rivals. The market is a carrier of the commodity economy; the commodity indicates the market and the market indicates competition. Competition is unavoidable for the survival and development of enterprises. Entrepreneurs should carefully observe the market competition situation and be prepared in advance.

7. Risk–benefit analysis

This part analyzes various potential risks the enterprise may encounter in future development and points out the promising profit outlook. Conducting a dishonest risk analysis is irresponsible for the entrepreneur himself as well as the funds provided by the investors. The risks associated with entrepreneurship include: technical risk, market risk, process risk, production risk, political risk, macro-environment risk, legal risk, policy risk, exchange rate risk, and of course, the biggest risk is always the "people risk," i.e. the management risk. Angel investors expect entrepreneurs to conduct a thorough and comprehensive analysis of the potential risks faced by the project, because on the one hand, a comprehensive analysis enables investors to know the risk awareness of the entrepreneurs and on the other hand, it provides investors with basis for risk evaluation. Every possible risk, no matter how trivial it seems, requires careful treatment so as to ensure safe investment.

Under the premise of conducting comprehensive analysis of various risks, the ROI and exit strategy proposal are also issues of concern to investors. Investors make investments for promising returns. For this reason, entrepreneurs should estimate the ROI for angel investors in their business plan.

8. Management team

Apart from good technology, having a good-quality product and being part of a booming market, a sound management team that is responsible for implementing the business plan plays a critical role in the success of an enterprise. When choosing potential investees, some venture capitalists believe the team is the most important factor for the business. They prefer an A-team with a B-plan to an A-plan with a B-team. A mediocre project run by a first-rate management team often succeeds in the end because a good team will consider the situation from an objective perspective and make appropriate adjustments to the original plan to make it more feasible and effective. An excellent business plan run by a mediocre team, on the other hand, often fails.

An outstanding management team often has the following features: (A) Common goals and values; (B) Complementing each other's advantages through quality, capability and experience; (C) Comprised of at least two to three people; and (D) United as one.

Luis Villalobos, the founder of Tech Coast Angels and winner of 2006 Hans Severiens Award, once pointed out that the key of angel investment is to select the right entrepreneurial team, and the right CEO of the entrepreneur team in particular. Villalobos believed that the CEO of the enterprise should be upright, selfless, hardworking and brave enough to take responsibilities and risks, have in-depth knowledge in business model, and pay attention to the details as well as the interests of the whole team.

For many angel investors, people are the most important factor. When they review investment projects, they tend to focus on the management team of the projects. This is quite similar to what venture capitalists do. Bill Unger, a famous venture capitalist, has six criteria for selecting entrepreneurs: He believes that a promising entrepreneur should possess the following characteristics:

(1) He has failed in the past and learnt his lessons in a bitter way. People who have experiences of failure will recall the painful experiences and learn the lessons. Entrepreneurs with such experiences tend to be more experienced, persistent and tenacious.

(2) People he hires should have experiences of rapid promotion in their career because an entrepreneur should be able to tell who has talents. They should be able to recognize talents. A successful enterprise relies on the people, i.e. a good team with executive capacity, in the end.

(3) The entrepreneur should have been engaged in different jobs because an outstanding entrepreneur should be flexible. The entrepreneur should be able to adjust his business model frequently to adapt to the ever-changing market. An entrepreneur who has been engaged in different jobs will therefore be more flexible to such changes.

(4) He should have work experience in small enterprises. We know that big firms have complex and complete organizational structure and employees are only familiar to their own departments or assigned jobs and lack the ability of big-picture thinking. However, people who have worked in small companies are often "jack of all trades" and may cope with various situations and coordinate between different departments.

(5) He is not afraid of details and trifling tasks; he might even be willing to clean the toilet. People who have grandiose aims but puny abilities will not be able to run an enterprise.

(6) He does not seek quick success and instant benefits. Entrepreneurship is arduous and time-consuming. People who lack patience and long-term plans will not succeed. Entrepreneurs who seek quick success and instant benefits not only lack patience and tenacity but also are shortsighted, and therefore, are not the first choice of angel investors.

(7) Many entrepreneurs do not specify the financing needs in their business plans, which implies that the more financial assistance provided, the better. However, an appropriate financing amount is good for the

development of the enterprise as well as the entrepreneur himself. How should one define the appropriate financing amount? An appropriate financing amount means the minimum amount required to support the normal operation of the enterprise, or the minimum amount of invested capital needed by the enterprise. Larger financing amount means more equity transferred and higher cost.

9. Financial plan

For an enterprise at seed-stage, a financial plan for future development should be created. For an enterprise at start-up stage, the financial statements for the past one or three years and the current financial statement should be provided, including balance sheets, cash flow statements, income statements and annual financial statements so that angel investors can analyze the financial position of the enterprise. Although income statement cannot reflect the actual situation of start-ups, it can be used to check whether the entrepreneur know the importance of financial management.

10. Attachment

Provide relevant proving documents, including market survey, market survey report and relevant references.

According to the requirements imposed by The US Small Business Administration, the above mentioned contents of the business plan may be summarized into four parts: company profile; marketing; financial plan; and management structure.

Searching for Angel Investors

I. *Who are Angel Investors*

Angel investors are called "business angels" or "informal venture capitalists" in Europe. They are affluent individuals who are willing to provide capital for start-ups and they are also professional investors. They usually make investments in exchange for ownership equity, but sometimes do so for convertible debt.

With money and passion, angel investors want to make profits and assist start-ups to realize their dreams by helping these enterprises financially. With their money and experience, they proactively participate in the development of a start-up while making money. In other words, angel investors are rich people with dreams and practical thinking. They are usually successful entrepreneurs, bankers, investors, senior executives, artists, athletes, movie stars, etc. With all the money they have, these people do not need to work any longer and can enjoy their life by traveling or vacationing. On the one hand, they cannot resist the temptation to participate in the innovative or entrepreneurial activities, or in the development of novel products or services. On the other hand, they do not want to or need to spend all their time managing the operations of a company like an entrepreneur. To many affluent angel investors, travel, vacation or gourmet foods cannot delight them or satisfy them spirituality. They need to do something "meaningful" and angel investment is their best choice, since they can take part in a business without being trapped in some specific duties and thus enjoy their own time and space. Angel investors do not advertise themselves. Instead, they work for what they are keen on working behind the scenes without being noticed.

Many successful entrepreneurs have become angel investors. One of them is Chris Sacca, the founder of Google. He became a millionaire in his early 30s and managing Google was no longer a challenge for him. Like other people who worked in Google since its early years, Sacca amassed a large fortune through the stock option trade and began to make angel investments. He often tells people that angel investment is one of the most interesting jobs in the world as it is challenging and might yield tremendous returns.

Many people think only the affluent could become angel investors, which might not be true. While many angel investors are rich people, for example, Paul Allen, the founder of Microsoft, H. Ross Perot, the founder of EDS and an independent presidential candidate, and Mark Cuban, a famous rich person and the owner of Dallas Maverick. Nevertheless, a lot of angel investors are ordinary middle-class people who have some wealth and are willing to help start-ups.

According to the London Angel Investment Association,[4] angel investors are mostly male (95%) aged between 45 and 65. In the United Kingdom

(UK) the average investment amount in one project by an angel investor was between £20,000 and 30,000, or about £27,500 (about RMB 300,000 at the end of 2008). One in two angel investors are willing to devote 25% of their personal assets at most to angel investment,[5] while others are willing to devote 50% or more of their assets to angel investment. Angel investors do not fear challenges or risks and are, thus, real angels for start-ups. They make investment not only for profits, but also for their personal interests.

Professor Scot Shane of Case Western Reserve University has proven that angel investors are different from what ordinary people believe they are. They are not really rich and most of them are blue-and-white collar workers. Many of them only invest in several projects and the investment totals less than US$10,000. Many of these investors have no time to manage the invested enterprises. Also, many of them lack the experience of investment and cannot focus on the invested project the way professional investors (i.e. venture capitalists) would. Thus, they need cooperation, education, and mentoring.

According to research done by Beijing Private Technology Entrepreneurs Association in 2007, angel investors in China could be divided into five categories: (1) foreign companies' representatives in China or senior executives; (2) foreigners, overseas Chinese and returnees who think China is a promising market; (3) domestic rich people and private entrepreneurs; (4) entrepreneurial and angel funds launched by the government; and (5) agencies such as angel investors clubs or angel investment management companies.[6]

II. *Overview of Angel Investors*

According to the Center for Venture Research of University of New Hampshire in the US, angel investors have an average age of 47 years old; their annual incomes and net assets are US$90,000–750,000. Most of angel investors have got bachelor degrees or finished further education. The mean amount of investment in each project is US$37,000 and most of the angel investment is over US$100,000. Angel investors are more willing to invest in places that they are familiar with such as places that they have settled down in. In fact, 70% of angel investors only invest in projects within a 50-mile radius around their homes or working places.

Angel investors want to make money, but they also want something more. Most angel investors are keen on starting up a business. Statistically, 90% of the angel investors like to invest in small enterprises or start-ups with fewer than 20 employees on average. Apart from equity investment, 90% of the angel investors also provide private loans or loan guarantee for the invested enterprises.

Compared with ordinary blue-and-white collar workers, angel investors are generally older, boast higher income and have received better education. They are also willing to take risks, and some even claim that at least 30% of the investment would not see any returns.

However, Chinese angel investors have unique characteristics. Angel investment is a novel concept in China, and is new to many people. Even though many successful entrepreneurs, financiers and senior executives have made angel investment in entrepreneurial enterprises — start-ups in particular — in exchange for equity, they do not have a clear definition about angel investment or its operation. These angel investors are learning while practicing. The specific conditions of Chinese angel investors will be detailed in Chapter 9.

III. *Definition of Accredited Investors*

Is there any standard to judge an angel investor? Who can become an angel investor? Besides personal interests, the most important key to an angel investor is economic strength. In other words, an angel investor could also be an accredited investor. The US Small Business Administration estimated that there were at least 250,000 American angel investors investing in promising enterprises for higher-than-average returns. To help potential investors avoid risks, the Securities and Exchange Commission issued the so-called standards for determining "an accredited investor."

According to the security acts in the US,[7] an accredited investor should be:

(1) A bank, insurance company, registered investment company, business development company, or small business investment company certified by the Small Business Administration;
(2) An employees' retirement scheme covered in the insurance scheme of employees retirement income and administrated by a bank, insurance

company or registered investment consultant firm, or an employees' retirement scheme boasting at least US$5 million;

(3) A charity organization, company or partnership with capital fund of US$5 million at least;

(4) A director, executive or common partner of a company selling securities;

(5) A company of which all directors are accredited investors;

(6) A natural person boasting net assets over US$1 million, individually or with his/her spouse;

(7) A natural person who boasts the individual annual income of over US$200,000 during the latest two years or the annual family income over US$300,000 and whose income is estimated to remain stable in the next few years; and

(8) A trust company with total commissioned assets of over US$5 million.

This definition is also adopted when people identify who is an angel investor. Generally, "accredited investors" as mentioned above are also accredited angel investors. According to Pankaj Mishra, Globevestor, an equity-based crowd funding platform in the US, among the 900,000 accredited investors in the country, 250,000 are active angel investors.[8] With the development of economy and the increase of people's income, the above-mentioned security acts are behind the times. In December 2006, the Securities and Exchange Commission amended its regulation about the natural person being "an accredited investor" to regulate people who participate in hedge funds and private investment funds. According to the amended article, as an accredited investor, a natural person should not only satisfy the abovementioned eight items, but should also have made an earlier investment of US$2.5 million. Moreover, the amount of investment (US$2.5 million) must be constantly adjusted according to the inflation factor.

In fact, the definition of "accredited investors" is only for reference and has no legal effects. In other words, an angel investor is not necessary an accredited investor. The government only suggests that an angel investor be an accredited investor. On the one hand, only accredited investors are capable of avoid certain risks. On the other hand, people with less income or net assets suffer greater risk and are likely to lose the ability to obtain living necessities in case of any failed investment.

An unspoken rule for angel investors is only investing in what you can lose. That is to say that an angel investor should never invest more money than he can lose. Let us make a hypothetical example: Both John and Peter are accredited investors and both of them have invested US$250,000. Unfortunately, the two persons' investment failed and all their money came to nothing. Unhappy as he is, John keeps working and enjoys his life, as if the money that has been lost is not a big loss. However, Peter regrets the investment and keeps blaming himself for making such a careless mistake. He keeps thinking, "Why haven't I used the money more wisely? I could have bought a yacht, a forest or some stocks..." Depressed as he is by this predicament, Peter cannot eat or sleep well because of the failure. According to the story, one can see that John should have invested more than US$250,000 while Peter should have invested much less.

In other words, angel investors should objectively determine their limits of investment. Different persons can bear different risks or failures, and thus their limits of investment varies.

In China, Shenzhen became the first city in 2009 to develop a registration system of angel investors. To accelerate the development of angel investment, the government also issued some incentive policies. For example, when registered angel investors contribute to some project, the government may also invest in the project with entrepreneurial guiding fund. Shenzhen made itself an example for local governments of other places around China.

With no limitation on the number of angel investors that can be registered, the registration system can cover every angel investor that satisfies the standards. To register in Shenzhen, an individual angel investor should meet the following conditions:

- The person should be honest, law-abiding, and have no records of offence against penal laws or Security Administration Punishment Act, or records of bad credit;
- The person should have strong economic capability and could bear certain risks, with the individual assets totaling over RMB 5 million;
- The person should have experience or skills about making investments, managing enterprises or the like, has made prior angel investments, or has sources of projects and social resources;

- The person should be recommended by the Angels Club of Shenzhen Private Equity Association, the Shenzhen Venture Capital Association, a venture capital enterprise registered in Shenzhen, a science and technology incubator certified in Shenzhen, or an influential organization or public institution person.

To register in Shenzhen, an institutional angel investor should meet the following conditions:

- It should be relatively reputable, possessing strong economic strength, capable of bearing certain risks, with the registered capital of no less than RMB 30 million;
- It should employ a senior executive with professional skills and at least two years of experience about entrepreneurial investment to administrate the investment, or it should hire some professional investment management institutions for the related work;
- It should feature experience of angel investment or sources of projects; it should be recommended by a referee as mentioned above.

Ways to Acquire Angel Investment

I. *Entrepreneurs Should Understand Angel Investors*

Sometimes, entrepreneurs would find it difficult to persuade a venture capitalist or an angel investor to invest in their enterprises. They complain about the ignorance of angel investors. However, the truth is they should question themselves and find out their own weaknesses. They should understand how an angel investor thinks or chooses a project. Why do some projects acquire angel investment more easily? What sort of projects will not win an angel investor's heart or investment? What makes it difficult for some projects to acquire angel investment?

To an angel investor, an entrepreneur often has the following lethal weaknesses when he/she asks for financing:

(1) The entrepreneur fails to prepare a complete business plan. One can never persuade an investor to finance the company without a painstaking

business plan. Experienced angel investors have read so many plans — so much so, that with one glimpse, they can figure out if an entrepreneur has tried his/her best to make the plan. An outstanding business plan is completed not with a pen, but with the entrepreneur's brain, insight, courage, capability and dream.

(2) The market is not promising or the enterprise's future is limited. Even with a good idea, an enterprise of a gloomy market will find it hard to offer the investor high returns.

(3) The entrepreneur overemphasizes the business idea but understates his/her capability of execution. Entrepreneurs are fundamentally idealists who tend to forget the obstacles they have to overcome to realize their dreams. Although dreams are important, the success of an enterprise depends on more painstaking work. A strong management team is the foundation for the success of a start-up.

(4) The entrepreneur underestimates the money he/she needs at the toughest time. According to the Bank of America, 79% entrepreneurs fail due to lacking capital. Many entrepreneurs lack financial knowledge and often know little about how much money they need to operate their companies.

(5) Many entrepreneurs prefer loans to investment that dilutes their equities. They do not understand that loaners only provide money while investors provide wisdom, experience and relationship as well. If entrepreneurs refuse to exchange capital with equity, it will be impossible for angel investors to make investment.

(6) Some entrepreneurs overvalue their enterprises. Sometimes, although an angel investor is willing to invest in an interesting project, the transaction fails because the entrepreneur requires too much. Like venture capital investment, angel investment is also a kind of transaction. Angel investors are buyers and entrepreneurs are sellers. Angel investors are buying part of the entrepreneur's equity with their money. (Angel investment is a kind of buyer financing which will be discussed in Chapter 9.) In other words, the buyer will only pay the money when they think the deal is appropriate. The buyer wants to pay less while the seller wants to earn more. These desires are understandable. However, two parties cannot complete the deal unless their estimated values of the enterprise are close.

(7) There is a lack of applicable laws — which is a really serious problem in China. The entrepreneurs need applicable documents and laws to protect their intellectual properties such as patents or trademarks.

(8) Entrepreneurs do not know how to manage cash. Most of the entrepreneurs are more like scientists than financers. They know little about financial affairs and do not know how to control costs and increase income. An enterprise is similar to a family. If you do not reduce expenditures, you might shoulder heavy debt even if your income is high. For these enterprises, angel investment would go for nothing and even the most brilliant idea will not be realized.

When entrepreneurs seek for angel investment, they should understand how the investors think and what they are worried about. The aforesaid eight weaknesses are some observed ones which might stop angel investors from making investment.

II. *Ways to Choose Angel Investors*

Entrepreneurs asking for angel investment and angel investors making investment are two sides of the same process. The deal can only be made out of the willingness of both parties. Angel investors are entrepreneurs behind entrepreneurs. They share the same goal with entrepreneurs, to develop an enterprise. From some aspect, the cooperation between an angel investor and an entrepreneur is similar to marriage. Once married, the two become a family. However, a marriage can only succeed with both parties' efforts. One party alone cannot form a happy couple. Like angel investors who assess entrepreneurs from many aspects, entrepreneurs also evaluate angel investors. This is a two-way selection: How can a start-up acquire angel investment? How should it choose an angel investor? The following aspects may be taken as reference.

1. Accredited investor

Firstly, entrepreneurs should find out if an angel investor is an accredited investor. Although a non-accredited investor may also be a viable option, entrepreneurs should choose an accredited one if they are not familiar with the investor.

2. Money with wisdom or not

Entrepreneurs should find out if an angel investor boasts certain experience and can support the enterprise with something more than money. Entrepreneurs should never underestimate the potential of an angel investor. They tend to believe it is easier to acquire angel investment than venture capital. However, this idea is no longer true. Entrepreneurs should prepare themselves mentally because angel investors are more and more similar to venture capitalists. Angel investors also require a fantastic team, a brilliant innovation and a promising market. Therefore, entrepreneurs need "money with wisdom." In other words, they need not only money but also other assistance from investors.

3. Investor and mentor

Entrepreneurs should often ask angel investors for opinions and guidance. Many angel investors make investment not only to earn returns but also to help a start-up. They are interested in participating in the development of an enterprise, and in sharing their experience with young entrepreneurs. They find their values and fulfill their spiritual needs during this process. Angel investors dislike arrogant entrepreneurs and often refuse to invest in enterprises run by such entrepreneurs. Therefore, entrepreneurs need to understand angel investors. Many angel investors have successful businesses and they make angel investment partially give back to society, the community or the group that has helped them to succeed. In a word, they make investment for both economic and social benefits. Their investment is not only to make profits, but also to help people with entrepreneurial spirits and to nurture scientific innovation that will benefit society.

Case II: Legal Aspects of Angel Investment and Financing Experience from a "Lawyer Angel"

WANG Jie: "Reasonable equity allocation in early-stage start-ups."

Time/site: August 5, 2014/Beijing, China

Wang Jie is a senior partner of Da Cheng Law Offices and the director of the firm's Xi'an branch. He is also the founding member of China Young Angel Investor Leader Association. Before joining Da Cheng Law Offices, Wang established Shanxi Fair Law Office and served as the director. During more than 20 years of practice, Wang and his team acted as consultants for many important financial and industrial enterprises, providing legal services in fields such as corporate legal matter, PE/VC investment and financing, IPO/listing, M&A and intellectual property rights.

A Lawyer as an Angel: Legal Service + Experience Sharing + Social Resource Network

Foreign experiences show that in addition to successful entrepreneurs and experienced high-net-worth individuals, participants of angel investment also include accountants, lawyers, doctors and professors, and the reasons of their participation boil down to personal interest, are job-related or expectations of financial returns. Wang tells us that as a law practitioner, he participates in angel investment for job-related reasons. He pointed out that in the early years, lawyers were primarily engaged in "litigation," and they were also called "litigators." Then, with China's implementation of reform and opening-up strategy, economic activities continued to rise and law practice was also growing. The market has begun to see non-litigation legal demand and the practitioners in this area were called "non-litigation lawyers." The legal matters of "financial investment" are a part of such non-litigation legal demand. A start-up cannot do without financing during the development process and will encounter legal regulations on equity and debt and this is where lawyers can assist enterprises. Whilst providing legal services for start-ups, lawyers might discover business opportunities and consider supporting the start-up as an

---

(Continued)

Case II: (*Continued*)

investor. This is particularly true after the opening of China's growth enterprise market in 2009. The public saw many angel investors and investment institutions gain huge profits through IPO exit. Armed with certain skills and social resources, lawyers can not only provide legal services for start-ups but can also share their experience to help start-ups grow. If they succeed, they will have financial and spiritual returns.

In fact, according to the requirements of industry ethics, lawyers are not allowed to invest in listed companies, which they have business relationship with. Wang believes that lawyers should never invest in a listed company to which they serve as the listed company is also a public company. The reason is that as a fair third-party, lawyers should issue legal advice to the public and this might lead to a conflict of interest. However, this is generally not an issue for investment in private company at the seed stage and angel investment stage. Start-ups in the very early stage may not require legal service, and sometimes legal consultancy and guidance can be provided pro bono for a good young team with a good business idea, or business model. Investment is possible if the investor recognizes the growth potential of the start-up.

Wang is prudent towards angel investment and will not invest in industry that he is not familiar with. Firstly, the angel investor should be familiar with the entrepreneur. There is a process for the angel investor to know the entrepreneur and become more familiar with him. Secondly, the angel investor should be knowledgeable about the invested industry. One must learn about and understand the industry when making investment decisions. He admits that he mainly invests in projects recommended by friends. They initially talk about the legal issues of the enterprise and may participate in investment if he believes that the enterprise has great growth potential. For unsolicited projects, he will first have an understanding of the founder (i.e. the educational background, work experience, hobbies) and then arrange a face-to-face interview with the founder to understand his moral qualities and character traits. Wang also stresses that he feels "uncertain" about a founder who is a fresh college graduate, as a founder should have work experience. He prefers founders who are about 30 years old, especially those who have suffered from failure, as they will know how to cherish and are experienced.

(*Continued*)

Case II: *(Continued)*

Common Legal Problems for Start-Ups: Equity, Employment, Intellectual Property Rights and Financing

Research has shown that most young entrepreneurs lack legal awareness and, due to inexperience, often fail to consult a lawyer when confronted with problems. Among factors contributing to the failure of start-ups, litigation is the most serious threat. Moreover, unpleasant contract dispute and plagiarism and imitation are also occasionally seen. In terms of legal problems encountered by start-ups, Wang, as senior legal consultant in the finance field and a practical angel investor, pointed out four common phenomena:

(1) *Equity allocation.* The founder and key employees are not clear about the development goals and current status/stage of the company. It is common that several friends or schoolmates establish an enterprise together and the equity allocation has not thought through. Generally, one of them will take the majority of the equity and the rest of the equity is allocated to others on an average basis. It is often true that unfair equity allocation at the early stage may not attract the founding team. However, with the development of the enterprise, a more competent member might not be able to manage the enterprise due to equity restriction, especially when the equity of each member is limited and equal. The allocation mechanism will result in "invalid decision-making." Wang suggests that the founders should define the role of each shareholder. There are also some members who are willing to transfer some of their equity to a more valuable person. This act will not only motivate the key employees, but will also promote stable development of the start-up.

(2) *Labor employment.* Nowadays, most founders are technical talents and are unclear about legal matters such as legal employment and signing labor contract. Under normal circumstances, as long as a company is established and labor employment is involved, the company will be subject to the regulation of labor law and a standard labor contract must be signed. In addition, the company shall also handle endowment insurance, medical insurance, unemployment insurance, industrial injury insurance, and maternity insurance procedures for the employee. However, many enterprises neglect these. Young people feel uncertain about future development,

(Continued)

Case II: (*Continued*)

or lack legal knowledge and awareness, are tired of red tape, or for the sake of saving costs — generally care more about take-home pay and less about taxes and invisible welfare. The law generally tilts in favor of the employee instead of the employer and the enterprise will suffer a great loss in the case of labor dispute.

(3) *Intellectual property right protection.* The founding team might sometimes be unclear about the scope and methodology for trade secrets and intellectual property rights. For example, what are the core components of the start-up that should be an invention or patent; which trademarks should be registered; and how should one protect network domain name and trade secrets? Generally speaking, the early-stage start-up will have some trade secrets (i.e. the core technology or industry trend which is frequently talked about), which lack protection. In particular, the start-up will suffer from horizontal competition with the dismissal of a core employee. This is called the "silence period" outside China. The purpose of this silence period is to prevent competitors from poaching the said employee, to lock the term of the period (generally two years) and to avoid potential loss (which can be hefty) caused by unfair competition.

(4) *Financing issues.* Take the value assessment as an example, founders of science and engineering background know well about the technology, but in regard of value assessment in the seed and angel investment stages, they either make subjective decisions or look for a reference. As for the term sheet, the contract also involves valuation adjustment mechanism (equity adjustment, repurchase agreement or cash compensation). Other examples include IPO legal shortcomings. Frustration during IPO application may occur when the enterprise fails to handle human resources and financial abnormalities in the middle and late stages of development (the company law proposes strict regulations on the registration condition, organizational structure, individual identity and financial information of the listed company).

In addition, there are other issues worth noticing. For example, when signing business operation and sales contracts, the founder generally does not ask a professional for negotiation or legal checking, which may result in an invalid contract or even cause the founder to incur losses.

(*Continued*)

Case II: *(Continued)*

Joining an Angel Organization: Sharing Insights and Risk, Expanding Social Networks

Wang Jie joined in China Young Angel Investor Leader Association (CYAILA) in the summer of 2013 and it was the first time that the authors of this book had the honor to meet Wang in a salon. He believed that everyone was restricted by the industry rules and limited insight on project judgment, and the understanding of start-up project and team also differed from each other. Members of CYAILA have participated in angel investment and it is a good thing that there is a group of friends to share insights with. In particular, CYAILA launched a "joint investment" mechanism. This mechanism helps to not only realize risk sharing, but enables the most excellent investors in the industry to "guide the path." And most importantly, the joint investment of experienced investors can exert positive influence on the project (in time, experienced investors can bring confidence to the next round of investors). Within one year of enrolling, Wang participated in six or seven salons and expressed his intention in several projects. After due diligence, he gave up some projects and finally invested in one enterprise successfully.

Currently, the country has witnessed a boom of angel investment clubs, associations and unions, most of which are inactive. However, with the support of several top investors like Xu Xiaoping, Yang Ning and Mai Gang, CYAILA has become the most influential angle investment organization in China through over one year of development. Apparently, it is not easy to run an organization. What is the secret of success? Wang pointed out that private groups require highly competent organizers and leaders who are highly influential in the industry, have good project sources (i.e. the insight to find high quality projects and high project judgment ability), and understand investment standards (founder groups, business mode and relevant indicators). Some investors come from institutions and have several investment cases and relevant work experience. And if the founding team proves to be competent and the due diligence results are reliable, the investment decision can be made. In addition, angel investment organization requires operational experience. The RMB 10,000 membership fee of CYAILA raises the entry level to certain point and qualification review is also necessary as angel investment is not only a financial issue, but also requires certain skills and expertise.

Notes

1. During our interviews and research, some believe that family members also belong to the scope of angel investors as their can provide emotional support to the founder. However, some oppose this idea and believe that family members who provide fund support cannot be regarded as angels. Angel investment should be seen as "business behavior" while investments made by family members should not be considered as such as it might be limited oral commitment and is not subject to formal agreements.

2. William Sahlman, 'How to Write a Great Business Plan,' *Harvard Business Review*, July–August, 1997.

3. Ibid.

4. London Business Angels, Raising Business Angels funding, 2008.

5. Julie Connelly, 'These Angels Like to Work as a Team,' *The New York Times*, November 14, 2007.

6. Research Report of the Environment for the Development of Angel Investment in Zhongguancun Science and Technology Park, Beijing Private Technology Entrepreneurs Association, July 2007.

7. United States Securities and Exchange Commission, SEC Rule 501 and Regulation D under the Securities Act of 1933.

8. Pankaj Mishra. 'Backed By Boost VC And Tim Draper, Globevestor Helps Start-ups In Emerging Markets Get Funded Online.' (March 18, 2014); available online at http://techcrunch.com/2014/03/18/backed-by-boost-vc-and-tim-draper-globevestor-helps-startups-in-emerging-markets-get-funded-online/.

Chapter 6

How Investors Can Get Involved in Angel Investment

Project Source of Angel Investment

I. *Entrepreneurship/Innovation Drives Angel Investment Development*

Generally speaking, angel investment is active in places where entrepreneurship and innovation are active. Start-ups tend to face financial difficulties early on in their development process due to lack of funds at the start-up stage, and VC investors generally invest at the middle and late stages. This creates an illusion that founders experience positive growth with angel investment or angel investment institutions. In fact, the opposite is true. Indeed, founders are like flowers and the angel investors are like bees. But bees will not come if there are no flowers.

In Britain, Cambridge University is an active place for founders and therefore the angel investment is also quite developed. In the US, Silicon Valley is the heaven for founders and angel investment, as VC investment also flourishes. In China, Zhongguancun is teeming with entrepreneurs and is the birthplace of angel investment.

The true inner driving force of angel investment development is entrepreneurship and innovation. Without entrepreneurship and innovation, there will be no need for angel investment — let alone angel investment development. Angel investment can only survive and flourish in places where entrepreneurship and innovation are active. Entrepreneurship and innovation bring the needs of angel investment and the intensity of this directly reflects the level of angel investment. This characteristic of angel investment is the same as VC investment. Entrepreneurship and innovation brings the need of financing, and the greater the need is, the more developed the VC investment and angel investment will be. Professors Paul Gompers and Josh Lerner from Harvard Business School noticed these issues in the 1990s.[1] They studied the financing process of VC investment funds and factors affecting this process. They discovered that the government is capable of promoting the development of VC investment from aspects of supply and demand. If promoting VC investment from the supplier's perspective, the government can directly establish VC investment funds or participate in private VC investment funds in the mode of "fund of funds." If promoting VC investment from a "demand" perspective, the government can introduce various policies to support the demand of VC investment. For example, the tax relief policies implemented by a government can spur the founder on, as well as encourage active participation of investors. The government and enterprise can also increase their input in R&D, which will also promote entrepreneurship, thus promoting the development of early VC investment. They discover that government policies promoting investment demand are more effective than supply policies.

In the west coast of the US, particularly in the Silicon Valley, VC investment is booming, as shown by active VC investment funding in early stage start-ups. This is closely related to the active entrepreneurship activities in the Silicon Valley. VC investment funds invested in early-stage project are the same with angel investment. This is a fact that entrepreneurship/innovation drives investment is also seen in China. The reason why VC investment and angel investment are active in Beijing, Shanghai and Shenzhen is because local entrepreneurship and innovation is flourishing. In some sense, it is the founders who drive the investment activities of the VC investors and angel investors.

Angel investment fills the capital cap between the 3Fs and VC capital during the financing process of the enterprise. Angel investment is only a link of financing chain during the growth process of the enterprise, instead of the whole chain. Its operation is closely related to previous financing, for example, the 3Fs and later financing like VC investment.

Figure 6.1 describes the position of angel investment in the enterprise financing chain. In the seed stage of a start-up, the 3Fs are important fund sources. In addition to 3F, angel investment, government subsidy and

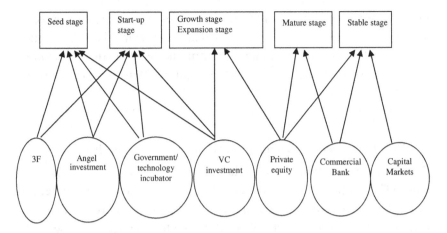

Fig. 6.1 Enterprise Life Cycle and Financing Mode.

technology incubator are also fund sources available for seed-stage start-ups. If the project is indeed excellent with huge development potential, the project may be favored by VC funds that focus on early-stage projects. When the enterprise enters the start-up period, angel investment, government subsidies and technology incubators are still primary fund sources and VC investments is also sometimes channeled into start-up stage projects. In fact, since the 1950s until 1980s, the primary investment area of VC investment was enterprises at the start-up stage. We divide angel investment in that period as below:

Project Source of Angel Investment

The success of angel investment largely depends on high quality projects and non-stopping deal flow. The term "deal flow" first originated in investment banking and refers to the speed of optional deal inflow. Later, this term was used by VC investors and angel investors as a group of deals.

In 2006, the founder and fund manager of the Band of Angels, Dr. Ian Sobieski was invited to a congressional hearing to describe the important role played by angel investment and to introduce the project source of the Band of Angels to congressmen. Dr. Sobieski believed that the deal flow of the Band of Angels came from two aspects: the first being the angel investor members of the Band of Angels as many of them are entrepreneurs or are closely related to entrepreneurs. The other source is the reputation of the Band of Angels. The more successful the Band of Angels, the more entrepreneurs would be encouraged to submit their business proposals and financing applications.

Generally, angel investment can come from the following sources.

1. Recommended by friends, relatives or family members

Recommendation by friends is the oldest and still most popular way today. This method is easy and practical with little costs. Of course, this method is also limited as it depends on the social connections of the angel investor. For experienced angel investors with wide social connections, this method is not only characterized by high success rates and low cost, it also helps deals struck quickly because of the existing relationships between founders and angel investors. This will help the founder win the trust of the angel investors in order to promote better cooperation. Of course, founders can also directly go to the "angel" they know about as angel investors are private investors with a large number of private assets (i.e. lawyers, accountants, and college professors). These angel investors generally lack proper investment opportunities but want to look for opportunities to attain positive financial gains. Therefore, they will be happy if the founders contacted them, and would willingly invest in their projects if they are of any interest to them.

2. Professional relationship: Lawyers, accountants, brokers, consultants, etc.

Like VC investment, angel investment also requires project assessment, investment decision-making, investment agreement signing, investment monitoring, realization of investment revenue and exit of investment capital. In this process, accountants, lawyers, auditors, consultants and brokers are necessary links. As a result, these professionals generally have good projects that require investment. On the other hand, a founder can acquire angel investors through accountants, lawyers or auditors they employ or are familiar with. Of course, these lawyers, accountants, auditors and brokers may be angel investor themselves.

3. The Internet: Angel investment through crowd funding platforms

With the wide application of the Internet, communicating information has become more convenient and fast. The world has become flatter and distances between people have been greatly shortened. The financing of start-ups also depends more on the Internet. On the Internet, founders and angel investors realize information sharing, communication and contact through special Internet platforms.

4. Project recommendations through individuals or conferences

Many intermediaries hold project recommendation conferences as a platform to attract investors and founders of high-caliber. These recommendations are found to be a quite practical source of good investment projects. In addition to project recommendations, other conferences — such as seminars, business proposal competitions and professional forums — are also good sources.

5. Angel investment associations, business angel networks and other angel investment institutions

In the past, angel investors used to just exist in a category that was individual, private and scattered. Since 2000, more and more angel investors have joined various types of angel investment institutions such as business angel networks, clubs or associations. They provide special intermediary services to make angel investment more systemic and principled; they also provide support and information to their members; they enhance the investment awareness of angel investors and improve investment environment. Angel investors find that by joining angel investment associations, they can easily invest in the founder as certain projects in the angel investment associations have been led by experienced members, thus reducing the burden for due diligence. With more and more angel investors joining angel investment groups, these groups have gathered like-minded angel investors and therefore attracted the attention of more founders. They can easily find angel investors who meet their requirements through these angel investment institutions. Angel investment institutions' websites can also attract potential investment projects.

Therefore, angel investment institutions are becoming an important project source for angel investors.

6. VC investment funds

Angel investment funds have received more business plans than ever. Although some projects have the potential, they are at the seed stage or start-up stage. For VC investors, these projects are not mature enough and it is too early to invest in these projects. The VC investment funds may refer these projects to angel investors or angel investment institutions. Generally, angel investment institutions have established close relationship with local VC investment funds.

7. Intermediaries

Generally, intermediaries can provide wide intermediary services of financing: from the preparation of business plan and providing information consultancy services, to contacting the angel investors directly on behalf of founders. They can act as important channels for founders searching for angel investors. However, the success of this method largely depends on the quality of the intermediaries as not every intermediary can meet the funding demands of founders. The market has intermediaries of varying quality and founders therefore should be cautious when choosing an intermediary. Founders should choose an intermediary with good comparative advantages, wide social connections, good reputation and no bad record in meeting the fundraising requirements of the project. Of course, these intermediaries may charge higher rates, but also ensure higher success rates.

After determining the intermediary, founders should set out funding and other relevant demands to enable the intermediary to look for suitable angel investors based on the requirements. Founders should also decide whether to entrust the intermediaries to help prepare the business plan or to provide other intermediary services, such as the study of the industry competition, market saturation and participation in the negotiation with angel investors.

Founders should, of course, pay for the services provided by the intermediaries. For founders of small and medium enterprises in the initial stage, the fee should be under strict control and the price of each service should be recorded in the form of a contract. Founders may appoint a special representative for information transmission and communication between the intermediaries and the founders so that the opinion and requirements of the founders can be transferred to the intermediaries in a timely, accurate and complete manner. When contacting the angel investors, the founders may also require the intermediaries to specify a representative to take charge of the communication between the founders and the angel investors.

This method of attracting angel investors through intermediaries has its advantages and shortcomings. The advantages are as follows:

(1) Intermediaries can act as the senior consultant of founders. Professional intermediaries have accumulated rich experience by handling large amounts of similar financing cases and have a large number of high-quality professionals who can provide advices and suggestions to founders. In addition, there are some processional issues which have to be handled by professionals during the process of angel investment, for example, the financing structure of the start-up, investment form of angel investors, shareholding proportion, convertible bond, re-dilution terms, and the final exit of angel investors. These issues should be handled professionally.

(2) They can save time for founders so that the latter can focus on laying the foundation of their start-ups such as establishing and improving various rules and regulations, and forming an efficient management consisting of high-quality professional talents; these are of critical importance for start-ups at the initial stage. Assisting founders in this aspect is what intermediaries are good at. For experienced intermediaries, they have accumulated precious information resources during the long-term business process and can quickly find angel investors who meet the requirements of the founder. Intermediaries can significantly save time for both founders and angel investors, and can accelerate the process of transforming idle capital of the angel investors into production capital.

(3) Intermediaries can provide diversified services to founders. Not only can they help contact angel investors on behalf of founders, but they can also use their information resources to provide a series

of supplementary services to the founder so as to help the founder solve accounting and legal issues, improve corporate management and business efficiency. A good intermediary will also provide follow-up services for founders and angel investors to ensure smooth cooperation.

(4) Intermediaries also tend to have high success rates. It is the rich experience, wide social connections, high quality talents and readiness to take responsibilities that ensure the smooth cooperation between founders and angel investors. Each takes what he needs and the success rate will be raised. Many successful cases have proven this point. Therefore, intermediaries have become an important way for start-ups to look for angel investors.

While the abovementioned advantages have value, the shortcomings of using intermediaries are as follows:

(1) The success of this method largely depends on the qualification and competence of the intermediary. Some intermediaries do not have the ability to provide services and may attempt to defraud. This obviously damages the interests of the founders.

(2) Attention should be paid to prevent the leakage of a business plan to the public or other competitors. As the intermediary may participate in the development of the business plan, an additional link of communication to outsiders is added — thereby increasing the possibility of business plan leakage. Business plans may involve many trade secrets such as the positioning of the start-up, its core technology, business management mode, investment return and financial planning. Once leaked, the founder may lose the competitive advantage and may be defeated or merged by others easily.

(3) The cost of hiring an intermediary is high. Intermediaries will charge a certain fee for the financing services they provide and the fee is high as the information is exclusive. The service charge general consists of two parts: basic service fee and financing commission. Before financing is successful, intermediaries will charge for specific services they provide (i.e. participation in the preparation of business

plan, information provision and related legal support). After financial funding is secured for the client, intermediaries will also charge a certain percentage of the total financing as their commission. For founders who lack funds, this can be quite a burden. Although the cost is generally higher than fixed expense before financing, the risk for founders lies in the pre-financing expense. This expense has to be paid whether or not the financing is successful. On the other hand, if this pre-financing expense is not charged, it may be unacceptable for intermediaries to assume all financing risks.

Pre-Investment Procedure for Angel Investment

I. Selection of Angel Investment Project

For angel investors, the selection criteria and process for projects are similar to those for VC investors. Let us compare and analyze the selection criteria and due diligence of VC with the precautions and selection criteria undertaken by angel investors when investment projects are selected.

For VC investment, there are five steps for project selection and due diligence.

1. Initial selection of investment project

The initial selection process is similar for angel investors (see Figure 6.2). For angel investors, the project source is generally that of acquaintances, colleagues, friends and angel investment alliances (such as associations). This is quite similar to VC investors who generally rely on the recommendations from others for project selection. If recommendations are not available, VC investors generally do not have the time to learn or know more about a brand new and unknown project.

However, if recommendations are available, VC investors may consider it if the project is similar to other projects they have previously invested in. VC investors can be divided into general VC investors and special VC investors. The former sets foot in all industries and fields as long as the project has development potential and is profitable, while

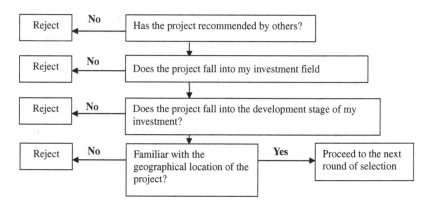

Fig. 6.2   Initial Selection of Investment Project.
Source: Authors' own compilation.

the latter only invests in fields or industries that they are specialized in. For example, VC investors focused on software industry generally are not interested in bioengineering projects.

Currently, with the deepened technology development and labor of division, special VC investors have further refined their investment field and portfolio. VC investors who only invest in software industry may limit their investment scope into management software or even further limit it to financial management software. Special VC investors on the other hand, with their restricted scope of investment, can focus on the studying the constant innovation to follow up to the speed of technology development. For special VC investors, they will generally recommend excellent projects, which fall out of the scope of their investment to other VC investors.

VC investment funds always determine the investment stage based on their own size and preferences: A large fund generally means limited project. This is because although the capital size managed by the fund is large, the number of fund managers available is limited. If a large fund invests in several small projects, they will lack enough fund managers to get deeply involved in the construction and development of the invested enterprise. Active post-investment participation in the invested enterprise is a prominent characteristic of VC investment. Assuming that one VC investment fund has US$1 billion of investment capital and has 10 fund managers, each fund manager will manage US$100 million. This limits their investment scale. If the average investment for each project is only US$1 million, they each have to participate in the post-investment management of 100 enterprises. This is not only inefficient, but also impossible. They have to expand the size of each investment to realize original efficiency. Assuming that they expand the average investment size by 10 times, which is US$10 million, and each investment manager manages 10 invested enterprises, their active participation in the construction of invested enterprise is feasible. The investment size of each project is also closely related to the investment stage. A large VC investment company only invests in enterprises in expansion stage or mature stage. This is because a large sum of funds is required in the late stage of enterprise development. VC investment fund with a small investment fund size and senior experience generally invests in projects in early periods. As we know, investing in early-stage projects, particularly technological project at seed stage, requires considerable judgment from the VC investor.

When considering an early-stage investment project, in addition to the investment industry or field, VC investors also takes an interest in the geographical location of the investment project. In the past, VC investors in the Silicon Valley restricted their investment to locations that were accessible within one- or two-hour drive. If the project was located in vicinities beyond this scope, VC investors may think that the post-management operations will be hindered and might give up the project. In recent years, VC investors have expanded their investment scope. Many Silicon Valley VC investors have expanded their business overseas and made investment in China, India, Israel and even Europe. Some VC investors have gradually changed from investing locally to globally. On the contrary, angel investors still maintain the investment behavior of traditional VC investors, limiting their investment projects within a certain geographical area. As angel investment is an individual investment behavior, after committing to a project, angel investors have to participate in important meetings in the invested enterprise. As a result, angel investors still follow the strategy of traditional VC investment and invest in projects that are not far away from their work place or domicile.

2. Assessment of project development potential

After initial selection, angel investors, like VC investors, will further analyze the development potential of the project, as shown in Figure 6.3.

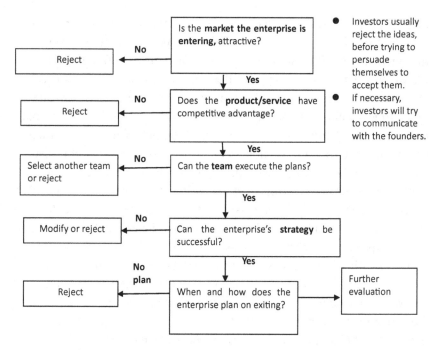

Fig. 6.3   Evaluating the Development Potential of a Project.

Different criteria are used by different VC investors to judge the development potential of a project. Some VC investors put market potential at the top of their list, as they believe a project will not be developed without a potential market. They also attach great importance to the start-up team. However, as long as the market prospects are good, the team can be supplemented or replaced if it performs poorly. Other VC investors believe that people are the most important asset. They think, based on their past investment experience, human capital matters; the success or failure of an investment hinges on people. Angel investors agree with this idea. They believe that the success of an investment depends on whether they have found the right person. A project may be excellent and has epoch-making significance, but if it lacks the right person to operate it, the project will fail.

For both VC investors and angel investors, whether we put market factor or the founder team as the top factor of consideration, the five factors in the above figure are keys to evaluating a project's development potential: Is the market that the enterprise is entering attractive? Does the product have competitive advantages? What is the start-up team's ability in implementing policies? Is the start-up's overall operational strategy feasible? And last but not least, has an exit plan for investors — when and how it should exit the market — been created? VC investors first reject everything when analyzing these five aspects before trying to persuade themselves into accepting the business plan, or simply adopt the "negation of the negation" analysis strategy. First, they assume that the market prospect of the project is not good, and then they reject the negative assumptions step by step based on the existing business plan or their research results. Similarly, they first assume a negative stance on the feasibility, quality or quantity of the product/service and then reject their negative assumptions step by step based on facts and data, and so on.

Among the above five questions, we will discuss market, product/service and team respectively. We will first discuss the questions of business strategy and exit. An enterprise's development strategy has always been a key to the success of an enterprise and is often ignored by enterprises and founders in particular. With the rapid development of China's economy, many Chinese enterprises including start-ups have to develop a feasible development strategy or competition strategy. However, Chinese enterprises generally pay little attention to the long-term development when developing a strategy. Many tend to pay attention to current market demand or development direction in recent years, but ignore the long-term strategy development — which is of critical importance. In addition, Chinese enterprises also lack a holistic perspective when developing strategy and might also develop a strategy as they go along. This current status is closely related to the rapid economic development in China and other uncertain factors. In addition, many start-ups only have a grand vision for the future but lack specific implementation steps. For example, many start-ups have the development strategy, which is to "become a TOP 500 in XX years" or "to go public in three years." However, they do not have a clear view on how to become a "TOP 500 firm" or how to go public. They have impressive slogans but lack specific implementation details. This type of enterprise development strategy is unrealistic and will not attract VC investors or angel investors.

Another important issue is the development of an exit channel for investors. In fact, investors attach great importance to the design of an exit channel. Start-ups should regard investors as their business partners, companions on the road of entrepreneurship, and should understand that investors share with them the entrepreneurship risks to a great extent by investing in the start-ups at such an early stage. In this way, investors (be it VC investors or angel investors) are also the founders and deserve the returns by taking such great risks. Although the returns are potential, the courage and boldness of the investors are valuable. At the initial stage of a start-up, in particular in the seed stage, the funds provided by the investors are key to success for start-ups. If founders only care about the success of their businesses and careers, and care little about the high risks assumed by the investors, they will think little for the investors and will not design proper exit plans for them. This type of founders is selfish, narrow-mined and will never been able to make great achievements. Investors will also not make investment in these start-ups.

Some start-ups only care about business growth and their personal success, and dream about going public one day. They are eager to acquire good financial backing and will, of course, hope that investors will see tangible results and feel confident about their start-ups. However, they never think about the issue from the perspectives of the investors and do not consider the interests of the investors. Founders should pause for a moment to consider the following questions: Why should investors invest in my project/ enterprise? Will the investors take great risk? Should investors be compensated for the risk they take? Should investors be rewarded for the fund invested in the initial stage of start-ups? As a founder, how can I ensure that the investors can attain rich investment return? How can I help investors exit in a proper manner at a proper time? If the founder does not think such questions through, he/she can hardly get any investments.

3. Market selection steps

Generally speaking, market decision-making can be divided into four steps, which are market life cycle, market capacity, consumer group and competition, as shown in Figure 6.4.

(1) *Market life cycle*

A market is like an enterprise and has a life cycle. The market's life cycle begins at birth and will undergo the following stages: young, maturity,

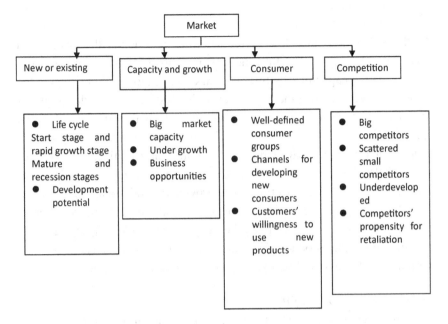

Fig. 6.4   Market Selection Steps.

old-age to death. The economic value of an enterprise can be seen from its position within a market and the prosperity of a market depends on its life cycle. Is the market a sunrise or sunset market? Is the market a rapidly growing market or downward market? Is the market a growing market or market that is already mature? For example, the VCD market was hot in the early 21st century but it is now being replaced by a growing DVD market. Technological development is ever changing in computer accessories. The earliest 5½-inch external floppy disk was replaced by 3¼ -inch floppy disk, which was in turn replaced by a small, easy-to-carry U-disk with a big storage capacity. Now, even the best external floppy disk does not have a market and even CDs are gradually being replaced. The law of natural science is ruthless and so is the life cycle of a market. The study in market life cycle by the investor is a key standard for making investment decisions. Generally speaking, being positioned within a sunrise market is an ideal and necessary condition for an enterprise to obtain financial backing.

(2) *Market capacity*

Market capacity is the basic factor determining whether the project can create economics of scale. Take the Internet market for example: China has a huge market capacity. The Internet market began to grow in China at the end of 1980s, and since the beginning of the 21st century, its development speed and force have become unprecedented in China's history. On July 23, 2015, according to the *36th Statistical Report on Internet Development in China* released by CNNIC, China had 668 million net citizens by the middle of 2015. The percentage of mobile users increased from 85.8% at the end of 2014 to 88.9%, reflecting stable growth. An additional 36.79 million net citizens joined the existing Internet community in 2015 and the Internet penetration rate was 45.8%. It can be said that the market capacity is huge for Internet-related products. In addition to the market capacity, we are also certain that this market has a great potential for development.

(3) *Consumer groups of the market*

A group refers to the aggregate of social members through long-term contact based on interaction and interdependency. A consumer group refers to the group formed by consumers with the similar consumption characteristics. Generally, a consumer group is formed based on the following factors: age, sex, personality, income, lifestyle, geological environment, interests and hobbies, and ethical group, religion, cultural tradition, political background, etc.

Founders often only have approximate rule-of-thumb estimation on the customer group for their products/service and they seldom delve into the details. A well-defined customer group is key a successful enterprise. In terms of customer group, the start-ups can judge from the following factors:

(A) Does the product/service have a clear consumer group? Where is the consumer group? For example, the consumer group of stylish, colorful and petite cellphones is young office ladies with a certain income. Young men with similar income and in the same age group may not be inclined to purchase this type of cellphones. Therefore, it is certain that this type of cellphone has a clear and existing consumer group.

(B) If the consumer group is clear but is not formed, the next question is how to develop an existing consumer group: Should it be done through advertisement, promotion or by other means? It must be cautioned that having a target consumer group is not a guarantee that this group will eventually buy your products, even if you know who to target.

(C) If the product/service is new the next question that the management team will have to consider is how can the enterprise cultivate a new consumer group? Would existing consumer groups be willing to try new things?

The above three questions must be thought through by founders before financing so that they can be prepared. This is because these questions will be asked by both VC investors and angel investors when they select start-ups that they want to invest in.

(4) Market competition

Different markets have varied forms of competition. Some markets have extremely intensive competition while others only face competition which is less so.

4. Product/service selection procedures

Quality and content are core factors to whether the product/service provided by entrepreneurs can capture the market. Entrepreneurs should understand that any product/service is likely to be replaced. The competitor can be an existing or potential one. As long as there is demand from the market, the product/service that you provide cannot be unique permanently. The practical value of your product/service, which has not been delivered by other products/services, can help you defeat the competitors. Figure 6.5 shows the product/service assessment of start-up enterprises.

As discussed above, new products/services can have a share in the market because they can provide value that cannot be offered by other products/services at present. Finding the market demand that is not provided is a challenge for entrepreneurs. The demand may have always existed, or might have come about due to economic development and social change, but only start-up enterprises established by entrepreneurs

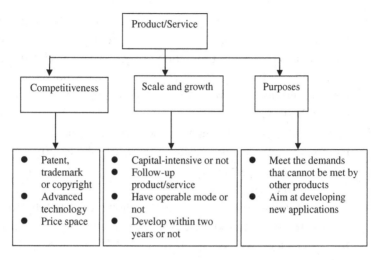

Fig. 6.5   Decision-Making Process of Products/Services.

with unique insights can seize the market gap and use new or innovative products/services to fill the gap. When investigating market niche, the investor should pay attention to the following aspects.

(1)   *Product/service competitiveness*

For science-and-technology start-ups, the core competitiveness of products/services is often associated with intellectual property protection, and the investor also regards intellectual property protection as an index of core competitiveness. For instance, do the start-up enterprises apply for a patent? After the patent has been granted, how long is its validity? Does the patent protect the core competitiveness of the enterprises? More importantly, are enterprises liable of infringing upon other people's patents? If the start-up enterprises are not science and technology enterprises, or if patent protection is not applicable to them, do they have registered trademarks? Are enterprises in dispute with other enterprises or individuals in terms of trademark or copyright? Are the projects still leading in the field of science and technology even if they are not protected by the patent, trademark or copyright? Does its leading position (if already in place) last for a long time and is it stable? How can the enterprise protect its leading position?

Favorable pricing is also an important factor that would make the enterprise's products/services more competitive. If a company does not have enough maneuvering space to adjust the price for its product/service, it will not be able to expand the market through price adjustments in the future. The more flexible the pricing is, the more opportunities a company will have to promote its products in the market.

(2)   *Scale and growth of product/service*

The scale of a product/service is also important. The competitiveness will be stronger with a larger scale. Take the mobile phone market for example: According to experts, between 2010 and 2012, China's mobile phone after-sales market has maintained constantly rapid growth, and the overall market scale was nearly RMB 12 billion with a compound annual growth rate of 20.1%. Customers' dissatisfaction towards mobile phone services also concurrently became more distinct. In 2013, among the complaints on communication products, the complaint about mobile phones became a hot issue. There were 47,849 complaints throughout the year, accounting for 71.2% of communication product-related complaints and 28.9% of home appliance-related complaints. Among them, the number of complaints due to quality issues reached a figure of 23,062, accounting for 48.2%; the number of complaints related to after-sales service totaled 15,395, accounting for 32.2%.

The complaints are mainly shown as follows: When there are problems with the phone, the maintenance provider often gives an excuse of lacking components, which results in the phone not being repaired for a long time, which in turn affects the customer's normal use. Within the period of "three guarantees,"[2] if a customer feels that his/her mobile phone has quality problems despite being repaired multiple times or replaced with a new one, the operator would have failed to fulfill corresponding obligations of the "three guarantees." The actual functions of new phones purchased by customers would therefore prove to be inconsistent with sellers' advertisements. Problems such as these, however, may produce opportunities, and opportunities may be silver linings for entrepreneurs. Naturally, there will be potential investment projects with broad prospect for development that would be selected and used by VC investors or angel investors if there is a gap in the market to be filled.

If the product/service is capital-intensive, angel investors will often have reservations about committing to that enterprise. Capital-intensive products/services refer to products/services for which capital cost, as opposed to labor cost, accounts for a large percentage of unit product cost. In other words, every worker occupies a large amount of fixed capital and variable capital. Generally, capital-intensive industries include steel industry, water and electricity, and large-scale manufacturing, such as electronic and communication equipment manufacturing, transport equipment manufacturing, petrochemical industry, heavy machinery industry, electric power industry, etc. Capital-intensive industries are an important pillar of a nation's economic development, primarily in basic industries and heavy processing industries, and they are also an important base for developing national economy and industrialization.

Although capital-intensive products/services are of great importance, they are often beyond the reach of individual angel investors. Apart from capital-intensive products/services, there are also labor-intensive and technology-intensive ones. Angel investors and VC investors tend to be inclined to invest in technology-intensive projects. Technology-intensive projects refer to projects that mainly rely on technology and intelligence factors during production, which are much more useful than other production elements. Generally, technology-intensive industries include microelectronic and information products manufacturing, aerospace industry, atomic energy industry, modern pharmaceuticals industry and new material industry. In China, technology-intensive industries — as represented by microelectronic and information products manufacturing — are developing rapidly and they have become leading industries that promote national economic growth. Base on China's experience, the development level of technology-intensive industries can determine a nation's competitiveness and its growth prospects.

(3) *Purposes of products/services*

The purpose of products/services is one of the keys that determines whether they are competitive. The most important factor pertains to whether the project can meet the existing demands in market, which cannot be offered by other products/services. Take Bluetooth technology as an example. "Bluetooth" used to be a name of a King of Denmark: Harald I Bluetooth (in Danish: HaraldBlåtand) (r. 940–985). He unified Sweden, Finland and Denmark during that period, which resulted in the fitting name for the new technology, as it symbolized unification. Its distinct feature lies with it being a short-range wireless communication technology. Despite its short-range, it can connect several digital devices in a cheapest way to form a network, such as mobile devices, fixed communication equipment, computer and its terminal equipment, and various digital data systems, including digital camera, DV recorders, and even various household appliances and automation equipment. Bluetooth technology acts like an invisible bridge that links various peripheral interfaces across a portable network. Its actual application range can be further extended to various household appliances, consumer electronic products, cars and other information household appliances. It has great development potential. Certainly, the potential of technology research and development is infinite, but there are huge technology competitive risks and any good technology faces a chance of being replaced by new advanced technology. For example, nearly all industries across the world have been affected by the rise of the Internet, mobile communication, social media tools and other technologies in recent years.

5. Management team selection

Whether an enterprise has a qualified management team is essential to acquiring angel investment successfully. Angels can evaluate the management team of an enterprise from four aspects, namely: relevant experience of an entrepreneurial team, relevant abilities, complementarity of an entrepreneurial team as a whole, and personal entrepreneurial determination and qualities of each member in the team (see Figure 6.6).

(1) *Relevant industrial experience of an entrepreneurial team*

Experience related to entrepreneurship of an entrepreneurial team is an important factor that should be studied by investors. Take a B2B Internet project as an example. Has the entrepreneur ever worked in B2B or similar industries? Does he have a good grasp of the development of the industry and its basic rules? Does he have personal connections in the industry?

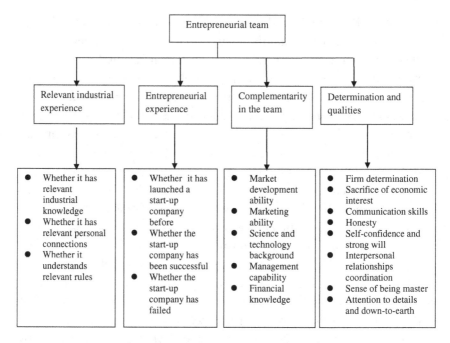

Fig. 6.6 Decision-Making Process of an Entrepreneurial Team.

Whether or not the entrepreneur has deep industry knowledge is also very important.

(2) *Relevant entrepreneurial experience of an entrepreneurial team*

The entrepreneurial experience of members within a team may not be related with the industry which this start-up business is involved in this time. No matter what industries, taking part in start-up businesses will always be a precious experience. Since the beginning of China's reform and opening-up, the Chinese have been in their element and very active in encouraging economic reform and have been striving to improve their personal economic status. The start-up business sector in China has grown vigorously. However, the country still lacks a real entrepreneurial atmosphere, in which success is applauded and failure is also tolerated. In Chinese history, there is a saying that goes like this: Victorious and you are the king; defeated and you are just a bandit. People always praise the winner, but tend to not understand the loser's situation and does not fully tolerate failure.

For VC investors, they not only help entrepreneurs with funds, but also help them with management, strategies, and designs of market development and exit channels; they can also offer help in business, and its ethics, thoughts and spirits. VC investors praise entrepreneurs for their success, but more importantly, they can tolerate their failure. As a venture capitalist, failure is unavoidable. You can try something and it could come to nothing, and then you can try again, but you had better not make the same errors. Making money is an operational objective for venture capitalists, but that is not their only goal. Reed Hastings, another venture capitalist, is a case in point. Hastings sold the company he invested in called "Pure Software" for US$750 million in 1997, but he did not take a break in his career. On the contrary, he invested part of the capital in "Educational Fund for New Schools," and enrolled in the Stanford Graduate School for Education to attain an educational qualification in pedagogy, with the purpose of pushing forward American education reform. Indeed, establishing new-type enterprises with great development potential is the real driver behind economic development, and venture capital often offers timely help for such start-up enterprises. Further development of China's economy requires greater levels of entrepreneurship, venture capitalist spirit, and the commercial atmosphere of encouraging success and tolerating failure. The help offered by VC investors to entrepreneurs can be applied to angel investors. Many angel investors have more respect for those who started their own business but failed in the end. Some angel investors specially invest in the entrepreneurs who start new businesses again after experiencing failure in prior start-up businesses.

Gradually establishing a new-type corporate culture is an important factor to encourage people to start new businesses and carry forward entrepreneurship, so that people can treat entrepreneurs' failure with a peace of mind. With every instance of success, failure also ensues. What people can learn best is not from their successful experience, but from the lessons of failure. People often think deeply when they fail and reflect on deficiencies. As long as they do not give up, they can start new businesses again.

(3) *Knowledge and complementary skills in an entrepreneurial team*

For investors, an entrepreneurial team with complementarity is an ideal team. Entrepreneurial team members should complement each other in knowledge and skills. Start-ups, especially science and technology start-ups, often have a team with strong technological capabilities but lack talents with management experience, financial background and market development ability. This kind of start-ups is incomplete and cannot really realize their entrepreneurial dream. An ideal entrepreneurial team should have various management talents, not only in science and technology, but also in corporate management and marketing. Only depending on science and technology strength can lead to technical breakthroughs, but entrepreneurship is a commercial activity in which entrepreneurs want to move science and technological innovation into market, and it is a process of developing science and technology innovation and industrialization. In the process, management talents, marketing talents and financial talents are naturally needed.

(4) *Personal determination and qualities of an entrepreneurial team*

Many investors think that personal determination and qualities of an entrepreneurial team are the most important factors when evaluating an entrepreneurial team. Investors may evaluate from the following perspectives:

(A) Do entrepreneurs have firm entrepreneurial determination? Do they consider their start-ups as the career that they should go all out to pursue? Do they have undivided attention? Do they pay the economic price? For example, do they invest in their enterprises? Does the investment include funds and other opportunity cost? For example, do they sacrifice their stable jobs and give up their high incomes? Are entrepreneurs bold leaders? Can they unite like-minded persons to develop their careers together? Can they listen to and take different opinions?

(B) The most important quality that entrepreneurs should have is honesty, including being honest to themselves. It shows whether they can be aware of and accept current realities, and advance courageously under existing real-world conditions.

(C) The ability of entrepreneurs to express their ideas is important. A good ability to do will allow them to persuade investors to provide financial support. It will also help entrepreneurs to organize and train other members in the management team, so that everyone can work towards achieving a common goal.

(D) Entrepreneurs should be strong and self-confident. Undoubtedly, there will be various difficulties and dangerous situations in starting new businesses. If entrepreneurs are not strong, it will be hard for them to overcome difficulties and to be persistent. Without persistence, no entrepreneurship will be successful. The strength will often come from entrepreneurs' confidence in their ability, experience and the career they are engaged in. Without the self-confidence, there will be no strong will and indomitable entrepreneurship.

(E) Whether entrepreneurs have leadership depends on their ability to surround themselves with different people. Working with various kinds of people is an important aspect to judge one's leadership.

(F) Entrepreneurs should have a solid sense of ownership and strong ambitions for their careers. They are active when doing business instead of waiting passively. If entrepreneurs only wait and lack initiative, they might be held back and will not be able to go all out to develop their careers.

(G) Entrepreneurs should start off with a detailed but realistic plan, rather than a grand blueprint. If entrepreneurs only consider themselves to be superior and indulge in empty talk, rather than focus on details and work step by step, he/she will not be a successful entrepreneur.

II. Project Evaluation by Angel Investors

The value assessment of an invested project by angel investors is a complex process. In some sense, the value assessment by angel investors is more of an art instead of a science.

Like VC investment, angel investment divides the assessment of invested enterprises into "pre-money valuation" and "post-money valuation" (or "pre-investment valuation" and "post-investment valuation"). Suppose some angels evaluate an enterprise as RMB 1 million, and they decide to invest RMB 500,000, which accounts for 33.3% of the shares. "Pre-investment

valuation" of the enterprise is therefore RMB 1 million and the "post-investment valuation" would be is RMB 1.5 million.
Thus:

Post-investment valuation = pre-investment valuation +
the amount invested
Shares held by investors = the amount invested/port-
investment valuation

According to the study conducted by the National Angel Capital Organization, the rate of return of angel investment can be estimated simply as follows. This method is produced based on years of investment practice and a set of data that can be referred by normal angel investors:

Annual rate of return is 7.20%, investment for 10 years = double return

Annual rate of return is 11.6%, investment for 10 years = triple return

Annual rate of return is 25.9%, investment for 10 years = tenfold return

Annual rate of return is 35.0%, investment for 10 years = twentyfold return

Annual rate of return is 115.0%, investment for 3 years = tenfold return

Annual rate of return is 46.8%, investment for 6 years = tenfold return

It seems that the higher the average annual rate of return is, the more the investment returns will be. The amount of investment return is also related with the investment horizon. It is worth noticing that although the higher the annual rate of return is and the more the investment returns will be, the two numbers are not comparable.

Angel investors usually adopt the following evaluation modes.

1. Simple mode: The rule of one-third

Investors hold about 30% of shares of invested enterprise (or a figure between 20% and 40%), which depends on the negotiation between investors and the invested enterprise. If investors think the enterprise has great development potential in future, they can hold 20% of shares, and the start-up business holds 80%. Sometimes, the rule of one-third is often defined as: One-third of shares belong to investors, one-third to entrepreneurs, and the remaining third belongs to the management.

2. Baucus mode

Baucus mode is as follows:

Table 6.1   Baucus Mode.

Evaluation Object	Valuation
1. Brilliant idea	US$500,000–1,000,000
2. Excellent management team	US$500,000–2,000,000
3. Strategic partner and the entry threshold of market	May be up to US$500,000
4. Completion of product/service sample	US$500,000–1,000,000
5. Board members with a certain quality	May be up to US$1,000,000
6. Existing sales	May be up to US$1,000,000
Total valuation	US$2.5–6 million

Source: Authors' own compilation.

3. Multiplier mode

Multiplier mode is simple; it involves multiplying a universal number in an industry by sales revenue or profit of evaluated enterprises. If the invested enterprise is in retail industry, investors will consider its stock in hand. Suppose that the multiplier of online shopping industry is 3, and the sales revenue of a newly established enterprise is RMB 3 million, so the valuation of the enterprise will be RMB 9 million according to multiplier mode.

4. VC investment mode

The evaluation mode of VC investment is based on several assumptions: Firstly, assume that the investment is conducted once without dilution.

Secondly, assume the internal rate of return (rate of return on investment required by VC investors) and exit time; the net earnings of the enterprise and PE ratio of the industry on exit. Thirdly, calculate future market value of the enterprise according to assumptions, and then convert the amount of investment in the enterprise into the future value on exit to figure out share ratio of the investment, namely valuation ratio after investing in the enterprise with the amount of investment. The market value of the enterprise on exit can also be converted into present value. Divide the present amount of investment by present value of market on successful exit to figure out share ratio.

Take the following assumed statistics as examples[3]:

Assumption 1: Internal rate of return of the investment is 50% and consider that as discount rate;

Assumption 2: Investment exits in 5 years;

Assumption 3: Net income of the enterprise is RMB 80 million after 5 years;

Assumption 4: PE Ratio of the industry is 20;

Assumption 5: Investment in the enterprise is RMB 3 million;

- Market value (V) of the enterprise in the fifth year is:

  PE Ratio (P/E) * price (P) = 300 * 20 = **RMB 60 million**.

- If the investment is RMB 3 million, the future value (FV) after five years is:

  $(1 + 50\%)^5$ * (RMB 3 million) = **RMB 22,781,250**

- Share ratio of angel investors is:

  Future value of investment (V)/future market value (FV) of the enterprise = 2278.125/6000 = **38%**

III. *Stock Dilution of Angel Investors*

Because the horizon of angel investment is early, follow-up VC investment or other capital may gradually dilute shares of angel investors who have invested at the early stage. Naturally, the earlier the investment has been made, the higher the shares are obtained with same investment amounts, which is one of the most basic theories based on finance and the risk-return relationship theory. Modification and supplement can be made according to the study of National Angel Capital Organization to adapt to the stock dilution in China's practical situation.

The dilution process can be analyzed according to the following assumptions (see Table 6.2):

(1) When angel investors invest in an enterprise, the enterprise doesn't have any operating income. However, because of its great development potential, angel investors think the enterprise has good investment value according to due diligence. So angel investors consider that the pre-investment valuation of the enterprise is RMB 2 million, and they will invest RMB 1 million. At this point, angel investors hold 33% of shares of the invested enterprise, and the post-investment valuation of the enterprise is RMB 3 million.

Table 6.2   Stock Dilution of Angel Investment (million Yuan).

Indicator	Angel Investment	Series A of VC Investment	Series B of VC Investment	Series C of VC Investment	Others
Operating income of invested enterprise	0	2	6	15	30
Pre-investment valuation	2	7	15	30	100 (Market value in exiting)
Investment amount	1	3	6	10	Angel investor's profit
Angel investment share	33%	23%	17%	13%	13%

(2) If the project performs well, VC investment will follow up. The first round of VC investment (Series A) invested RMB 3 million, however, the invested enterprise now has already had some operating income, so pre-investment valuation has been improved to RMB 7 million, and post-investment valuation reaches to RMB 10 million. After input of VC investment, the stock dilution of angel investors is 23%. The distribution relation of stock right after investment: VC investment accounts for 30%; invested enterprise (including RMB 1 million angel investors have invested) takes up 70%, which make stock dilution of angel investor reach: 33% × (70%) = 23.1%, about 23%.

The second round of VC investment (Series B) puts in RMB 6 million, while pre-investment valuation of invested enterprise is RMB 15 million and post-investment valuation is RMB 21 million. (It is noted that angel investors and VC investors in the first round have been regarded as shareholders of the invested enterprise and share enterprise value of RMB 15 million), the Series B investment of VC investments accounts for 28.6% shares (28.6% = RMB 6 million/(RMB 15 million + RMB 6 million)), and angel investor's shares once again be diluted, the process of which is similar to the above: (23.1% × 71.4%) = 16.5%, about 17%. The third round of VC investment (Series C) puts in RMB 10 million, when pre-investment valuation of invested enterprise is RMB 30 million and post-investment valuation is RMB 40 million. In Series C, VC investors account for 25% share (RMB 10 million invested/(RMB 10 million + RMB 30 million) = 25%), and the initial investment shares of angel investor are further diluted into: 17% × (1 − 25%) = 12.75%, about 13%.

(3) It is assumed that if invested enterprises have been listed successfully, the market value will reach RMB 100 million. The market value of the angel investor's initial input of RMB 1 million now is RMB 13 million (RMB 100 million × 13% = RMB 13 million), which is 13 times of the amount invested originally. The rate of investment return should be based on the exit limit, and the shorter the investment limit is, the higher the rate of investment return is.

Post-Investment Management of Angel Investment

I. *Characteristics of Angel Investment in Post-Investment Management*

In terms of engaging in the management of invested enterprises, with special characteristics, angel investment differs a lot from VC investment in many ways. After the investment, an angel investor's requirements might differ from another according to different situations. Some angel investors insist on occupying a seat on the board of directors, while the others are indifferent; some require further engaging in the management, while the others would not want to; some might ask the founders to send a weekly report, while the others might just require a quarterly or annual report. For the choice of investment tools, some might just want common stock, but most of them would add other terms on common stock, such as the right of veto and liquidation preference. If using preferred stock, most requirements are convertible. Generally, angel investors will require taking a part of invested enterprise stock right ranging from 5% to 25%. Some angel investors are more demanding, such as asking convertible bond or redeemable preferred stock. For investment return, angel investors also greatly differ: From 30% internal return rate to 5 times or more of return.

II. *Confirmation of Investment Terms*

VC investors usually like placing risk control on invested enterprises through additional provisions of investment terms. These investment terms often include a variety of additional provisions, such as anti-dilution provision, the term of convertible preferred stock, the term of share change for accident and others. However, angel investors always hold common stock only and do not require convertible preferred stock, in order to prevent the situation that once an enterprise fails, there is risk of liquidation. Certainly, as angel investment should invest earlier and the investment risk is higher, with the same amount of investment, they will acquire more shares.

Angel investment taps into the means to control high risk at the early stages of investment and development. In general, the earlier an investment is made, investing the more shares the angel investor will gain. It is because the earlier one invests, the higher the risk one will undertake. Investors always expect to acquire a higher equity ratio to compensate for higher investment risk. The higher the risk is, the more future expected returns investors will request. For example, one might invest RMB 1 million to an enterprise. If one invests in the enterprise within a year of its establishment, you may get 30% shares; at the second year of its establishment, you may get only 20% equity from the same RMB 1 million; at the fifth year, only 1 % share can be gained from the RMB 1 million, and so on.

On the other hand, the higher potential risk of the invested enterprise is, the smaller the average amount of investment made by angel investors is. If this kind of enterprise wants to obtain investment of angel investors, it usually needs the joint investment of angel investors.

III. *Control of Investment Risk*

Angel investment tends to take the same measures on the risk control as VC investment. For example, they take the pattern of joint investment to reduce the investment risk. However, generally, angel investment tends to focus on personal trust, which is different from VC investors who attach more importance to formal, organized, institutional risk control measures. VC investors usually employ the pattern of stage investment as an important means to control investment risk. But angel investors barely adopt this kind of risk control mechanism.

Similar to VC investment, angel investors often adopt the pattern of joint investment to avoid investment risk as well. Unlike VC investment, the application of joint investment by angel investment is more frequent, and the number of participants is also larger. Andrew Wong found that there are 12.2 angel investors on average participating in the process of angel investment in each round, and the median value of the number of angel investors investing in each round is 8.[4] That is to say, in angel investment, there is an average of more than 12 angels jointly investing in each investment project, and normally, there will be 8 angels jointly engaging in each round of investment. Based on personal understanding, personal experience, personal intuitive feeling to entrepreneurs, personal investment preferences, or combination of other reasons, these angels, to some extent, hold similar opinions on the prospect of invested enterprise.

Angel Investment Can Engage in the Management of the Invested Enterprise

Most angels will actively engage in the management of the invested enterprise. In their opinion, if entrepreneurs only want their money, they have no interest in participating. Only those entrepreneurs who need both the money and experience from angels, they will get the real help from angles' experiences and suggestions. Some VC investors compare the participation of invested enterprise management to "life-cycle investment:" namely, after investment, engaging in the whole growth process of invested enterprise, from seed stage, start-up stage, post-start-up stage, development stage, mature stage to the final exit. The investment process a growth process that all enterprises will undergo.

1. Get involved in the board of directors

Although angels have a chance to be involved on the board of directors of invested enterprises, they do not require to make this involvement as one of their investment terms. In addition, as the enterprise that the angel investor invests is often not mature, or would have been recently established, the board of directors of the enterprise would usually not have been set up. As a result, angel investors seldom become members of the board of directors as a means of controlling the enterprise. VC investors however often become members of the board of directors to reduce principal-agent costs and they see it as a necessary institutional arrangement to control risk. However, angel investors do not adopt this kind of management mode. Angel investors do not attach such importance to the board of directors as VC investors. According to the study of Steven N. Kaplan and Per Strömberg,[5] VC investors typically account for 37% to 47% of the seats in the board of directors of invested enterprises. Angel investors, on the other hand, tend to only take up 18% of the seats.

2. Management arrangement

Angels pay more attention to, and take active part in the management arrangement of invested enterprises. Generally, if key positions of invested enterprise management need to be replaced, angel investors often want to get information in advance, or get involved in the management directly. Sometimes, angel investors will actively require invested enterprises to reshuffle their management arrangement.

3. Market development

Angels usually help the invested enterprises a lot in market development. Because numerous angels used to be successful entrepreneurs or excellent managers themselves, they have rich experience in market development. With years of accumulation, they boast extensive business relationships. All of these are non-capital-related, yet extremely precious "treasures" angel investors embrace.

4. Refinancing

Although angels provide timely and critical help in their career, entrepreneurs often feel that at a certain stage of enterprise development, the investment scale of angel investment is often not enough to help them expand further. So enterprises need to refinance, and at such a juncture, angel investors are usually the most like-minded assistants for invested enterprises. Angel investors usually help invested enterprise refinance through their business relationships with partners in the past, lawyers, trusted accountants, or their own personal relationships with friends, relatives, classmates and colleagues. Although refinancing is one of the most important steps that angel investors contribute to helping invested enterprises, most enterprises supported by angel investment will still find it hard to obtain VC investment.[6] In fact, VC investment agencies are critical to the identities of start-up shareholders, therefore whether or not VC investment agencies select the enterprise depends on the background and reputation of angel investors, and the invested enterprise that has been invested by well-known angel investors is generally seen as a "quality project signal" and is more likely to get the opportunity of follow-up financing.

V. *Advice for Angel Investors*

Angel investment is an investment activity with high risk. As an angel investor, one must have enough knowledge of investment risks. When making investment decisions, if one feels uncomfortable, one should consider giving up investing. Sometimes, the intuition of angel investor is right. Here are nine suggestions for angel investors.

1. Determine the maximum investment norm

As an angel investor, you should create your own economic conditions for cash flow and put your risk tolerance capacity into consideration before making any investment decisions. If you are a married investor, think about whether you would need to negotiate or discuss with other family members about this potential investment project. As mentioned above, the maximum investment an angel investor puts in should be the maximum amount of loss you can accept, considering your economic status, family's opinion, psychological endurance, tolerance to risk, and so on. With an objective and calm analysis of your own investment capacity, determine whether you can invest or not, and determine the upper and lower limits of the amount of investment. If you feel that it is difficult to coordinate/discuss with family members, if your financial capacity is insufficient, or if your psychological tolerance to risk is not enough, you should not consider investing in that particular project at that point of time.

2. Understand the entrepreneurs' mentality, personality and ability

Entrepreneurs tend to be optimistic in nature. Based on this kind of optimistic nature, they usually overestimate the development prospects of their own enterprise, and are too optimistic about factors such as market evaluation of their future market, product design and the production process, and might easily ignore the estimate of difficulty. If you think that the entrepreneur's optimism is excessive, or if his/her entrepreneurship idea is impractical, you should not consider investing in that project. Investing in an enterprise also means investing in an entrepreneur, which is not just investing in a certain type of technology or project. If you think the personal character of the entrepreneur is morally contentious, do not further pursue details about the project. In addition, the unity (or lack of it) within the management team is of great significance. If each member of entrepreneurial management team is intelligent and capable but they have different ideas on development prospects, what the business model should be, and have different strategies in mind, you should not consider pursuing this project further.

3. Gain a better understanding of the business model of start-ups

If you do not have a thorough understanding of the model, it is best to not consider investing in it. If you have any doubts about the business model, you must actively propose solutions to what you might deem to be problematic. If you are not content with the solutions that have been proposed by the entrepreneurs/founders, you should re-consider your decision to invest. Generally, when start-ups apply for angel investment, they have little, if any, operating income. What they project in their proposal to angel investors is often expected income. The expected income of start-ups often resembles the shape of a "hockey stick'" (see Figure 6.7). At first, it develops slowly, but after a period, it changes suddenly — showing a linear upward trend. If you find that the "hockey stick" projection does not correspond with the current developing status of the industry the enterprise is entering, you should not consider investing in the project.

Fig. 6.7 The Expected Income of Start-ups in the Shape of a "Hockey Stick".

4. Have a clear understanding of an enterprise's financial status

Check the cash flow of the enterprises — not only its annual cash flow, but its monthly cash flow as well. If the monthly cash flow cannot explain the trend of annual cash flow, it is better to further communicate with the entrepreneurs. If you find obvious vulnerabilities in cash flow, you should not consider investing in the project any further. In addition to considering an enterprise's cash flow, much attention should also be placed on the enterprise's expenditure. Angel investors should take a closer look at the expected expenditure of an enterprise, and analyze whether its expenditure budget is proportional to its expected development. The initial budget of many start-ups is reasonable, but if its expenditure does not increase with its development, problems will occur. Do pay special attention to the enterprise's debt situation: If the enterprise falsifies its real debt situation, do not consider investing in it as this highlights the lack of trustworthiness of the entrepreneurs.

5. Consider the market, product/service and competitiveness

If entrepreneurs are too optimistic about the enterprises' market prospects, angels should communicate with them actively to make them adjust their forecasts. If entrepreneurs estimate that the market prospects are unrealistic, you should not give their business proposal further consideration. Angels should also check the price positioning of the enterprise's products and/or services. If the market positioning of an enterprise is for high-end customers, lowering the price of the product or service will lead to the decline of an enterprise in the long run. On the other hand, if the market positioning of an enterprise is for low-end customers, higher prices will naturally damage the enterprise's competitiveness. If you find the entrepreneurs' price positioning to be quite different from its market positioning of products and services, you should re-consider your decision to invest in the enterprise.

Whether a product/service possesses development prospects depends on its competitiveness, especially its science and technology competitiveness. For science and technology start-ups, science and technology competitiveness is the key. Consider the following questions: Does the core technology of an enterprise have development prospects? Are there barriers to entry as far as core competitiveness is concerned? Will it be easy for the product/service to be eliminated by competitors? Are the entrepreneurs mentally prepared for technological competition? If you think that the entrepreneurs have exaggerated the product's/service's technological competitiveness, or that the product/service relies on existing science and technology, and ignores the potential or actual competitors, do re-consider your decision to invest in the start-up. In connection with the competitiveness in science and technology, angel investors are also concerned about the protection of intellectual property rights. Whether science and technology start-ups possess certain abilities to protect intellectual property rights, such as patents, trademarks and copyright. If the enterprise has been suspected of infringing on intellectual property rights, investors should not invest any further in the project.

6. Value assessment

Angels usually invest in start-ups, especially enterprises at the seed stage, but assessing the value of such enterprises is difficult to some extent. If investors think that the enterprise has development potential, one should ask experts to make a formal value evaluation if they have a strong willingness to invest. If the assessment results show little or no resemblance to the entrepreneur's self-assessment, however excellent the project is, investors should consider giving up the project immediately.

7. Exit channel

Angel investors should pay attention to whether entrepreneurs conceive an appropriate, reasonable exit channel for investors. If entrepreneurs only want to achieve individual success and make money for themselves, and do not consider any compensation for investors with regards to the capital that has been invested and the investors' risk tolerance, investors should give up the project immediately.

8. Pay attention to details

Angel investors should not neglect details. Sometimes they might be extremely interested in the project, satisfied with its management team, market prospects, cash flow forecast and other aspects, but they and entrepreneurs might hold different opinions on details — even trivial ones. In such cases, investors should try their best to communicate with entrepreneurs and seek common ground on major issues while leaving aside minor differences in order to secure a partnership more quickly. However, if entrepreneurs fuss over details and would not compromise even after investors have made concessions, the latter had better give up immediately.

9. Make timely decisions

Angel investors should invest when the opportunity has arrived, and give the project up when the opportunity has turned out to be untimely. In essence, invest quickly, but decisively let the project go to prevent a further incurrence of losses.

Exit Strategies for Angel Investment

I. *Significance of Exit Strategy for Angel Investment*

The exit is the last step of angel investment as well as the key point where the angels get a return on their investment. The exit serves both as a finishing point of previous angel investment and a starting point of new angel investment. The angel investment capital increases along with the growth of the invested enterprises. However, the absence of appropriate exit channels prevents the book value from being cashed out.

The meaning of exit to the angels is similar to what it means to the venture capitalists. As mentioned earlier in Part One, venture capital can be divided into four stages while the angel investment has three stages. Exit, however, is an end to the first cycle as well as a start of another cycle for both investment modes.

Similar to VC investors, angels seek to make a profit out of the investment rather than being engaged in the long-term operation of the enterprise. Angels will exit from the invested enterprise after a period of investment management, which means that they will transfer their shares in the enterprise to other entities or institutions. The exit mechanism is the core of angel investment. This is because angel investment is characterized by high risk and high yield, i.e. angels are willing to take big risks only for big returns and the key to securing big returns is withdrawing and cashing out the investment in time. Once angel investors have made an exit, the angel investment cycle has been completed. Professional angel investors may then invest their private capital fund into a new round of capital appreciation activities. From this perspective, the exit of angel capital is of critical importance to the success of an angel investment.

II. *Exit Mode for Angel Investment*

Angel investors may learn from VC investors in terms of the latter's exit mechanism. However, given that the start-ups are of special development form and face a special economic environment, the exit for angel investment is quite different from that for venture capital, thus requiring further investigation into venture capital from a legislative perspective.

In China, a complete and comprehensive legal system for venture capital has not been established. The Interim Measures for the Administration of Start-up Investment Enterprises issued by National Development and Reform Commission serves as the legal guideline and there are several venture capital-related clauses scattered in basic laws such as the General Principles of the Civil Law of the People's Republic of China, the Contract Law, the Company Law and the Securities Law. According to the Interim Measures for the Administration of Start-up Investment Enterprises, the shares held by shareholders of start-up invest-ment enterprises may be transferred through listing, equity transfer agree-ment, buy-back by the invested enterprise, etc., to realize capital withdrawal. This is similar to the exit mode for angel investment. Exit for investment can be categorized into three categories: Successful exit, failed exit and flat-out exit. Given that the angel investors face considerable investment risks, and a relatively long investment horizon is required, a flat-out exit can be viewed as a failed exit.

The successful exit for angel investment includes: initial public offering (IPO), financial merger and acquisition, strategic merger and acquisition, and management buy-back. If the invested enterprise liquidates its assets, the exit fails. In addition, some mediocre projects might also make the investors hesitant. Terms such as "walking-wounded project" and the "living-dead project," for instance, refer to projects that are "chicken ribs;" tasteless but wasteful to discard.[7] Under such circumstances, the invested enterprise might give a mediocre performance, and not declare bankrupt, leaving investors in a dilemma of whether they should continue to provide support for the enterprise.

Among all options, going public is the first choice of the angel investors and the entrepreneurs. Through IPO, the enterprise may make a profit that equals to a multifold figure of the original investment and sometimes, the figure might be even a hundred times of the original investment. Merger and acquisition and entrepreneur buy-out are the most common exit channels. Although they are the most realistic exit channels, their yield rate is lower than that of the IPO. As for bankruptcy and liquidation, which signals total failure, the loss incurred can only be compensated with the profit made out of successful exits. Should the enterprise become a "chicken-rib investment," the investors will suffer. The IPO and merger and acquisition are the most common exit strategies used by European investors as well as American investors. For angel investors, the latter strategy is more often used. Considering that the investment is made at an early stage, the angel investors may exit when the invested enterprise is subject to refinancing. For example, the angel investor may exit when the VC investors enter the fray. On the other hand, the earlier the investment is made, the longer the investment horizon and the poorer the liquidity of the investment capital will be. In case the angel investors require turnover of capital, they may turn to merger and acquisition, buy-back or right offering instead of waiting for the IPO.

It can be seen from Figure 6.8 that:

(1) Invested enterprises generally favor merger and acquisition. Using IPO as the way out is rarely seen in countries with relatively developed capital markets like the US or in countries with an emerging capital market like China.

(2) Few enterprises turned to IPO even in late 20th century and early 21st century, when the Internet bubble prevailed and the stock market flourished. Most of the enterprises adopted merger and acquisition as their exit strategy.

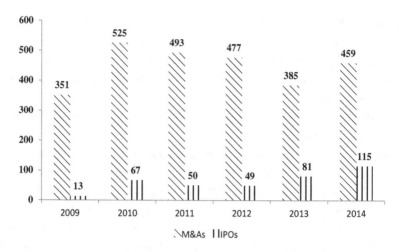

Fig. 6.8   Exit for American Venture Capitalists from 2009 to 2014.
Source: NVCA Yearbook 2015.

(3) The figure shows the exit situation for venture capitalists. Under general circumstances, however, the angel investors favor the IPO less than the venture capitalists.

III. *Expected Return on Angel Investment*

Generally, the earlier the investment is made, the higher the risk associated with the investment and the prospective earnings will be lower. Since the angel investment applies to the early stage, in particular the seed stage of an enterprise, it is naturally characterized by high risk and high potential gains. In 2011, the Venture Capital Research Center of the University of New Hampshire conducted a survey on angel investors who invest in software and high-tech industry in New England. According to the survey, the average annual rate of return of angel investors of five years was 65.5%. Making a profit equal to seven times of the original investment in seven years is desirable for the angel investors. However, the average annual rate of return of seven years was 32%. Robert Wiltbank and Warren Boeker surveyed 3,097 investment projects carried out by 539 angel investors from 86 angel investment institutions, among which, 1,137 successful exits have been accomplished.[8] According to the result, over half of the angel investment cases went down the drain. In general, the average investment amount of angel investment is US$191,000, the profit is US$295,000 and the internal rate of return is 27%, which means the investors make a profit equal to 2.6 times of the original investment amount in 3.5 years.

In 2012, CYzone, a well-known domestic entrepreneurial magazine, published the Report of Angel Investment of 2012, which was the first survey report targeted at Chinese angel investors. As mentioned in the Report, Chinese angel investors have witnessed gradual development and made great contribution to Chinese start-ups. In addition, the return on angel investment has been decent. Among all Chinese angel investors, less than 10% of the investors saw negative ROI, more than half of the investors witness a ROI of above 30%, 18% of the investors enjoy a ROI of above 200% and some star enterprises even make a profit equal to dozens of times, sometimes even 100 times of the original investment amount. Compared with foreign angel investors, domestic angel investors expect shorter investment horizons and wish to receive the returns as early as possible.

Notes

1. Paul Gompers and Josh Lerner, 'What Drives Venture Capital Fundraising?' *Brookings Papers on Economic Activity. Microeconomics* (July 1998): 149–192.
2. This refers to China's lemon law, known as "san bao" (三包). It gives customers "three guarantees" within a certain period of time if the products they have bought are defective: guaranteed to be repaired or replaced free of charge, or fully refunded.
3. Liu Manhong, 'VC Investment and VC Investment Management,' Course Notes, Renmin University of China, 2007.
4. Andrew Wong, 'Angel Finance: The Other Venture Capital,' Working Paper, University of Chicago, 2002.
5. Steven N. Kaplan and Per Strömberg, 'Venture Capitalists as Principals: Contracting, Screening and Monitoring,' Working Paper. University of Chicago, 2001.
6. Brent D. Goldfarb, Michael D. Pfarrer and David Kirsch. 'Searching for Ghosts: Business Survival, Unmeasured Entrepreneurial Activity and Private

Equity Investment in the Dot-Com Era,' Working Paper. School of Business, University of Maryland, 2005.

7. In the *Annals of the Nine Provinces* used by Pei Songzhi in his *Annotation to Annals of Emperor Wu, Book of Wei, Records of the Three Kingdoms*, "At that time, the King wished to return to his palace and said, 'Chicken ribs.' All officials and servants were confused with the order. Yang Xiu, the Official in charge of Documents, started to pack by himself. People were surprised and asked how he could know the intention of the King, and Yang responded, 'Chicken ribs are something regrettable if you throw them away but tasteless if you eat them. And the King used chicken ribs to describe Hanzhong, thus I know the King wants to return."

8. Robert Wiltbank and Warren Boeker, 'Returns to Angel Investors in Groups,' Working Paper, SSRN, November 1, 2007, available at http://papers.ssrn.com/sol3/papers.cfm?abstract_id=1028592.

Chapter 7

How Third Parties Can Strengthen Angel Investment

Individual investment model has shown limits in terms of information acquisition, the spreading of risk, efficiency of investment, etc. In contrast, angel investment derives a combination of group-based and institutionalized investment models from the individual investment models. The emergence of group-based and institutionalized investment models has helped speed up the appearance and development of the angel investment service providers.

Angel Investment Service Provider: Match-Maker Between Entrepreneur and Angel Investor

Most individual angel investors are part-time investors. They are mainly confronted with the following problems: limited project sources and quantities; limited individual financial strength which makes it difficult to diversify the investment; limited time to conduct detailed background checks such as due diligence; lack of investment experience and knowledge; and high failure rate. To overcome these issues, the angel investment service providers can be seen as a solution/response under specific timeframes and conditions.

I. *Category of Services Provided by Angel Investment Service Providers*

Angel investors mainly engage in project sourcing, project screening, preparation of investment contract, post-investment participation and exiting. Angel investment service providers can play an important role in all five activities.

1. Project sourcing

Most angels search for projects through the trustworthy networks of investment relationships that were established by them. Some angels however might have no powerful networks of investment relationships, and may turn to the intermediary service agencies for sourcing out and screening projects. Angels mainly obtain information related to the projects via the following channels: (1) direct contact with entrepreneurs; (2) angel investment groups and intermediary service agencies; (3) venture capitalists; (4) legal advisors, accountants, consultants, investment bankers, etc. Generally speaking, trustworthy angel groups and intermediary service agencies, followed by personal connections (such as those mentioned in (4)) tend to be reliable bodies that might introduce high-quality projects. New angel investors particularly value the function performed by angel groups and intermediary service agencies and view them as the major channels to obtain projects.

2. Project screening

Angels will conduct due diligence against the enterprise as per certain criteria to screen the project after acquiring information related to the project. The due diligence can be divided into preliminary and in-depth due diligence from the perspective of content and dimensions. Preliminary due diligence mainly focuses on project source, geographical factors, and industry properties, while the in-depth due diligence covers the start-up team, market potential, business model, the product and the technology involved. Generally speaking, angel investors are only capable of conducting preliminary due diligence independently while in-depth due diligence requires a team effort. For average angel investors, the cost of establishing their own angel investment team is relatively high, and therefore, they often entrust angel investment group or intermediary angel investment service agency to perform in-depth due diligence.

3. Preparation of investment contract

Angels will prepare investment contract and negotiate with start-up on the specific terms and conditions after thorough due diligence and screening.

The negotiation will mainly focus on following aspects: first of all, the arrangement of types of investment securities. The start-ups have three major types of securities: common stock, convertible bond and preferred stock attached with several rights; secondly, anti-dilution clause and protective clauses; thirdly, ownership proportion and control (angel investors often hold 5% to 25%, generally 10% of the ownership of the enterprise during the start-up stage); and last but not least, both parties will negotiate on clauses such as key employees and exit mechanism.

Mature angels often choose to prepare the contract independently based on their abundant experiences of investment negotiation while new angel investors are more likely to listen to the analysis and suggestions made by the angel investment service providers to prepare the contract. Some angels may even hire angel investment service providers to assist them with the negotiation of contract terms and conditions.

4. Post-investment participation

Different angels play different roles and participate in different degrees in start-up management. The passive angels are often not members of the board and they rarely take part in daily management of the enterprise. Instead, they have an eye on the investment and operation of the enterprise through the reports provided by the enterprise regularly. On the other hand, active angels are usually experts with abundant work experience and areas of specialty and are thus able to offer value-added services to the enterprise. Generally, they play the role of director or consultant to the enterprise. The post-investment participation becomes diversified along with the emerging and development of angel investment service providers. The angel investment service providers will deliver development analysis report of the target enterprise to their clients on a regular basis and present their clients with the start-up's management plan.

5. Exit

Angel capital increases along with the growth of the enterprise and an appropriate exit channel is required to cash out the increased angel capital. Major exit strategies include IPO, merger and acquisition, buy-back, asset liquidation, etc., among which, IPO and merger and acquisition are the widely used. IPO often brings abundant payback to the investors. This is because the value of the shares held by the investors may increase rapidly thanks to the leverage of the security market. However, IPO has certain drawbacks. First of all, IPO requires a lot of preparation, which is cumbersome, and the exit cost is relatively high. Meanwhile, exiting laws prohibit principal shareholders from selling their stock within a certain period. This means the angel investors cannot fully exit within a relatively long period of time after IPO and their gains are entirely rely on the market performance of the share stocks. Thus more and more investors turn to merger and acquisition as their way out.

When angels choose merger and acquisition, the angel investment service providers will help them search for the most desirable buyers, working out a reasonable merger and acquisition model, finding the golden exit opportunity and developing a strategy of negotiation between the angel investors and new potential investors.

6. Training of angel investor

Past successes show that start-up investment brings an enterprise the most benefits. However, professional skill and remarkable insight are necessities; otherwise, blind investment is no different from throwing money away. If one wants to set foot in angel investment, there is some basic knowledge he/she needs to acquire. For this reason, angel investment service providers develop various training courses for the abovementioned angel investment activities and hold salons based on the focus of angel investors to discuss development status of the industry.

II. *Experience of American Angel Investment Service*

American angel investment service providers become mature gradually after development of nearly half a century and they provide angel investors with the six professional services mentioned earlier. Angel service providers in the US mainly consist of angel investment network platforms, angel investment groups, universities and angel investment forums.

1. Angel investment network platform

Existing angel investment network platforms draw more and more attention from investors and entrepreneurs because they have clear advantages and results of integrating resources and improving efficiency. Since this kind of platforms provides investors with angel investment services and entrepreneurs with start-up services, they are service providers for angel investors as well as start-ups.

The most developed Internet platform in the US is Gust, formerly known as AngelSoft, established by David S. Rose in 2004 (it was renamed Gust in September 2011). Currently, Gust is a global platform for start-up financing and its headquarters are in New York. Gust has set up a R&D center in Vancouver, Canada and a European office in Paris, France. The platform has received support from world leading angel investors and venture capital associations and promotes the development of over 1,000 investment institutions in 65 countries. Over 160,000 start-ups have established contact and partnership with over 45,000 independent qualified investors through this platform.

Gust has evolved into a global platform providing searching, screening and management of investment projects. With support to investment relationship received from Gust, entrepreneurs with professional skills have the chance to join hands from initial marketing to successful exit. It can be seen from the above that the services provided by Gust cover five of six major angel service categories. One merit Gust has is that it can provide angels with global view and enable them to search and screen projects without being subject to national or geographic restrictions.

There are some angel service providers in China that are similar to Gust, such as AngelCrunch. AngelCrunch is an online start-up investment community founded in November 2011 that provides various kinds of guidance on product, user experience, financing and equity. AngelCrunch breaks the pattern in which promising projects are snapped up at a very early stage and it gathers high-quality projects on the platform. Investors using AngelCrunch may recommend projects to each other and many investors may play the role of leader or follower in the area where he has home field advantage. Win-win cooperation not only results in resource complementarity but also lowers the investment risk and increases the growth rate of the invested project. Through AngelCrunch, investors may screen projects according to their investment style and focus and get accurate personalized project recommendations.

Compared with its American counterpart, the development of Chinese angel investment network platform is imperfect, which is reflected on severe geographic restriction on project sourcing the Chinese angel investment network platform is subject to. Without being geared for the international market, Chinese angel investors have difficulty finding excellent foreign start-up projects whereas foreign investors can find Chinese start-up projects easily through platforms like Gust. In this way, the project channel of Chinese angel investors is squeezed.

2. Angel investment associations and groups

(1) *Industry association — Angel Capital Association (ACA).* ACA is a non-profit organization established by Kauffman Fundation in January 2004, providing members (angel investment groups and individual angel investors) with services like information exchange, dialogue and communication, and education and training. ACA has established long-term partnership with American universities to provide its members with research data and consultation services. Besides, ACA holds annual conferences and allows American, as well as global angel investors, researchers and institutions an offline platform to learn from each other and communicate. ACA has also set up an Angel Capital Education Foundation (ACEF). The Foundation aims to provide potential and existing angel investors with education and training so as to enable them to better utilize their fund and reduce investment risks.

(2) *Angel investment groups* (including investment institutions and investment service providers). There are numerous angel investment groups in the US, for example, the Las Vegas Angel Investors, the Common Angels, the New York Angels, the Sand Hill Angels and the Golden Seeds Angels. Similar to the angel investment network platforms, angel investment groups also supply angel investors with project searching, project screening, investment contract preparation, post-investment participation, and exit services. However, angel investment groups offer advantages in post-investment participation and exit

services. Besides, angel investment groups furnish the sixth category of service mentioned earlier (training for angel investors). Combined with the investigation and survey conducted by the editors in Silicon Valley, Sand Hill Angels and Golden Seeds will be further analyzed:

- Sand Hill Angels was set up at the end of 2000 with over 100 active angel investors and is specialized in investment in the field of IT, Internet, life science and clean energy. As one of the Top Five American angel investment clubs, Sand Hill Angels is vastly superior in its professional investment procedure. The Club will establish an independent partnership for every investment project and have the member who makes investment in the project act as the shareholder. In this way, the ownership structure is clear and convenient for post-investment participation and exit.
- Golden Seeds was founded by Stephanie Newby, a senior Wall Street investor, in 2005. Golden Seeds targets female angels and entrepreneurs and provides them with better financing channel and value-added services. The establishment of Golden Seeds gives female angel investors the same reputation and rights their male peers have enjoyed for a long time.

Compared with American angel investment groups, Chinese angel investment groups have just emerged. Although some angel investment groups such as the China Young Angel Investor Leader Association have been set up, the role of the angel investment group as an angel service provider has not been fulfilled, the services provided are limited to the provision of project channel and the training function is restricted to inviting well-known angel investors to give lectures.

3. Angel investment training institutions (i.e. universities)

Generally speaking, universities are classified as start-up service providers, which aim to provide entrepreneurs with business and technical assistance. Universities, however, also serve as angel service providers in America. As mentioned above, American angel investment groups cooperate with universities to supply angel investors within the group with relevant training.

Many business schools of the universities invite famous angel investors or venture capitalists to be their guests to give lectures to students or potential investors about angel investment and prepare them for undertaking such investments. Take Stanford University as an instance. As everyone knows, Stanford University is within Silicon Valley and provides America with a steady flow of technology talents. Meanwhile, Stanford invites noted venture capitalists in Silicon Valley to offer courses related to investment not only to students and entrepreneurs but also to angel investors. Mr. John Glynn, a second generation venture capitalist and partner and managing director of Glynn Capital Management, which was founded over a century ago, is one of the guest lecturers/professors.

Similar to the model adopted by Stanford, many Chinese universities such as Peking University also provide angel investors with similar training course.

4. Angel investment forum

Angel investment forum is a unique kind of angel service provision model created by America and has played a critical part in the development of American angel investment. It can be seen as the milestone that signifies that angel investors have become standardized and professionalized. Famous angel investment forums include Angel Forum and keiretsu forum (K4).

Angel Forum was founded by Mrs. Carol Sands in 1997. All 16 founders of Angel Forum are wealthy entrepreneurs who have gained success and reputation in business and participated in IPO of at least one company, and have abundant experiences of and strong motivation for start-ups. Angel Forum has a standard model of operation that has been adopted by venture capital companies, including the screening/review and due diligence of target project, and post-investment management. Carol Sands believes that the only difference between a professional angel investment team and a venture capitalist is that the latter invests with other people's money while the angel investor invests with his own money. A more desirable advantage enjoyed by angel investors is that the investment made by them is the return they have received their successful start-ups, which means the experiences of start-ups accumulated by them enable them to provide the invested company with various valuable and instructional assistance. K4 is the largest angel investment website designed to unite individuals and small enterprises to create a fresh force of investors. Currently, angel service providers in the angel investment forums are absent in China and experiences and lessons may be learnt from America to set up relevant institutions to provide similar services to angels within China. Angel service providers have arguably improved the overall efficiency of angel investment. Since Chinese angel investment has not yet matured, investors should pay more attention on the construction and development of angel service providers while strengthening the angel investment groups to serve both as an angel investor and an angel service provider. Considering that the concept of angel investment has not been popularized in China, the source of angel investment project is limited and the specialization level of project screening is relatively low. Angel investment institutions should hence offer services with emphases on investment training, project sourcing and project screening to angel investors.

Start-up Service Provider: Improve the Development Efficiency of Angel Investment Industry

Start-up services cover start-up orientation, consultation and assistance, and therefore plays a critical role in helping start-ups and entrepreneurs seek external help, while reducing the start-up risk. Start-up services offer great help in terms of connecting angel investors and facilitating the integration of resources. All these in turn reduce the risk of failure confronted by angel investors, and indirectly improve the development efficiency of the industry.

I. *Categorization of Services Delivered by Start-up Service Providers*

Start-up services are characterized by diversification. The services vary along with the fields that start-up talents may come from. In addition, different social and economic environments and the position of the enterprise in the development process all affect the categorization of start-up services. Based on the current situation, start-up services are in urgent need of vertical expansion. According to the categorization by the magazine

Chinese Talents in 2013, start-up services are divided into investment and financing service, technology platform service and quality enhancement service.[1] This categorization is adopted here.

1. Investment and financing service

More and more people have chosen to start their own business in China in light of the rapid development of its economy. However, numerous entrepreneurs fail to realize their dreams due to limited sources of funding, which have motivated some start-up service providers to provide entrepreneurs with investment and financing services. Major types of exiting start-up service providers which offer investment and financing services include: special funds for development of science and technology and guidance funds that support entrepreneurship, which have been established and funded by the government. For this type of funds, a special project review unit will be set up to review the project proposals submitted by entrepreneurs. Angel investment funds set up by high-tech development zones and technology incubators also provide investment and financing services and they often act as investors, angel service providers and start-up service providers at the same time.

Besides the government-led start-up service providers, the private start-up service providers afford entrepreneurs more sources of financing, crowd funding and joint investment in particular, with its emergence and rapid development. We will take the crowd funding mode adopted by AngelCrunch as an example to elaborate on new financing channels here. AngelCrunch, founded in November 2011, is currently operated by Tianjin Sheng Bang Investment Co. Ltd. It is the first domestic platform to publish crowdfunding rules for angel investors, and aims at giving full play to the efficient and transparent Internet and helping entrepreneurs and angels establish connections quickly. The basic procedures of crowdfunding are: (A) Investors join AngelCrunch; (B) Entrepreneurs submit projects online; (C) The analyst team of AngelCrunch reviews the project; (D) Investors look through the projects and AngelCrunch recommends projects to investors; (E) Entrepreneurs and investors make an appointment to discuss; (F) Entrepreneurs and investors conclude contracts. Since its official launch in 2011, AngelCrunch has financed RMB 250 million for over 70 SMEs and many successful projects have evolved from angel financing to first round and even second round financing. Successful examples include DiDi Taxi, Menstrual Cycle Helper (DAYIMA Helper), BreadTrip, Huang Taiji, etc. Up to now, over 8,000 start-up projects have been registered on the AngelCrunch platform and over 1,000 enterprises have been reviewed and licensed. In addition, the number of entrepreneur members has exceeded 22,000.

2. Technology platform service

Product design, processing and inspection are essential to the start-up process. Some design procedures, processing and inspection equipment may cost the entrepreneurs and their backers several million yuan. If these costs are borne by the entrepreneurs entirely, the financial burden on their shoulders will inevitably affect the start-up process and may even result in idle equipment and waste. The development of public technology service platform may solve this problem effectively. The public technology service platform can build up a public technology support system designed to provide SMEs with development training, promoting technology and design, processing and testing of the product in an area where the degree of industrial concentration is relatively high with certain industrial advantages. Public services like R&D of new products, product testing and inspection, and technical expertise training may be provided through the public technology service platform, which will not only satisfy the development need of SMEs but also improve the overall performance of the products within the industrial clusters and bring about positive spillover effects on local industries.

Some science and technology parks have paid more and more attention to the construction of the open technology service platform and the provision of services to SMEs:

Case 1: The Test Platform of Shenzhen Software Park and China Software Testing Center (CSTC) joined hands to provide various kinds of software and hardware testing environments. This measure overcomes the inadequacy of technology support system confronted by many software enterprises which value the software quality but lack special testing tools and complex testing environments and provides IT enterprises in Shenzhen with all-rounded third-party services.

Case 2: The governments funds the state biotech and pharmaceutical industrial base of Zhangjiang Drug Valley. It practices market-orientation operation and adopts the separation of establishment and management and market operation. The government is responsible for providing the initial infrastructure, instruments and equipment while the Shanghai Pharmaceutical Valley Business Management Co. Ltd., a semi-nonprofit business of the industrial base, is liable for daily operations, and mainly supports the development of innovation-based SMEs.

Case 3: The Wuhan National Bioindustry Base is the second national industrial base constructed in East Lake High-Tech Development Zone, following to the State Optoelectronic Information Industry Base. The industrial base covers an area of 1600 Mu (1Mu equals to 0.0667 hectares) and hosts a bio-industry R&D area, incubation area, pilot test area and Biotechnology Research Institute, Animal Experimenting Center, Enlarged Experiment Platform and special incubator — all of which constitute the technical support and public service system for bio-industry development and incubation. Among them, the Biolake of Optics Valley has six servicing platforms of bio-industry technology support, public services, business incubators, information resources sharing, investment and financing, and talent introduction and successfully plays the role of public technology service platform. Given the gradual perfection of infrastructure and supporting functions, a number of world leading innovations were created here.

Apart from the Technology Park, some private start-up service providers strive to create technology platforms such as Innovation Works and Legend Star. The open classes for product given by Innovation Works are often taught by world-class experts to provide specific training on the products launched by the entrepreneurs.

3. Quality enhancement service

Currently, the quality promotion services supplied by start-up service providers include open classes, salon sharing and small-scale forums. An example of an open class and start-up experience sharing session held by Innovation Works includes a venture capital investment salon held by venture capital investment circle, Online Q&A for Cycle of Venture Capital Investment, exchange salon and Garage activities organized by Garage Café. Apart from these services, the government, the media and some private institutions have organized various large-scale activities such as innovation and entrepreneurship competitions and conferences, aimed at creating an effective project display and information exchange platform for technology-based SMEs. They have also actively channeled more and more social resources to support innovative entrepreneurship and promoted the development of innovative SMEs. One of the most influential activities is the "Black Horse Activities" held by The Founder. Take the Black Horse Competition designed to select innovation-based growing company for investment and financing as an example. This competition also serves as a development platform, a display platform and a trade platform for start-ups. Besides the Black Horse Competition, there is the Black Horse Camp, a high-end comprehensive start-up service platform designed for the founders of growth-type enterprises to provide with learning, financing, promotion, cooperation and consultation services. In addition to the Black Horse Competition and the Black Horse Camp, the Founder also launched a high-end entrepreneur club called Black Horse Club, which features training, communication and mutual help and unites entrepreneurs to study together, centralize the resources and increase the success rate of start-up.

II. *Experience of Starting Businesses and Services in America*

The function of government, colleges and universities, incubators is deemed very important in US, which has provides policy services counseling and entrepreneurship service. Main practices include:

1. Government departments

The US government has established the US Small Business Administration (SBA), which is designed for the small enterprises — especially start-up enterprises. The aims of the SBA are to provide support, consultation, help and protection, to maintain the competitiveness of free enterprises, maintain and increase the economy of the country. At present, the SBA has 3,000 employees to provide services for the small enterprises and start-up enterprises, with 300 in Washington, and others in 70 offices around the country.

SBA has adopted many measures to provide services for entrepreneurship: The first is to provide the face-to-face or online courses for the start-up enterprise and small enterprises on education, information technology, technology assistance and training. The web portal of SBA has a total of 45,000 pages, with 1.8 million clicks each week, covering every kind of policies and service procedures and translated into many languages.

The second is to help the small enterprises to get purchasing contracts from the government. The federal government spends about US$200 billion every year in procurement. The procurement office of the SBA provides help to the small enterprises to get purchasing contracts through coordination with the government, which turns out to be successful. In 2008, Shanghai Pharma Engine, which is a state-specialized bio-pharmaceutical incubator, got 22% of the total US federal procurement budget and in 2012, the percentage reached 23% (as required by the Congress). The Office also provides outsourcing opportunities, outward bound and training to small business.

The third is to perfect the policy for promoting the development of small enterprises. The SBA has a policy supervision office, with the chief advisor being appointed by the President directly. The office's primary mission is to supervise the executive condition of relevant acts, to assess the negative effects to the small enterprises of each policy, to collect advice from everywhere to promote the development of small enterprises and to decrease the burden of those small enterprises. It is said that the office can save about US$10 billion for small enterprises each year.

The SBA also established a volunteer team with 13,000 individuals who provide help for small enterprises in the areas of policy and management for free. About two-thirds of the volunteers are retired administrative staff. This team has a history of 48 years of providing voluntary service for small enterprises for about 1.5 million hours each year and saving hourly consulting fees of about US$200 for the small enterprises. Some institutions, private sectors and local governments also provide the entrepreneurship instructing service. They provide guidance for the entrepreneurs through the establishment of Small Business Development Centers (SBDCs), Women Business Centers (WBCs), Counselors to America's Small Business (SCORE).

2. Colleges and universities

Colleges and universities are the perfect places for entrepreneurs, especially Harvard University on the east coast and Stanford University on the west coast. This book will take Stanford as an example and show readers how higher education institutions in the US provide relevant services to entrepreneurs.

The teachers of business school and engineering school of Stanford have set a series of entrepreneurship education courses. They have merged the entrepreneurship and courses together; focusing on the basic courses by breaking the block between the majors and combining basic courses and major courses together to reinforce the liberal education of students. They have also increased the integrated courses and set up an interdisciplinary curriculum of science and technology, and social sciences. The courses include those in liberal arts, science and engineering, which help meet students' need in studying entrepreneurship.

Over 20 courses on entrepreneurship are offered in Stanford, introducing how to start a business, including the financing, searching for resources, staff employing and so on. The Stanford business school has set up a series of entrepreneurship courses, such as "Entrepreneurship Management," "Entrepreneurship Opportunity Assessment," "Entrepreneurship and Its Financing," "Financing Management and Entrepreneurship Finance," "Management of Enterprises in Their Growing-up Phase." Those courses are very popular and more than 91% of the MBA students choose at least one entrepreneurship course. Every year, about 2,000 students take part in the technology entrepreneurship program course. Every entrepreneurship course has a good atmosphere of interaction of students and teachers.

The teaching in Stanford has resulted in the emergence of a good practice system. Stanford places a lot of emphasis on the training of students' capacity for scientific research and occupational skills, and requires students to take all kinds of research lectures, some of which can be counted as credits. Stanford encourages students to take part in scientific research activities and allows them to participate in joint-operated projects beyond the university.

As is well known, the majority of the successful entrepreneurs in Silicon Valley are from Stanford, which enables the university to make full use of this resource pool to set up courses of entrepreneurship training. Indeed, Stanford often invite successful alumni entrepreneurs to gives lectures in entrepreneurship in the university.

3. Incubator (accelerator)

According to the National Business Incubation Association (NBIA), "incubator" and "accelerator" are interchangeable but accelerator is increasingly considered a more fashionable term. However, in our opinion, those two words have subtle differences. An accelerator mainly deals with enterprises in their growth phase and an incubator deals with enterprises in their start-up period. To some extent, enterprises served by an accelerator are mainly from those served by an incubator. In addition, an incubator provide more "hardware" (such as workshops, office spaces, telephones, printers) than "software" (such as consultation services, training, team construction, product development, market evaluation training). On the contrary, an accelerator provides more "software" than "hardware."

The incubators in America, as a typical entrepreneurship-facilitating agency, provide three kinds of services on financing, technology platform and quality enhancement to the entrepreneurs at the same time. We take Y Combinator (YC) as an example in financing service. YC was established by Harvard graduate Paul Graham in 2005, and it focuses on enterprises in their start-up phase only and provides necessary services for them. Usually, YC will invest a small amount of money (no more than US$20,000) into the company and hold a small portion of its shares (about 6%). YC provides funding to those enterprises "in batches." Therefore, YC is sometimes known as the earliest, or one of the first incubators. Since its establishment, YC have invested in hundreds of science and technology enterprises, such as the famous Reddit that has been merged by Kondner; Dropbox, valued at US$4 billion; and Airbnb (a bulletin board system of traveling house leases). After two other Silicon Valley old hand, Ron Conway and Yuri Milner, joined YC, every enterprise invested by the YC has been able to receive a convertible bond worth US$150,000.

In the technology platform arena, we can take AngelPad as an example. AngelPad is an incubator set up by Google in 2010, which aims to provide help in product development and financing for the enterprises to become more successful. Meanwhile, AngelPad also provides authentic Google training and support. For quality enhancement, we take Capital Factory as an example. Capital Factory is famous for its excellent instruction team, which includes Joshua Bear, the founder of Skylist, Jeremy Bencken, the founder of ApartmentRatings. Apart from the help of experienced instructors, the enterprises receiving the help of Capital Factory will also get an investment of US$20,000 and a series of hardware support (in exchange, Capital Factory gets 5% of each enterprise's share). The duration of incubation lasts from late May to early August every year. During this period, the enterprises will get support from the instructors in a group or one-to-one. The Demo Day is usually in September.

Colleges and Universities: Entrepreneurship, Education and Competition

I. *Introduction of College Entrepreneurship Education in China*

Since 2002, the entrepreneurship education in China's universities and colleges has entered a phase of diversified development with the guidance of the government. It has formed a pattern where the establishment of pilot education programs, introduction of similar projects from abroad and related government policy support together push for the development of entrepreneurship education in China's higher education institutions.[2] First, nine universities, including Tsinghua University, Renmin University, became pilot universities of entrepreneurship education in 2002. In 2008, the Ministry of Education set up 30 new pilot areas of human resource training in innovation and entrepreneurship. Second, under the auspices of the Chinese government, entrepreneurship education programs from overseas, such as Start and Improve Your Business (SIYB) and Know About Business (KAB), were introduced into China between 2004 and 2005. The Ministry of Education then reinforced the importance of entrepreneurship education in a number of its official notices and announcements. Those three policies have greatly helped promote the development of entrepreneurship education in China.

1. The education department should promote the entrepreneurship education

The Ministry of Education started the entrepreneurship education pilot program in 2002, choosing Renmin University, Tsinghua University, Beijing University of Aeronautics and Astronautics, Heilongjiang University, Shanghai Jiaotong University, Nangjing institute of economics, Wuhan University, Xi'an Jiaotong University, Northwestern Polytechnical University as the pilot universities. The entrepreneurship education can be divided into three types. The first is in-class teaching, strengthening the importance of school education and forming the knowledge structure the entrepreneurs need. The knowledge acquired is intended to lay the foundation for real entrepreneurship projects in the future. For this, courses like "Entrepreneur Spirit," "Venture Investment," "Entrepreneurship Management" have been offered. The second type focuses on promoting students' hands-on knowledge and skills in starting a business. To this end, the universities have established entrepreneurial parks for college students, taught them how to start a business and provided support in finance and services. For example, Beijing University of Aeronautics and Astronautics has professional teachers for the study and research of entrepreneurship education, and the university has set up a special institution called the Entrepreneurship Management Training Institution for them. Meanwhile, the university also established a Venture Capital Fund of RMB 3 million to invest in its students' stage enterprises after entrepreneurship assessments have been conducted.

The third step is comprehensive education, which combines the two types mentioned earlier.

2. The KAB project of Central Communist Youth League and University Union

In order to help youth during employment, the International Labor Organization has developed a new project called Know About Business, whose aim is to strengthen college students' awareness and ability of entrepreneurship. The KAB constitutes of a series of training materials and unique teaching methods, which focuses on the education and training of starting a business. At present, more than 20 countries have adopted this project. In order to solve the problem of low employment rate and the lack of ability of employment, the United Nations, International Labor Organization and World Bank has form the Youth Employment Network (YEN) in 2001. The aim of the YEN is to create jobs for youth and provide advice and support for them during their employment. The YEN clearly puts the promotion of young people's employment ability, the equality of opportunity of woman and man, entrepreneurship spirit and the creation of new jobs as four priorities for all the countries.

To introduce the KAB in China, the Central Committee of the Chinese Communist Youth League and China Youth Federation held a discussion with the International Labor Organization in January 2005, and finished the translation and editing of *Know About Business: Basic Entrepreneurship Rules for College Students* at the end of the year. In 2006, YEN opened the pilot program on KAB in six universities in China through the All-China Youth Federation. This project had trained about 300 teachers from 22 provinces and 149 universities. As for the courses opened in those pilot universities, most of them are optional courses, which provide systematic and scientific training for the students.

3. The entrepreneurship education project opened by universities

From 1997, many universities reformed their education mode from traditional economic management training to entrepreneurship training and they came into a period of independent exploration in this field. During this period, many had attained good results. For example, Zhejiang University opened the course of "Innovation and Entrepreneurship Promoting," which chose a number of upper class engineering students with a good knowledge in engineering and management to receive training in the promotion of awareness, quality and skill on managerial control, innovation and entrepreneurship. Fudan University implemented the entrepreneurship education program into their daily teaching schedule, which allowed the students to gain knowledge and acquire skills of entrepreneurship. It also set up a special fund to support the students to take part in social science practices of entrepreneurship, and provide special instruction to students who want to start a business. East China Normal University set up an "Entrepreneurship Education Course;" Wuhan University used "innovation, entrepreneurship and entrepreneurship education" to promote education quality and foster talents. Nankai University, Sun Yat-Sen University also opened entrepreneurship management courses and how to develop small enterprises courses.

Apart from universities and colleges, vocational schools also placed special emphasis on entrepreneurship education. Wuxi Vocational Institute of Commerce was the first to establish "Entrepreneurship Streets" and the first to establish a vocational training group Jiangsu Commercial and Trading Education Group, which led to the development of many companies like Jiangsu Education Market, Wuxi Decoration Company, and Mengzhidao Information and Technology Company. It also established an entrepreneurship education park of "entrepreneurship teaching + entrepreneurship modeling + entrepreneurship practice." The school cooperated with enterprises to establish modeling platforms for corporate planning, registration and operation. The school also made an effort to develop the 3D virtual software with enterprises' features to allow students to experience the real entrepreneurship. Meanwhile, the school introduced the SYB (Start Your Business) program and piloted the Wuxi SYB training project to promote students' skills in starting a business and operating a company. The school also encouraged students to start their own business. In the first half of 2006, there were more than 20 companies, innovation studios and business environment simulation centers owned by the students in the 1,800-square-meter entrepreneurship park. After experts conducted the training sessions and assessed their design proposals, the students could start their business in the park. The park is the education base of teaching and production; the platform for special skills training and a bridge connecting students and society. Another example is Zhejiang Vocational College of Commerce's "Real Entrepreneurship Education in Real Environment," which has been praised as "the ground breaking program of China's higher vocational education; the pioneer of China's higher vocational education." Rather than sitting in a classroom, the students would engage in real entrepreneurship practice and all pre-proposal issues that they face should be solved by themselves (i.e. conducting a market survey before the project is made, the commercial planning, the application of the product/service in real market conditions etc.). The school would then appoint experienced teachers to assess the reports. After their reports have been approved, the students should register the company to get a license — conditions which reflect real-world ones. Students should do everything related to starting a business. Over the last two years, 69 projects have entered the entrepreneurial park in 4 batches, with 353 students directly involved and another 3,000 students within the school community indirectly involved. While one enterprise dropped out mid-way, the remaining 68 enterprises all achieved profitability and reached a sale of over RMB 3.5 million.[3]

II. An Overview of Entrepreneurship Education in the United States

American entrepreneurship education began in the 1960s. The US is the pioneer and most successful performer in this field. Its development goes through the process that begins with course teaching, then professional teaching, then followed by degree teaching that focuses on different types of training: from vocational to systematic training. Some major features are shown below.

1. Multi-channel financial support

American entrepreneurship education receives strong financial support. The US National Science Foundation has established the institution implementing Small Business Innovation Research Program (SBIR) to encourage people to start their own business after acquiring knowledge of how to do so. Entrepreneurship education also wins extensive support from all walks of life, including the Coleman Foundation, Kauffman Entrepreneurial Center, the National Federation of Independent Business (NFIB), and New Mexico Business Development Center. Every year, those foundations provide a great deal of entrepreneurship education funds to colleges and universities in the forms of prizes from business plan competitions, theses and so on. The American VC investment has also provided practice bases and sufficient funds for entrepreneurship education.

2. Diversified entrepreneurship education institutions

The major institutions generalizing entrepreneurship education in American include SBA, Youth Entrepreneurs of Kansas and the Kauffman Entrepreneurial Center. Many colleges and universities in the US have their own entrepreneurial centers, whose major function is to transfer research achievements from teachers and students to enterprises. The distinguished "Silicon Valley" is gradually growing up on the basis of achievements transformation of teachers and students from Stanford University. There are a great variety of entrepreneurship education institutions in colleges and universities, such as the entrepreneurship education centers which exist on some campuses, which are responsible for formulating and implementing curriculum plans, outreach and developments plans that promote entrepreneurship education. Entrepreneur associations have also been formed by outstanding entrepreneurs, which contribute to current efforts to teach about entrepreneurship and provide opportunities for students to acquire angel investment when starting their own business. Think tanks have also been established and they are composed of external enterprise senior managers who put forward suggestions for entrepreneurship education. Other kinds of associations that exist in partnership with education institutions include entrepreneurship societies, family business research institutions and so on.

3. Various curriculum systems of entrepreneurship education

The first entrepreneurship education curriculum for higher education institutions in the United States was born in 1970. In 1980, the first entrepreneurship education major for undergraduates was set up. At present, more than 500 colleges and universities provide entrepreneurship education curriculums and degree programs, and the curriculum system of entrepreneurship education from primary school to university and even to postgraduate has taken shape. Although there are various types of education in American higher education, none of the education program or teaching practice can cover the entire spectrum of entrepreneurship education. Over the last 20 years, the curriculum for innovation and entrepreneurship education in colleges and universities had developed rapidly. In 2008, over 5,000 entrepreneurship-oriented courses had been set up in two-year community colleges and universities that offer four-year degree programs. Innovation and entrepreneurship education programs of some colleges and universities are shown in Table 7.1.

III. An Overview of Entrepreneurship Competition in Chinese Universities

Usually, innovation and entrepreneurship competitions on campus are regarded as important ways of practicing/implementing entrepreneurship education programs. Based on key events in the development history of entrepreneurship education, the real implementation of undergraduate's entrepreneurship education practice in China can be traced back to the first undergraduate entrepreneurship plan competition in Tsinghua University. In May 1998, Tsinghua University held the first undergraduate entrepreneurship plan competition in China. The university also organized a variety of lecture trainings and entrepreneurial salons, which contributed to popularizing entrepreneurial knowledge.

Among numerous domestic entrepreneurship competitions, the "National Undergraduate Academic Science and Technology Competition," also called "Challenge Cup" in short, is considered the most influential one. "Challenge Cup" is a nationwide extracurricular academic practice race for undergraduate. It is jointly organized by the Central Committee of the Chinese Communist Youth League, Chinese Association for Science and Technology, Ministry of Education and the All-China Students' Federation, and the first competition was held in 1998 in Tsinghua University. The race consists of two parts: "Entrepreneurship Plan

Table 7.1 Innovation and Entrepreneurship Education Programs of Colleges and Universities in the United States.

Colleges and Universities	Innovation and Entrepreneurship Education Programs	Relevant Content
Arizona State University (ASU)	Innovation space	The interdisciplinary program includes two semesters, taught by teachers from the field of enterprise design, visual and communicating design, engineering entrepreneurship, industrial engineering, marketing and so on. Students in advanced classes shall put forward and show their own product design, with the aim of transforming it into commodity.
	Entrepreneurial program for performing arts	The program helps students to establish interactive art enterprises, form a concept within the media market and provide real art entrepreneurship experience for would-be entrepreneurs.
	Master's degree in medical care innovation	Different from traditional nursing treatment, the program intends to allow nursing and non-nursing majors to consider the systematic problems of nursing from multiple perspectives, such as commerce, leader, technology and so on.
Stanford University	Biological design program	As a part of the "Biology Community" in the university, the program intends to provide training about biological design process for students, researchers and teachers.
	Creation and innovation course	Through work discussions, case studies, team activities, field practice and class instructions from experts in this field, students learn more about entrepreneurship and innovation.

University of Maryland, Baltimore	Incentive and activation program	This program tries to commercialize technology venture investment through pragmatic entrepreneurial training.
University of Miami	Nature and foundation of entrepreneurship	This course crosses management department and religious study department, including reading, case study, guest lecture, independent research.
University of North Carolina at Chapel Hill	Freshman seminar	Freshmen are divided into several groups, discussing topics they interested in with teachers.
	Introduction to VC investment	The two-semester course is jointly taught by commercial college and technology development office and it aims to help faculties and students carry out their commercial or non-commercial VC investment plan.
	Challenge	This is a student-guidance-oriented entrepreneurial plan competition.
University of Rochester	Kauffman entrepreneurship year	It helps students realize their entrepreneurship dreams within one year.
University of Wisconsin-Madison	Entrepreneurship training camp	The five-day program focuses on introducing technology entrepreneurship to postgraduates majoring in medicine and engineering, training them to grasp opportunity to commercialize and other entrepreneurial skills.
Washington University in St. Louis	Own Your Business	It provides undergraduates with real entrepreneurial experience in a free market, and helps them establish or purchases enterprise during their campus life.

Source: Department of Higher Education, Ministry of Education of China, *Global Entrepreneurship Education*, Higher Education Press, 2012.

Competition" and "Extracurricular Academic Science and Technology Works Competition," which are held alternatively every two years.

The biennial tradition of "Challenge Cup" has led to increased interaction and communication between universities and society, and between undergraduates and existing enterprises. The competition draws much attention from media, experts, entrepreneurs and VC investors, and has become a major event for all walks of life in China. This competition is significant for popularizing entrepreneurial knowledge and promoting entrepreneurial activities among undergraduates, piquing undergraduates' interest in entrepreneurship, and, according to its official website, has been successful in "advocating innovation spirit, creating entrepreneurial atmosphere and transforming ideas into achievements."[4] Students who win prizes in the competition also win more opportunities that help in future employment.

How the Government can Formulate Public Policies to Promote the Development of Angel Investment

The development of angel investment requires a sound external environment, which is largely created by the government, because the government has the resources to improve the nation's investment environment, create investment platforms and encourage angel investors to invest more actively. The rapid development of angel investment market of some developed countries in North America and Europe is closely related to the positive and effective government incentive measures that are in place. In summary, the Chinese government can promote the development of angel investment in the following three ways.[5]

I. Support the Building of an Angel Investment Network

The angel investment network plays the role of medium in angel investment market, which reduces the search costs of enterprises and angel investors effectively, and encourages them to link up. The traditional angel investment network is to introduce investment opportunities to investors through regularly published brochures, or to allow entrepreneurs to be introduced to private VC investors directly through trade fairs. With the development of computer networks, the angel investment network is inextricably linked to the Internet. There are a large number of angel investors' networks in countries, whose VC investment markets are well-developed, such as the US, Canada and the UK. Most of the networks are run by government sectors or non-profit organizations, but a minority is established for commercial purpose.

In the early 1990s, the UK set up the first angel investment association in the world. The Netherlands, Finland and Belgium followed suit and established their own associations in 1995, 1996 and 1999 respectively. Throughout the 1990s, Europe 66 angel investment associations were set up in Europe, and this led to the formation of EBANs. Between 2000 and 2008, there were 298 members in EBANs. France, Germany, Spain, Britain and Sweden are the top five countries in the association number board, possessing 66, 38, 37, 35 and 22 associations respectively. In 1988, the European Union (EU) (then known as the European Economic Community) launched a three-year program to support the establishment, feasibility research and spread of angel investment associations. The EU also encouraged the establishment of angel investment associations by using regional funds.[6] New science and technologies, such as the Internet, have endowed the traditional way of accessing angel investment with new vitality, and angel investment association is playing an irreplaceable role in the world.

II. *Tax Incentive Policies*

The flourishing of the angel investment market in the US has benefited from the support and encouragement of government policies, with the market first emerging nationwide unorganized, then developing into self-organized groups and finally the current government-led stage. Besides the tax preferences offered by many states, the SBA (which is part of the US Federal Government) established ACE-Net (Angel Capital Electronic Network) in October 1996. Small businesses whose financial gap ranging from US$500,000 to US£5,000,000, can publish their business plans via this platform, thereby allowing investors to discuss and communicate with entrepreneurs. In recent years, due to the federal government's pursuit of higher employment rates, angel investors can make use of the investment tax credit policy for small businesses. According to this policy, investors do not have to pay any capital gains tax, even if gains were generated before the implementation of the act. Some state governments have also issued taxation reduction policies in favor of angel investors. For instance, since 2010, Minnesota has reduced 25% in taxes for specified investors whose headquarters are located in this state and who invest in small businesses.

In 1996, the Netherlands also adopted a taxation-reduction program to promote angel investors to invest in young companies and investors warmly received this move. The program stipulated that the investor must provide a loan to the new company. The amount of tax deduction of interest on loan belongs to the investor; if there is any loss in the loan, the investor could deduct it from income tax. With regard to the entrepreneurs, they received a loan with a maximum amount of EUR 22.15 million, and the loan interest rate is 0.5% lower than that of the bank at the same time. In 1994, Britain implemented Enterprise Investment Scheme (EIS) that stipulated a series of taxation reduction policies to stimulate individuals to invest in some particular types of high-risk and non-listed small companies, helping them to raise external capital for developing.

III. *Support the Training and Education of Angel Investment*

A serious problem for angel investors (particularly for potential angel investors) during the establishment and development of angel investment programs is their lack of knowledge of the investment process, so that they cannot take those opportunities efficiently. In addition, although angel investment associations can draw the attention of enterprises and potential investors well, it cannot arouse massive angel investors and promote the investment of those investors to reach an anticipated level effectively. Therefore, the establishment of institutions that aim to train angel investors has become an effective measure to promote the development of angel investment in other countries, which can also be an effective supplement for angel investment association. For example, the state of Nebraska in the US has set up special funds to supplement educational expenses for angel investors.

With the development of angel investment in China, the government should gradually define its role in this field and introduce policies, laws and regulations on angel investment and play a major role in shaping the angel investment industry and take the lead in establishing closely related angel investors group, information networks and so on.

Case III: Entrepreneurship Service Agency — Yonggang Modern Business Incubator, Ningbo

ZHU Li: "The Pattern of 'Incubator + Angel' Conforms to the Development Trend of Privately Operated Business Incubator."

Time/site: June 18, 2013/Ningbo, China

Mr. Zhu Li is an office manager of the public relations department in Ningbo Yonggang Modern Innovation Service Center, and concurrently holds the position of government supervisor in the enterprise customer development department of Yonggang Modern Holding Group.

The Ningbo Yonggang Modern Innovation Service Center (hereinafter referred to as the Innovation Center) was established in October 2008, and it is a science and technology business incubator engaged in investment attraction, science and technology incubation, investment and financing, entrepreneurial platform construction and other services under Yonggang Modern Holding Group. As the only private science and technology business incubator in Ningbo's national high-tech zone, Yonggang Modern has been supported largely by municipal and district governments since its establishment. In October 2011, Ningbo Yonggang Modern Innovation Service Center passed the experts review organized by the Science Technology Department of Zhejiang Provincial Government. The center was identified as a "science and technology business incubator at (the) provincial level," becoming the first private science and technology business incubator at provincial level in Ningbo.

Service Pattern: Professional Incubation + Entrepreneurial Platform + Angel Investment

Referring to the service pattern of Innovation Center, Zhu points out three aspects: The first is professional incubation. They are a privately operated agency and by relying on the government, the Center can cooperate with

(Continued)

Case III: (*Continued*)

industry associations and professional agencies by providing them with entrepreneurship consultation. The Center seeks to become a platform, providing powerful support and guarantees for the establishment and development of enterprises according their actual needs. The Innovation Center has professional talents, adopting the incubation service system of "Liaison Man + Instructor + Entrepreneurship Mentor." As the only science and technology business incubator in the high-tech zone, the agency has adopted the fiscal taxation policy introduced by the local government, which has created a sound policy environment for start-up enterprises. The second is the Center's entrepreneurial platform. In terms of encouraging undergraduates to start their own business, Yonggang Modern Group has established the Small and Micro Business Pioneer Park for college students. With a small amount of rent, students can have access to office facilities, Netcom communication equipment, public meeting rooms, business receptions and other services. In terms of helping youth to start their own business, the Innovation Center cooperates with the Ningbo Youth League Committee and All-China Youth Federation to establish the Youth Start-up Base, aiming to provide entrepreneurial youth with all-around "chain-type" entrepreneurial resources. In terms of developing a professional business incubator, the Innovation Center has constructed a green and professional business incubator that is reliant on the energy-efficient and environment-friendly regional advantage in the high-tech zone, and integrating relevant institutions for professional talents. The center aims to become the largest energy-efficient and environment-friendly demonstration base in Ningbo. Recently, the green business incubation building underwent further construction to enable it to provide services such as products exhibition, science and technology research and development, detection and authentication for energy-efficient and environment-friendly businesses. The third is angel investment. Yonggang Modern set up a seed fund of RMB 3 million at the end of 2009, providing financial support for outstanding established enterprises. As of 2015, two excellent companies have received funding from this seed fund.

The Development Model of Privately Operated Business Incubator Requires Innovation

Research shows that science and technology business incubators usually present four types of models: the first being the property business model, which

(*Continued*)

Case IV: (*Continued*)

Cultivate Quality Project in Universities, Attract Angel Investment, Conduct Joint Projects

The industry is keeping a close eye on the problems of entrepreneurship faced by undergraduates, and many angel investment projects originate from undergraduates' original inspiration and entrepreneurial plans. When it comes to the effective way of university resources docking with angel investment, Chen Hang considers that university is a vital spring of science and technology and the innovative spirit shall be activated by the use of resources effectively, turning the university into an innovative "Spouting Spring." In this regard, MIT is a successful case. There is a special entrepreneurial center in the college to provide assistance for teachers and students, helping them to transform the advanced technology in lab into mature entrepreneurial programs. He elaborates further by stating that there are three steps of "incubation process" in MIT's entrepreneurial center. Firstly, it provides relevant entrepreneurial courses, inspiring students to figure out their surroundings and potential start-up ideas, and helping them build a team to carry out their entrepreneurial plans. Next, it encourages and helps students related to entrepreneurship to organize and launch entrepreneurship competitions, creating an entrepreneurial environment. For example, MIT-CHIEF has largely been supported by the entrepreneurial center. By participating in the entrepreneurship competition, an entrepreneurial team can help create a complete business plan. Finally, the entrepreneurial center will provide resources to foster excellent entrepreneurial programs. Over a long period like a summer vacation, through full-time devotion of the whole team and intensive training provided by the entrepreneurial center, the program is able to develop at a much faster rate. An entrepreneurial program has taken shape generally after going through the above three steps. By this time, it can already attract angel investors through road show. As always, angel investors favor high-quality entrepreneurship and innovation projects. The quantity of projects from college students is never an issue, but it is not the case in terms of quality. Therefore, universities should cultivate more projects with potentials, attract more angel investors to enter campuses and participate in these projects.

Features and the Future of MIT-CHIEF

MIT-CHIEF is the first forum with a Chinese background that has themes of science and technology, innovation and entrepreneurship. Held annually

(*Continued*)

Case IV: (*Continued*)

at MIT, it attracts a lot of support and help from the institute, famous entrepreneurs of China and other countries and well-known organizations in New England. After a few years' development, the forum has become the most influential forum related to China along the east cost of the US. At the same time, the forum has established a sound cooperative relationship with China's science and technology zones, business incubators and VC investment agencies.

It has been noticed that teams participating in the entrepreneurship competition called "Pitch to China" in the forum are not limited to the state of Massachusetts, but from other states as well. During the 2012 edition of the competition, 52% of the participant teams came from Massachusetts, 32% from other US states, and 16% from China. The areas that those entrepreneurship teams are involved in are also much diversified. That year, the mobile internet group, the medical treatment and health group and the network group — the three hottest innovation fields — each had 28, 26 and 25 teams respectively.

Chen indicates that compared to other entrepreneurial competitions across the world, MIT-CHIEF is aimed at the China market. When it comes to projects screening, there will be six entrepreneurial projects chosen from over 100 projects through a four-month period of strict selection and two rounds of elimination, and they are entitled to participate in the finals in November. Among the judges in the competition, there are investors from China and America, professors in the relevant fields, successful entrepreneurs, business incubator managers, lawyers, marketing experts and so on, such as Li Xiaojun, partner of IDG Capital, Xu Xiaoping, senior partner of Zhen Fund, Jia Shilian, co-consultant of GSR Ventures, Yuan Yue, chairman of Horizon Research Consultancy Group. Besides, MIT-CHIEF adheres to the college entrepreneurial culture, pays attention to the incubation of start-up projects and assigns entrepreneurial mentors for select projects. MIT-CHIEF's entrepreneurial mentors include Wu Ying, founder of UTStarcom, Canice Wu, chairman of Plug and Play Tech Center which is a famous business incubator in America, Cheng Datong, partner of Huashan Capital, and Dave Feinleib, partner of Mohr Davidow Ventures and author of *Why Start-ups Fail: And How Yours Can Succeed*. In the meantime, MIT-CHIEF also regularly organizes activities

(*Continued*)

Case IV: (*Continued*)

related to entrepreneurship. Now the entrepreneurial environment with MIT-CHIEF features has taken shape, and those entrepreneurial teams selected from the entrepreneurship competitions also possess considerable market competitiveness.

Encourage Angel Investors to Pay Attention to Social Enterprises

Chen has his own understanding about angel investors. In his opinion, each investor strives to pursue a higher rate of return on investment, but people who excessively do so cannot be called angel investors any more. In China, the real angel investors are in the minority, as most investors still tend to invest in projects that can reap a lot of profits within a short period of time. Social enterprises, therefore, have often been neglected. Chen hopes that angel investment in China can pay more attention to long-term social value rather than short-term economic interest. He believes angel investors should invest more in social business, and take into consideration what the Chinese society needs. In fact, in 2013, MIT-CHIEF hosted a panel discussion on social business, studying the development and positioning of their entrepreneurial activities.

As a leader of one of the associations and societies in his university, Chen has his own understanding about management. He believes that people is the key in organizational management. The most important point is that one must recruit members who have motivation for and interest in this particular organization or project; otherwise, organizatioal management is prone to failure. Chen further emphasizes that the most important thing for non-profit organizations is for its members to have a sense of ownership. Each member should be able to play an active part in the process, instead of working for work's sake. In fact, the above two points also apply to those newly emerged angel investment associations within China.

Furthermore, in regard to the public policy about angel investment, Chen admits that China requires more open policies, such as in taxation, which will in turn, allow angel investors to play in a more free field.

Case V: Education and Training of Angel Investors–Angel Camp

Angel Camp: The Cradle of the Qualified Angel Investors

Angel camp is the first non-profit program that aims to train angel investors in China. In 2014, proposed by Xu Yong, the assistant to the general manager of China Gold Group and Tong Weiliang, founder and partner of Phoenix Tree Capital Partners put forward a proposition, angel camp was jointly established by ZACA, China Youth Angle, Angel 100, Legendstar, Asia America Multitechnology Association, Innovation Works, Gobi Partners, China Renaissance K2 Ventures, Innovation Angel, Qingsong Fund, Huachuang Shengjing Investment, Silicon Valley Bank, Zero2IPO Group, Sina Micro Ventures, AngelCrunch, Fuho Capital, China Venture, Beijing Zhongguangcun Finance Group, among others, which aims to spread "correct" concepts of angel investment, share angel investment experience and optimize the investment environment. The construction of authoritative and pragmatic curriculum system in the field of angel investment would hence fill the gap in area of training for the Chinese angel investment industry.

Student Enrollment: Value Orientation is a Top Priority

With regard to the enrollment conditions, angel camp pays close attention to "soft power" and professional quality. Xu Yong, the initiator and executive vice-dean of angel camp, points out the following six aspects:

(1) *Value orientation.* The students signing up agree with the value of angel camp, treat the industry of angel investment with honest, responsible and serious attitudes, and are willing to make contributions to entrepreneurship as well as input time and energy into the activities that are part of the camp's program.

(2) *Investment strengthening.* Students shall have annual income over RMB 500,000 or disposable liquid investment of over RMB 5,000,000.

(3) *Strong willingness for investment.*

(4) *Psychological preparation for losses.* Students should be prepared for this and understand angel investment cycles.

(*Continued*)

Case V: (*Continued*)

(5) *Participants' time allocation.* Students shall adhere to the regulations of angel camp, participating in the training sessions accordingly.

(6) *Relevant expenditure.* Angel camp is tuition-fee-free, but students shall pay for their own transportation, boarding and lodging, teaching materials and class activities, and these expenditures shall be collected and managed by the class committee in the form of class expense.

With regard to the selection of students, Xu emphasizes that successful entrepreneurs and enterprise senior executives will be prioritized first, because it's wise to provide training resources for them. Through a strict selection process, the first angel camp selected over 30 students from more than 200 applicants, including nearly 10 senior managers of listed companies, persons in charge of high-speed growing start-up enterprises, a few professional investors. Except six to seven people, most of them come from Beijing. Angel camp hopes to attract credible and grateful applicants who are ready to help entrepreneurs give back to society, so that the atmosphere among students can give off "positive energy" and the interaction between students and mentors will be promoted. In this way, students will receive much more assistance from mentors.

Curriculum System: Theory Guides Practice, Emphasize on the Combination of "Principle and Method"

With regard to curriculum system, Xu indicates that the training covers the key content in the field of angel investment, including project selection criteria, risk aversion method, core provision of investment agreement stipulation, popular industries analysis, practical operation and regulations of joint investment and so on. The training also puts emphasis on the combination of "Principle and Method," and strives to combine knowledge system and investment practice efficiently. The major features of course in angel camp are:

(1) The lineup of mentors is strong and dean in charge is enthusiastic. Over 50 mentors that angel camp has invited are renowned top angel investors, including Honorary Dean Xu Xiaoping, the founder of Zhen Fund, Dean Luo Zhuo, the partner of TusPark Ventures, Dean Yang Ning, the founder

(*Continued*)

Case V: (*Continued*)

and partner of LeBox Capital, Dean Qiao Qian, the Chairman of Angel 100 and so on. It is the first time that so many renowned investors have gathered to offer joint support for one program. These mentors have abundant investment experience, successful cases and social resources. In order to guarantee the course quality, one of the Vice-deans will be invited as the mentor in charge each class. Before each class, the Dean in charge will have thorough communication with other mentors. In this case, the mentors will prepare carefully in advance to guarantee the quality. Vice-deans in charge of curriculum include Mr. Tong Weiliang, the founder and partner of Phoenix Tree Capital Partners, Ms. Tao Ning, the CEO and partner of Innovation Works, Mr. Lu Gang, the standing vice-president of Legendstar, Mr. Li Zhu, the founder and partner of Innovation Fund, Mr. Li Hansheng, the founder and partner of Huachuang Shengjing Investment, Mr. Li Songbo, the partner of Sina Micro Ventures, Ms. Fu Xinghua, the managing director of Zero2IPO Group and so on. In each course, there will be about 10 experienced investors participating in project discussion and sharing investment experience.

(2) The training courses are scientific, pragmatic and systematic. The one-year training can be divided into two parts: In the first half of the year, students will be trained monthly, while in the second half of the year, students will be arranged for one-to-one interaction with mentors and discuss group projects. The monthly intensive training consists of three parts, that is "project road show and discussion" on a Friday afternoons (students will be divided into four groups and each group recommends an excellent project), a knowledge-based course on Saturday mornings (such as industrial tendency, legal knowledge, investment knowledge etc.) and theme sharing on Saturday afternoons (the research of industrial experts, experience sharing of first-tier angel investors etc.). Starting from angel investment, the curriculum discusses its trend, methodologies, identification and checking of good and bad investors, covering the core contents of angel investment systematically. Moreover, the curriculum introduces important knowledge under each special topic. For example, on July 5, 2014, Vice-Dean Fu Xinghua delivered a lecture about Chinese VC investment and angel investment, giving a panoramic view to students, and Ms. Lin Ying, the general legal

Case V: (*Continued*)

officer of Innovation Works, introduced 10 key provisions of angel investment "Term Sheet" to students. On August 9, 2014, Vice-dean Tong Weiliang gave a lecture on "Internet, Value and Trend of Investment in 2014," Vice-dean Li Zhu gave a lecture on "Joint Investment Trend and Opportunities," Xu Qian, the general manager of Fosun Ventures, delivered the speech on "Angel Investment Appraisement," Gui Shuguang, the founder and partner of Landsangels, delivered a speech on "How to Judge a Project from Business Plan," and Yang Xiaolei, the vice-president of ChinaVenture, gave a lecture on "Joint Investment Procedures" and so on.

(3) The project road show and discussion is solid and profound, and the joint investment regulations with "angel camp character" were born. The projects recommended for road show come from students' offline resources and online project platform resources such as AngleCrunch, 36 Kr, VC etc. All the students are divided into four groups, and each group shall recommend 5 to 10 projects. Through group road show and discussion, each group selects the best project to participate in the monthly class road show. These projects are not "mock projects". Instead, they are real ones that requires financing, and some students have intentions to invest in them. During road shows, students will discuss and listen to mentors' comments on the spot. On the afternoon of July 4, 2014, "Jade Hibiscus," "Yi Jin Jing," "Thumb APP" and "Juker" participated in road show; in the afternoon of August 8, 2014, "Blue Track," "Gear Mach," "This is the Three Kingdoms," and "Ishow" participated in the road show. Furthermore, the road show activities are distinctive in that mentors not only simply look at these projects, but also help students to analyze and review them. For example, during the road show, after the teams of recommended projects are introduced, the reasons for recommendation are given, the questions are posed by judges, mentors in charge of each project will give out detailed opinions, comments and instructions, such as investment opportunities in the project's field, feelings towards the character of the entrepreneurs, investment value of the project, risks and some remaining problems etc. — this kind of "reviews" is quite unique and it has seldom been seen elsewhere. In order to further train students' ability in project selection, angel camp also works out a precise project grade sheet

(*Continued*)

Case V: (*Continued*)

designed for students, including favorable timeframes, places, support of people, estimated value and intuition. After listening to the profound comments from mentors on partial projects, students re-consider their investment intent and avoid incurring any losses. Of course, some projects are determined as promising projects by mentors and students. Through the thorough investigation with camp participants, the joint investment comes into being. The first joint investment project has attracted nearly 40 mentors and students. Except for the leading investor, the investment of other participants ranges from RMB 10,000 to RMB 50,000.

Training Features: Emphasize Angel Investment Culture, Form Public Welfare Effect

Compared to other types of investment, the "original intention" of angel investment lies in helping start-up enterprises to develop. Xu has deep understanding of it and indicated that angel camp attaches great importance in the cultivation of "angel original intention" culture, that is, respect for entrepreneurs should not only be promoted, but an innate love for entrepreneurship and willingness to help entrepreneurs should also be present. The culture turns angel investment into something with high risk, long period and low probability, and it is not the speculation or industry making money merely. Several organizations and institutions jointly launch the public welfare training, and those participants should possess the spirit of honesty, sharing and mutual assistance. Xu also stated that the establishment of angel camp has been supported by many organizations and institutions. Innovation Works, Gobi Partners, ChinaVenture and many other enterprises have opened numerous resources, which have aimed to create real mutual assistance and a shared platform. Meanwhile, some unexpected achievements emerge during the process of training. For example: the close interaction among students, self-organized responsible investigation of projects, the sharing of the entrepreneurial experience and reflection on angel investment; the positive response from participants makes it possible to participate in joint investment of high-quality project with less fund. As what Xu said at the open ceremony of angel camp in June 6, 2014, "Angel camp is a public welfare organization which needs 'love.' With love for angel, entrepreneurs and entrepreneurship,

(Continued)

Case V: (*Continued*)

participants can put down their 'internal ambition' to 'experience life' with a peaceful mind."

In reality, angel investor training is facing a great shortage. Although the number of active investors in China is small, the potential number of angel investors is massive. Compared to traditional investment like stock or real estate, angel investment gets involved in entrepreneurial projects at an earlier period and faces higher risks, which put forward high demands on the insight and professional ability of investors. Through training and education, more high-net-worth people can know about, comprehend and participate in angel investment. So, can the training of angel investors operate under a commercialized model? Xu considers that: as long as the goal and direction of training are to cultivate more angel investors, both public-welfare training and commercial operation are feasible. After all, the scale of angel investors in China is too small, so training and educational programs are necessary. He further indicated that current venture capitalism and private equity possessed relatively mature training and education systems, and investment theory and evaluation models of enterprises in middle and late stages have formed some certain regulations. These regulations however may not be suitable for angel investment. There are too many uncertainties existing in early-stage projects, and the entire angel investment industry is still growing. Furthermore, the development history of renowned institutions like Innovation Works and Zhen Fund has been short thus far, so it's necessary to gather more investment experience and industrial resources and allow students to know about different investment types and strategies. The organizers and executors of angel camp are willing to make a promise, to continue conducting training by way of public welfare.

Notes

1. *Chinese Talents*, No. 6, 2013.
2. Shang Yingmei, Fang Lin and Ma Chenglong, 'Study on Entrepreneurship Education and Its Current Status in Higher Education Institutions,' *Modern Education Science*, No. 1, 2013. (In Chinese)
3. Wei Lihong and Chen Zhongwei, 'The Comparison of Entrepreneurship Education Modes and Entrepreneurial Talents Training,' *Teaching Research*, No. 3, 2009. (In Chinese)

4. For more information, please visit http://www.tiaozhanbei.net/.
5. Deng Chao, Zheng Yuanting and Wang Changdong, 'Comparison on How Different Governments Promote the Development of Angel Investment and Its Lessions,' *Inquiry into Economic Issues*, No. 1, 2010, 129–133. (In Chinese)
6. Rudy Aernoudt, Amparo San José and Juan Roure, 'Executive Forum: Public Support for the Business Angel Market in Europe — A Critical Review,' *Venture Capital*, 2007, 9(1): 71–84.

Part III
Angel Market in China

Chapter 8

Market Conditions of Angel Investment in China

In China, angel investment began at the end of the 20th century and its development accompanied the development of Internet and high-tech enterprises. In recent years, more and more entrepreneurs and industry experts have participated in this field. At the same time, with the development of normalized and institutionalized investment, more and more VC firms are paying attention to the early stage deals, setting up special angel investment funds. Also, there are some high-net-worth individuals that constitute as an angel group by joint investment. Apart from individual angel investment models, many other models like joint investment, institutional investment, combination with business incubator and crowd funding have all undergone extensive exploration and practice. With regard to government support, central and some local governments stress policies that "encourage developing angel investment," "support to develop angel institution," "establish angel investment funds" and so on.

The History of Angel Investment in China

The *Report of Development Environment for Angel Investment in Zhongguancun Technology Park* issued by Beijing Non-governmental Science Technology Entrepreneurs Association in July 2007 indicated that, "The earliest angel investment in China originated from the 1986 'National High-tech R&D Program (863 Program)' and 'China Torch Program,' which was introduced in 1988. The government invested in these two angel investment programs at the seed stage." It can hence be deduced that the government spearheaded the earliest angel investment

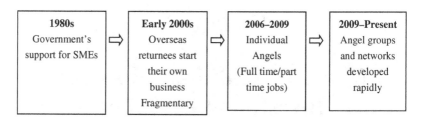

Fig. 8.1   The Development of Angel Investment in China.

programs in China, which is a major unique feature of the field within China.[1]

Since 2000, the development of the Internet, information technology and other high-tech areas created a boom in global entrepreneurship and early investment. Some overseas returnees started their business at home and tried to conduct "angel investment" domestically. They helped more youth to start business, drove the successful local S&T entrepreneurs to engage in angel investment, and supported the start-up businesses with their own funding, industrial experience and connections.

Between 2006 and 2009, the size of angel investment expanded, and more domestic investors began engaging in angel investment or tried to establish angel investment funds. On the other hand, traditional VC firms and PE firms attempted to establish special angel investment funds one after another.

Since 2012, angel investment in China has developed dramatically, and its tendency of systematization and institutionalization is distinct. Some local governments issue normative documents to promote angel investment. See Figure 8.1 for a summary of the development of angel investment in China.

The Market Characteristics of Angel Investment in China

I. *The Total Scale of Angel Investment*

Most of the studies focus on qualitative description and statistics features in these reports about angel investment in China. In the early 2000s, Beijing Software and Information Service Industry Promotion Center, Internet Labs and *New Economy Weekly* issued the first domestic Industrial

Research Report on Angel Investment 'Research Report on Angel Investment in China' (2006), which showed that the seed investment accounts for 17% of aggregate Venture Capital in 2006, reaching RMB 1.054 billion mainly in TMT industry (technology, media, telecommunication). A few years later, institutions like Research Center of Zero2IPO Group (2011, 2012, 2014), ChinaVenture Capital Research Institution (2011), CYZONE, Zhongguancun Management Committee (2013), China Business Angel Association (2013), ChinaVenture Research (2013) and several academic groups, did surveys and analyzed the issues of angel investment in China. Currently, public angel investors in China that are available for statistical studies in the national market are no more than 3,000, and active angel investors in Zhongguancun[2] account for half of that. Since 2008, 79 Angel Investment Funds have been revealed to the public, with over 50 Angel Service Platforms like associations, clubs, alliances, and networks.[3] In terms of trade scale, according to the latest report issued by ChinaVenture Research: The trade scale of Angel Investment has been on the rise annually over the last five years; in 2004, domestic Angel Investments have built up a momentum until 2013, and the numbers and scales of investment cases are increasing.[4] ChinaVenture Research has made the statistics according to the information disclosed: 317 Angel Investments cases in the first half of 2014 had a total investment of RMB 4.226 billion. The investment scale has exceeded that of the whole 2013 year (see Figure 8.2).

II. *The Operation Models of Angel Investment*

Before 2000, the angel investment mainly came from fragmentary investments of individual angels; between 2001 and 2008, angel investment in China started to develop with individual investors as main investors. However, institutional angel investments like Investoday and Zhen Fund have surfaced; after 2009, angel investment has been developing rapidly, and more and more new angel groups, institutions and networks emerged (see Figure 8.3).

I have divided the current angel investment operation modes into six categories: The first consists of individual angels and this category has the highest potential to get into the business of angel investment and the upward trend of angel investments shows that there will be more high

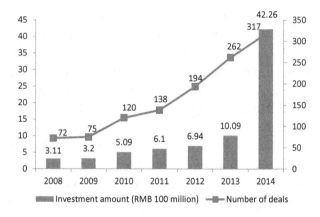

Fig. 8.2   Angel Investment Scale in China (2008–2014).
Source: Report on Angel Investment in China 2015, ChinaVenture.

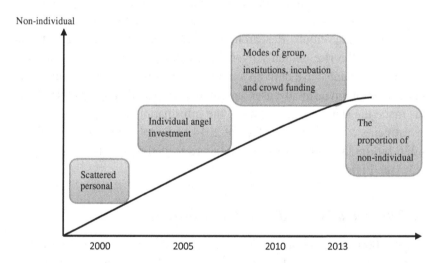

Fig. 8.3   The Changing Operation Modes of Angel Investment in China (2000–2013).

net worth individuals making such investments in the future. Angel investment groups form the second category: they exist in the form of clubs, alliances and other organizations, and act as communication and exchange platforms for angel investors and start-ups. Usually, members of angel organizations adopt joint investment to gather funds, make advantages complementary to each other, and lower investment risk. The third category consists of angel investment funds — they are like venture capital funds that are focused on the early investment stages, and they transform scattered funds and informal operation into sustainable funds, and provide professional investment management advice. The fourth category is angel investment incubator/accelerator. Some investment institutions not only provide funding support, but also afford incubation space and other services for start-ups. On the other side, some incubators provide seed funding for young enterprises in exchange for a few shares, so as to achieve some integration in their investment, and the incubation and management of the enterprise. This new operation mode can lower the investment costs and reduce investment. The fifth category is a venture capital platform: the funds through which big high-tech companies and government can support start-ups in specialized fields, such as "safe" venture capital funding for companies like Tencent, cloud funding for Alibaba, and Weibo's development fund of Sina. The sixth and last category is that of an angel investment online platform. The year of 2013 was called "the first year of Internet Finance." Crowd funding modes were created in angel investment field, and this mode has gradually become a service platform (see Figure 8.3).

III. *The Regional Differences of Angel Investment*

In America, although some states have a higher concentration of venture capital activity, angel investment is by no means distributed evenly. However, the differences in active levels of angel investment between different states are related to indicators like the foundations of local industry, how well off a state is, the overall economic situation, the numbers of universities, local enterprises and management talents located in a state.[5] In China, angel investment of Zhongguancun in Beijing has taken the lead and the number of individual angels accounts for 60% of the national total. These angels are successful entrepreneurs, senior managers or professional investors. They enjoy high media exposure, with certain influence and fame within the angel investment industry. Survey findings show that: (1) Angel investment in Shanghai is active, and the investors are scattered. Most of them prefer TMT field; (2) most investors in Jiangsu and Zhejiang are potential "angel investors," who attach more importance to investing in traditional industrial upgrades related to local industrial characteristics; (3) Shenzhen is the most active region of angel investment in the south of China. Unlike Beijing, most investors in south of China are part-time angels; (4) angel investors in Hong Kong are rational, and prefer investing overseas and Chinese mainland deals; and (5) angel investment in the mid-west region, typically Wuhan and Chengdu, are mainly supported and guided by the government, despite the fact that local angel investment is in its early stages.

The Main Form of China Angel Investment

I. *The Attitude, Behavior, and Characteristics of Angel Investors*[6]

Research has shown that: (1) The average age of angels is 41; (2) most of the angel investors are male (88.57%), and have high education backgrounds (48.57% with a masters and above); (3) the majority (68.57%) work in the field of finance have experience of starting business (57.14%) and work as company superior managers (54.29%); and (4) most investors (62.86%) are engaged in angel investment with the aims of getting more economic returns or have invested based on their own personal interests (60%).

1. Funds and deal sourcing

The funds for start-ups derive mainly from the investors' start-up accumulations (37.14%), family wealth (31.43%), and personal salary (25.71%). As for the deal sources, relatives and friends recommendations make up 54.29%, the forum activities of angel investment make up 51.43% and start-ups channels form the last part of deal sources (see Figures 8.4 and 8.5).

2. Investment scale

In terms of invested projects, the number of invested deals is few because most angels only started investing in recent years. 43.75% of them have invested in less than five projects, and the total amount of investment is half

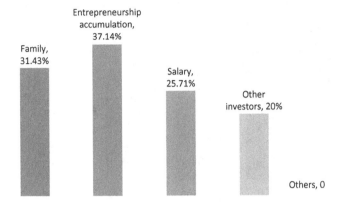

Fig. 8.4   Sources of Funding for Angel Investees.
Source: Authors' own compilation.

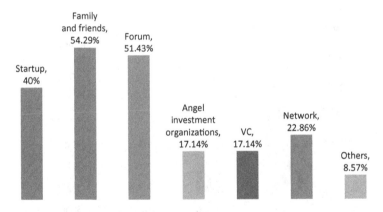

Fig. 8.5   The Project Sources for Angel Investors.
Source: Authors' own compilation.

and half (50% = RMB 5 million, 50% = below RMB 1 million) (see Figures 8.6 and 8.7).

3. Investment preferences

The research concluded that: (1) Most people (56.25% of respondents) hold shares of 5–10%; (2) TMT (57.14%), energy conservation (34.29%) and biological medicines (20%) are popular industries, while Beijing

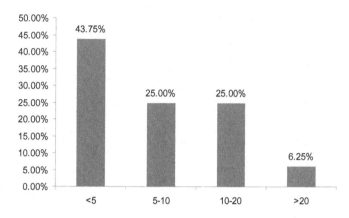

Fig. 8.6 Investment Scale Distribution (project number/unit).
Sources: Authors' own compilation.

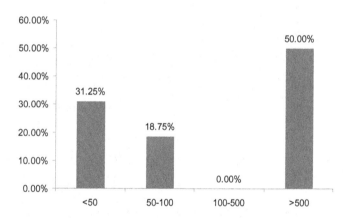

Fig. 8.7 Investment Scale Distribution (Investment Total in Ten Thousand Yuan).
Sources: Authors' own compilation.

(48.57%) and Shanghai (42.86%) are the most investment-intensive areas; (3) the decision-making periods of angel investors are short, and 70% of them cost no more than three months from the time deals are discovered, to the stage of final investment; and (4) three main indicators of deal screening and due diligence are industry investment (31.43%), team quality and ability (31.43%) and market prospects (25.71%) (see Figure 8.8 and 8.9).

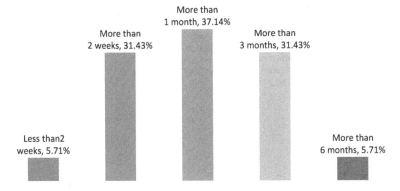

Fig. 8.8   The Decision-Making Period of An Angel Investor.

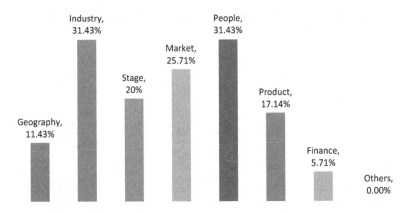

Fig. 8.9   Indicators for Screening Project and Conducing Surveys.

Source: Author's own compilation.

4. Investment strategy

Investment strategies tended to be quite diverse: Over 80% of investors made field investigations for the invested teams; over 90% of investors have the experience of joint investment with relatives and friends (54.29%) and members of angel organizations (51.43%) as the partners. All of them will sign the investment treaties, mainly in forms of equity transfer (71.43%), anti-dilution (60%), and bet clauses (54.29%) (See Figure 8.10). Over 90% of investors oversee and manage the affairs after the investment and over 80% of investors will join the board of directors of the company invested (See Figure 8.11).

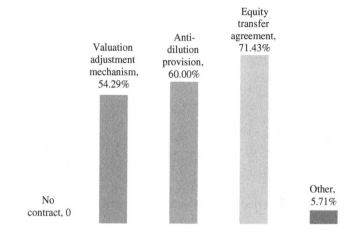

Fig. 8.10   Varied Conditions For the Signing of Investment Treaties.

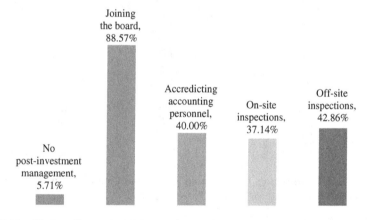

Fig. 8.11.   Various Strategies of Overseeing and Managing Investees after Investment.

II. *The Investment Style of Angel Investors*

Active angel investors in China have different investment styles due to their different professional backgrounds, commercial skills and characters.[7] For instance, entrepreneurs like Lei Jun, Zhou Hongwei, Xu Xiaoping and Zeng Liqing have established business themselves, so that they understand the requirements of a start-up enterprise and are capable of offering effective assistance; while for the enterprise senior executives like Kai-Fu Lee, although they do not have enough entrepreneurial and investment experience, they possess fund, industrial relationship and other resources, so that they are important parts of angel investors as well (see Table 8.1). Angel investors also tend to follow a general principle: "Invest only in familiar fields." However, this industry at its current age also encourages the way of "joint investment," "co-investor," "fund," "incubation," "crowd funding" and so on to solve the problems of limited social resources, unfamiliar industrial background, insufficient investment experience, etc.

III. Classification of Angel Investment Organizations

With the expansion of angel investment, the formation of angels is also changing. Angel groups or angel fund companies could share risks and resources. So individual angel investors start to form groups or institutions of investment and various for-profit or non-profit agents are established. Based on Linde and Prasad,[8] the organizations and institutions of angel investment are divided into the following four types:

1. Angel investment companies

This type of angel investors is also called "Super Angels." Generally, these institutional angels use the typical VC structure and focus on early-stage investments. Except for some government funds, angel investment companies are usually established and funded by several angel investors together. They are also managed by angel investors or hired professional general partners who will screen and evaluate projects and make investment decisions for the angel investors. Based on the types of limited partners and founders, angel investment funds can be classified into four groups: (1) funds established by famous angel investors, such as ZhenFund by Xu Xiaoping and Shunwei by Lei Jun; (2) angel investment funds established by venture capital institutions, such as Fuxing Fund by CDF-Capital and the seed funds by Northern Light Venture Capital; (3) angel investment funds established by the government, such as

Table 8.1 Background and Investment Style of Famous Angel Investors in China.[8]

Investor	Background	Investment Style
Lei Jun	Currently serves as founder, Chairman and CEO of Xiaomi Technology, Chairman of Play More Games Network and Kingsoft. A renowned angel investor in mainland China.	Part-time angel; pays attention to people and team; invests in start-ups in early period; an entrepreneurial investor; participates in post-investment activities; invests in acquaintance
Xu Xiaoping	Currently serves as founder of Zhen Fund; founder and former Chairman of New Oriental Education & Technology Group; former Dean of New Oriental cultural development academy.	Full-time investor; pays attention to people; invests in many strangers; seldom manages enterprise after investment and does not interfere enterprise developments.
Zeng Liqing	Currently serves as Chairman of the board of Decent Investment. One of the former five founders of Chinese famous Internet enterprise — Tencent.	Full-time investor; invests in start-ups in early period; an entrepreneurial investor; the amount of investment is between RMB 2 million and RMB 10 million; participates in post-investment activities; invests in acquaintances.
Ji Qi	Currently serves as founder and chairman of the board of Huazhu Hotels Group, CEO of Powerhill Investment; former president of Ctrip, former CEO of Home Inn.	Invests casually; the amount of investment is no more than USD 1 million; accounts for 10% or 20% of total shares without conducting systematic investigation and assessment; seldom manages enterprise after investment and does not interfere enterprise development.
He Boquan	Currently serves as founder of Investoday. Former founder of Robust Group.	Only invests in familiar industries; external business model is mature but lack of successful domestic sample; invests in start-ups in early period; an entrepreneurial investor; participates in enterprise management after investment; pays attention to honest and contract spirits of start-ups.

Name	Bio	Investment
Cai Wensheng	Founder of 265.com, which was founded in 2003 and acquired by Google in 2007. After 2007, he conducted network investment, investing in dozens of excellent website successively and turning into a distinguished angel investor in China.	Invests in start-ups in early period quickly; pays attention to the number of users; the amount of investment is between RMB 0.5 million and RMB 5 million; prefers to invest in deals with small funds at an early stage; refuses money-consuming deals.
Lv Tanping	Currently serves as Chairman of Authosis Ventures; an entrepreneur and angel investor with over-20-year experience; former founder of Legend Computer Ltd. (Hong Kong); founded APTG Ventures in 1997 and Authosis Ventures in 2000; set up new VC investment fund — Start-up Capital Ventures with several partners in 2005.	Prefers to invest in deals in the industry of TMT; a part of investment for making profits, while another part for helping others to start their business; pays attention to people.
Yang Xiangyang	Currently serves as Chairman of Shenzhen Resources Investment Development Co. Ltd. and Chairman and President of Yuanxing Bio-Pharm Science & Technology Co., LTD. He is an entrepreneur and angel investor with more than 20 years of experience.	Concentrates on the field of biology and medicine; the amount of investment is large; the return period of investment project is long.
Kai-Fu Lee	Currently serves as Chairman and CEO of Innovation Works. He was the former senior executive in Apple, SGI, Microsoft, Google and other IT companies.	The investment model of "Angel + Incubation" not only provides financial support, but also offers supporting service; institutionalized operation; prefers to invest in asset-light deals; concentrates on the field of TMT

Source: Authors' own collation and Li Xiaoyan, *Why Should I Invest in You*, Beijing: China Commercial Press, 2012.

Entrepreneurial Angel Investment Fund of Chengdu Hi-tech Industrial Development Zone and Ningbo Angel Investment Guidance Fund; and (4) angel investment funds established by new incubators such as Legend Star and STEP Angel. For the development of angel investment, institutionalization is the new trend. From 2008 to 2015, the number of the newly raised angel investment funds was increasing year by year. The total amount of fund raising decreased by 14.3% in 2013, which means the scale of angel investment funds was shrinking. However, under the new power of mass entrepreneurship and innovation in China, early-stage investing increased sharply after 2014 (see Figure 8.12).

- The Entrepreneurial Angel Investment Fund of Chengdu Hi-tech Industrial Development Zone was founded in June 2012. It is the first entrepreneurial angel investment fund fully financed by the government in China. The first-round fund was raised at RMB 80 million, all from the management committee of the zone. The fund is entrusted to CDHT Hi-tech Entrepreneurial Investment Co., Ltd., a wholly owned subsidiary of CDHT Group — a state-owned sole corporation under the jurisdiction of the zone. The CDHT Hi-tech Entrepreneur Investment utilizes the fund to support entrepreneurial and innovative enterprises,

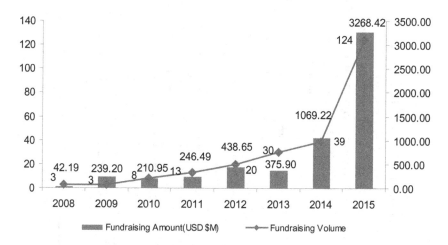

Fig. 8.12   Trend of Collection of Angel Investment Funds (2008–2013).
Source: Zero2IPO Research (2015).

engages in equity investment, adheres to market-oriented operations, and professional management. The detailed procedure includes incubation and screening, project establishment, due diligence, investment decision-making, investment implementation, post-investment management and exit. According to the estimation, all investment would be done in the next three years and the invested projects would exceed 60. It is said that angel investment funds would finance an entrepreneurial company differently at different stages, with no more than RMB 2 million in principle. Generally, no person would be sent to manage the invested company after investment and the fund would exit according to the condition of the company.

- ZhenFund was established in 2006. It was founded by long-time angel investors, Xu Xiaoping and Wang Qiang, to encourage young people to start their businesses and make innovation. In 2011, ZhenFund and Sequoia Capital China formed the strategic cooperation partnership and invested USD 15 million separately to establish a new angel investment fund. ZhenFund in Era 2.0 was dedicated to entrepreneurial deals at the stage of angel round. Since 2006, Zhen fund has invested in around 200 start-ups. These start-ups included those related to e-commerce, mobile network, education and training, commodity and medication. Among these start-ups, Jiayuan.com, Jumei.com and Light in the box were the well-known successful cases.

2. Angel investment clubs

For many individual angel investors, angel investment is just a part-time job. These investors face the following problems: limited deal sources, limited personal fund, limited time for making tedious jobs like due diligence; insufficient experience and knowledge resulting in high rate of failure. As a result, some angels jointly establish groups or organizations of angel investors like clubs, unions or associations, so as to collect sources of projects, make regular assessments and communicate on a regular basis. Members of such organizations could share experience regarding to industries and investment. When members are interested in some suitable deals, they could conduct due diligence together and each of them could do some work according to their schedules and experience. They may also make investment together to increase the amount of contribution and share risks. Nowadays, there are several angel clubs established in some cities, such as Shanghai Angel Capital Club, Ningbo Angel Capital Club, Wuhang Angel Capital Club, and North China Angel Capital Club. However, these clubs are not active, because members have different backgrounds and internal management is poor. Among these organizations, some are relatively more active, for example:

- China Young Angel Investor Leader Association (CYAILA) is a union of active angel investors.[9] The members will share information and make decisions together. CYAILA was founded in January 2013. The association only welcomes honest, kind-hearted individuals, or partners of institutions and representatives of enterprises who are keen on angel investment. To join the association, these people should have invested RMB 100,000 in at least two projects over the last three years. Now, there are 60 members and 80% of them are full-time angel investors. The association promotes the concept of "co-investment, win-win cooperation and openness" and encourages more people to make angel investment. The organization features monthly salons where members would recommend fantastic projects for road shows. By June 2015, the group had organized over 20 road show activities, and one of three start-ups got angel investments through this group.
- Angel 100 of Zhongguancun Private Equity & Venture Capital Association is an association for part-time angel investors. Also founded in January 2013, the organization was the first angel investment service platform that officially registered in China. Among the 20 sponsors of the association, most people are from CEIBS, CKGSB, Tsinghua University, EMBA of Peking University and Zhongguancun. The association features themed dinner parties, entrepreneurial forums, enterprise visits and meetings with professional investors.[10]

3. For-profit angel investment service institutions

These institutions not only make investments but also offer consultant services such as project screening, due diligence and so on. They also provide intermediary services and charge people for these services. These institutions are generally divided into two types. One is "incubation angel investment institutions" similar to Y Combinator in USA, for example, Innovation Works, STEP, Inno Valley and other "angel + incubator" institutions. They screen out seed deals and make investment, provide enterprises with seed funds (RMB 500,000–5 million) and get a few shares (5–25%). Then, these institutions will provide value-added services such as working space, Consulting Services, entrepreneurial training, communication, and follow-up investment. The other type is "angel online platform" similar to "angel + funding" network companies like Angellist and Kickstarter of USA. Angel Crunch, VC.CN and Dajiatou belong to this group. They are platforms bridging angel investors and entrepreneurs and make profits with member fees, service fees, public activities, etc. Established in November 2011, Angel Crunch is the first website of crowd funding in China. By June 2015, the website had launched over 50,000 start-ups and accommodated around 2,800 certified investors. About 400 start-ups had got the investment, totaling RMB 4,000 million.[11] Some famous APPs for smart phones won their first rounds of financing on this web site, such as Didi Taxi, Xiachufang and Dayima.

4. Non-profit angel investment service institutions

These non-profit institutions are dedicated to delivering information between angels and enterprises. An example is the China Business Angel Association (CBAA), which governed by the China Association of Technology Entrepreneurs of the Ministry of Science and Technology of the PRC. Established formally in June 2013, CBAA is the only Chinese member of World Business Angels Association (WBAA, an authoritative angel investment organization in the world). CBAA focuses on building an efficient platform for angel investors to collaborate with each other, share resources and develop together. CBAA provides services including online information, research publication, forums and salons, project docking, training & certifying and entrepreneurial services. By June 2013, its members totaled 141, 132 being individual members and nine being institutional members.[12] Another example is Shanghai Angel Capital Club

(SACC) in East China. Founded in November 2008, SACC is now guided by Torch High Technology Industry Department Center of Ministry of Science and Technology, and launched by China Association of Technology Entrepreneurs, Shanghai Venture Capital Association as well as Shanghai Technology Entrepreneurship Foundation for Graduates. SACC aims to gather angel investors around China, professionalize angel investment and further perfect the environment of venture capital. As one of the major initiators, STEFG would try its best to support SACC with its funds, resources, etc. SACC spends most of its funds on daily operation, annual activities, member communication, etc. Angels Canton (AC) in South China is also an example. Established in June 2013, it accelerates the development of angel investment in Guangdong, and is a comprehensive angel investment organization that provides training courses, industrial research and consultation services about financing. Most of its members are angels, successful businesspersons, professional investment institutions, private investment institutions and individual entrepreneurs in Guangdong, Hong Kong and Macao. AC closely cooperates with individual and institutional angel investors at home and abroad, gathers various resources and has an efficient platform for sharing, education, communication and collaboration. It launches online and offline activities such as investment symposiums, entrepreneurial meetings, entrepreneurial training courses, project promotion meetings, forums, etc. AC also bridges entrepreneurial ideas and capital, helping early-stage entrepreneurial teams to get financial and managerial support. It guides people to make proper investment as well, explores and nurtures entrepreneurs, increases the success rate of starting businesses or making investment and creates a favorable environment for entrepreneurs.[13]

Case VI: RenownedAngel Investor — Xu Xiaoping and "ZhenFund"

Xu Xiaoping: "Entrepreneurs Must Be of Integrity, Commitment and Persistence"

As one of founders of New Oriental Education & Technology Group, Xu Xiaoping is known to be a mentor to young Chinese entrepreneurs. Today, he is one of the most well-known angel investors in China and he takes angel investment to be part of his mentoring career.

Background

Xu Xiaoping, Yu Minhong and Wang Qiang were seen as the "three carriages" of New Oriental Education & Technology Group. When the Group was listed in 2006, Mr. Xu started to support young entrepreneurs and was entitled "The Most Honorable Angel of 2010" and "Chinese Angel Investor of the Year 2011."

Xu believes that an entrepreneur must have many merits. The most important three merits are integrity, commitment and persistence. Integrity is a must. Commitment is also a key, and an entrepreneur must devote all he/she has to his/her business. An entrepreneur should also be persistent, succumbing to no obstacles and retrying after analyzing the failure and making adjustment, since there is always a possibility of success.

In order to encourage the youth to start businesses and make innovation, Xu established ZhenFund in 2006. Like New Oriental School that helps the youth study abroad, ZhenFund aims to assist overseas students to start businesses back in China. ZhenFund is willing to help young people who have a global vision and understand the ethos behind ZhenFund to start their own businesses. ZhenFund has invested in nearly 200 companies including Jiayuan.com, Lightinthebox, Jumei.com, RYB Education Institution and Langkoo. This makes ZhenFund one of the investors that invest in the largest number of early-stage projects.

Performance

Compared to another angel investor, Lei Jun, who only invests in people he is familiar with, Xu believed contributions could be made to both familiar and

(Continued)

Case VI: *(Continued)*

unfamiliar people: "I will make investment if your smile is touching and your idea is convincing." Xu mentioned that his favorite entrepreneurs are those who devote everything to their dreams.

At the beginning of 2008, Lightinthebox, which was invested by Xu in 2006, won two rounds of venture capital and its overall estimated value increased 20-fold in just two years. Xu finally harvested the fruits of angel investment and became more determined to continue the career of angel investor.

As a famous website for selling foreign goods, Lightinthebox was founded by Guo Quji, the former senior manager of Google China. When starting his business, Guo called Xu and introduced his commercial plan. After 20 minutes, Mr. Xu said he didn't understand the idea. But Xu thought Guo was a dependable entrepreneur. Thus, he asked two questions: How much did Guo want? How many shares could he (Xu) get? The next day, Xu invested USD100,000. Guo said that that key call changed his life. "Before that call, we have met less than five times. If he said we needed to communicate one or two times more, I may have quit."

Another outstanding investment of Xu is about Jiayuan.com, an online dating platform built by Ms. Gong Haiyan. Gong first met Xu at a cafe in 2007. After an hour of talking, Xu appraised of what Gong had experienced before: Working in a factory, studying again to enter Peking University and then Fudan University for further education, and founding the dating website to find her Mr Right. Xu decided to make investment at once. In 2011, Jiayuan.com was listed in NASDAQ, USA. After years of investment, Xu enjoyed the first fruits of exit strategy. Gong once said on her blog, "The Adorable Xu Xiaoping", that when Xu was talking, you could do nothing but listening. However, chatting with him was nice. He could always find your softest point and strike your response.

By far, Xu has invested in over 200 projects such as Jumei.com, SAIL-ONG and RYB Education Institution. According to the estimation, these companies value far more than USD 1 billion. Xu once joked that his investment could be judged by his wife's looks: The first year — angry, the next year — annoyed, the third year — mildly annoyed, and the fourth year — happy.

(Continued)

Case VI: (*Continued*)

Features

Entrepreneurs tend to recognize Xu as the most welcomed investor. He makes investments based on quick decisions and seldom reads financial reports. If an idea does not interest him within 30 minutes, he will turn it down. At the end of 2012, Ms. Gong quit Jiayuan.com and started 91 waijiao. This time, Xu also made investment without any doubt. He never quits the investee halfway because he believes that one should never recede after he/she starts something.

Shen Nanpeng, the founder and managing partner of Sequoia Capital China, remarked, "Mr. Xu is one of the most successful angel investors in China. He has a unique view, and is eager to make early-stage investment and yields a lot of results. He is recognized by many entrepreneurs and Sequoia Capital China takes him an ideal partner of seed investment. ZhenFund co-founded with Mr. Xu will be a platform helping more early-stage entrepreneurs realize their dream. We also believe that assisting early-stage entrepreneurs is very meaningful and is an important social mission for any sound investor."

ZhenFund has no long investment provisions, but one page of articles. This new agreement excludes protective rights such as seats at the Board of Directors, the veto right of directors, the right of participating in clearance, preferred dividend, the right of redemption, the right of drag-along and anti-dilution as well as the whole set of delivery terms. Xu said although the comprehensive and complete contracts could protect both investors and the invested, ZhenFund greatly simplified the contract to meet Chinese conditions.

Xu said, "Early-stage entrepreneurs usually do not understand the relevant laws. They take this set of rules that are completed over 100–200 years in the West as restriction on them." Therefore, Xu would only sign simple contracts with entrepreneurial teams at the stage of angel investment. He might use complex contracts with entrepreneurs at the stage of A round investment or at even later stages.

He thought entrepreneurs should learn from the contracts about angel investment instead of resisting them or following to their own rules.

Source: Internet data, including those from Baidu, ZhenFund, China Venture, The Founder and CYZONE, compiled by Wang Jipei (a doctoral candidate of the School of Finance, Renmin University of China).

Case VII: Renowned Angel Investor — Lei Jun and "Shunwei Capital"

Lei Jun: "Investing in Familiar People, Contributing to People Instead of Ideas, and Doing No Harm But Offering Help"

Born in 1969 at Xiantao of Hubei Province, Lei Jun is the founder, President and CEO of Xiaomi and President of Kingsoft. He is also a well-known angel investor in China. In December 2012, he won the prize of "Annual Pioneering Person in Chinese Economic World." In October 2013, the 60th anniversary of All-China Federation of Industry & Commerce, China Business, the editor committee of Huashangtaolue, and China Federation of Industry & Commerce Publishing House co-launched the report "The Power of Private Business and Brilliant Chinese Dream — 100 Businesspersons Contributing Most to National Industries," to demonstrate the power of private economy, private businesspersons' achievements and their contribution to China. Lei Jun is among the listed business persons. On December 12, 2012, he won the titles of "Annual Person in Chinese Economic World" and "Top 10 Economic Leader." In February 2014, Lei Jun, the founder of Xiao Mi, was listed in the Hurun Global Rich List for the first time owning to his fortune of RMB 28 billion, ranking 57 in China and 339 in the world.

Background

Being an angel investor, Lei Jun has invested in many enterprises, including over 20 entrepreneurial enterprises such as Zhuoyue, Xiaoyaocd.com, Shangpin, Lexun, UC, Duowan, Lakala, VANCL, Letao, Keniu, Haodf and GWC. He also founded the angel investment fund — Shunwei Capital.

Shunwei Capital was established in 2011. According to Zero2IPO Pedata, it raised USD 225 million for the first round of funds and USD 315 million for the second round of funds. Lei Jun is both the founding partner and the president, and Xu Dalai is the founding partner and the CEO. Shunwei Capital is a USD venture capital fund. LPs are top institutional investors around the world, such as internationally famous sovereign wealth funds, family funds, funds of funds and university funds.

(Continued)

Case VII: *(Continued)*

Shunwei focuses on Internet-related industries in China, and invests in mobile network, E-commerce, social platforms, etc. It mainly invests in excellent entrepreneurial companies at early or growth stages. According to INVESTIDE, Shunwei mainly make A Round and B Round investment.

Performance

At the first China Angel Inventor Conference, Lei Jun said, "There are two keys to success. One is an outstanding entrepreneur. The other is a good chance — wind gap." Lei Jun has mentioned this phase many times at different places. He believes that "at a wind gap, even a pig could fly". In November 2011, Lei Jun remarked at TechCrunch Disrupt that among the 20 companies he had invested in, VANCL was the most successful one. In 2007, Lei Jun had invested RMB 100 million in VANCL, a B2C platform for clothes sales and several rounds of financing were made after that. On February 11, 2014, VANCL declared the completion of another round financing at USD 100 million.

In 2000, Lei Jun and Chen Nian co-founded Zhuoyue, which was sold to Amazon in 2004 at the price of USD 75 million. After the sale, Chen Nian left the company due to managerial dispute with his new boss. In 2005, Chen Nian founded WOYO, a platform for trading properties of online games. Lei Jun also invested in the company, but it went bankrupt before long. However, in 2007, Lei Jun found Chen Nian again. The two men then co-founded VANCL.

According to Lei, angel investment is investing in the people you trust. When the people received funding, most of them had nothing but ideas and some didn't even have any idea. When he was answered the reason of the investment in VANCL, Lei Jun said, "Because the founder is Chen Nian. I don't care if it's VANCL or something else." "'C' stands for Chen Nian, 'L' stands for Lei Jun and 'VAN' represents vanguard and vessel. When Chen Nian and Lei Jun work together, they will always be the pioneers in the world of E-commerce." Chen Nian also made similar comments on his collaboration with Lei Jun.

VANCL did not fail the two. According to the media, VANCL was valued more than most of the other enterprises in which Lei Jun has invested, and its value topped USD 5 billion in 2011.

(Continued)

Case VII: (*Continued*)

Features

Lei Jun summarized his entrepreneurial experience with three words: "Following the trend." In other words, one should spare no efforts in what the trend allowed and never go the other direction since there were hundreds of ways towards success. As an angel investor, Lei Jun follows three principles: Investing in familiar people, contributing to people instead of ideas, and doing no harm but offering help. When choosing start-ups, Lei Jun usually considers four keys: the larger picture and direction of the enterprise, a "verified" smaller direction/vision provided by the investees, a fantastic management team and high returns. His investing is focusing on familiar people, and he only invests in friends and friends of friends.

Lei believes that the values of angel investment lay in three factors: (1) It provides starting funds — highly valuable as the first entrepreneurial investment; (2) it enables sharing of experience, human resources and integrity — creating strategies, grasping more solid directions, introducing engineers and gathering founders; and (3) it comes with added integrity — "I have your back," making you dependable.

About the important concept of investment, Lei emphasizes doing the right thing at the right time. For Lei Jun, to start a business, one should choose the biggest market within his/her capacity because only large markets could accommodate large enterprises and if the direction is wrong, precious resources will be wasted; and starting a business is also about the right time, dedication and perfection, the three keys to top in a vertical market.

Source: Online data including those from Baidu, Shunwei, JRJ, Sohu Finance, TMTPOST, The Founder, CYZONE, compiled by Wang Jipei (a doctoral candidate of the School of Finance, Renmin University of China).

Case VIII: Private Angel Investment Institution — Chen Shiming and "Ningbo Boleyuma"

Chen Shiming: "Building the Eco-system for Angel Investors and Helping Entrepreneurs by Integrating Resources"

Time/site: June 17, 2013/Ningbo, China[14]

Mr. Chen Shiming is the founding partner and general manager of Ningbo Boleyuma Co., Ltd., Secretary-General of Zhejiang Sunflower Development Center, Deputy Secretary General of Second-generation Entrepreneurs Association of Jiangdong, Ningbo, and the entrepreneurial mentor of Ningbo Volunteer Team of Entrepreneur Mentors. Before that, Chen was the managing director of a joint venture, and completed the whole procedure of ISO9001 certification for the company; he has also established and invested in innovative modern service enterprises like Bole Commercial College, Honey Comb and Fashion Mindo. He is familiar with the operational management and establishment of commercial pattern of entrepreneurial enterprises, good at integrating various social and market resources needed by start-ups and exploring commercial value of start-ups in high-tech and innovative modern services industries. Therefore, he is capable of helping innovative start-ups establish their core competitiveness and develop themselves.

Boleyuma is an institution providing high-tech and innovative modern service enterprises with financing and incubation services. It is dedicated to finding, assisting and nurturing good entrepreneurial teams and cradling more excellent entrepreneurs and start-ups with deep cooperation such as successive, effective training, personnel introduction and re-financing. In Chinese, the company's name refers to the chances for boosters and horses meeting each other. As this name shows, the company is neither the booster nor the horse, but a platform for them.

Keys to Avoiding Risks of Angel Investment: Only Investing in Familiar Industries/People + Taking the Lead in Investing & Co-investing

Chen believed that the key to avoiding risks of angel investment was only investing in familiar industries because only in this way could an investor

(Continued)

Case VIII: (*Continued*)

judge if an idea was marketable, valuable or promising. This meant investing in the familiar industries and the familiar people. He further explained that all starters were less experienced, and unlike VC or PE, angel investing usually face more risks and difficulties. So investing in familiar industries or people could help to reduce risks. He also said that Boleyuma had invested in many start-ups of modern services related to human resources, education, property management, etc. These start-ups are of light assets, low cost and risk. He also mentioned that since 2012, the industry of angel investment had witnessed good environment, policies as well as new angels. Angel investors were ready to take risks, but they should also take measures to avoid risks, especially when it came to unfamiliar but promising ideas. Angel investors could hire professional teams to manage funds. As managers, these professionals could perfect the decisions made by investors. However, the final decision was made through voting by investors. This was the evolution from individual angels to institutional angels. According to Chen, two patterns would be used comprehensively. One is using the lead-investment mode in the familiar industries. The other is investing in unfamiliar but valuable start-ups through equity-based crowd funding "Bole Co-investment" (i.e. to make industrial leaders be lead-investors and let the rest make co-investment), which allow people to invest in promising but unfamiliar projects and helped to enlarge Bole Co-investment, the online equity-based crowd funding platform of Boleyuma. Thus, more investors with certain financial and investment capabilities could contribute to the construction of innovative and entrepreneurial cities, and enlarge commercial values by collaboration and sharing.

Eco-system: Angel fund + Bole Co-investment + Bole Business School + Training Camp

Recent researches showed that institutionalization and group co-investment became the trends, and many for-profit and non-profit organizations like clubs and unions were emerging, including China Young Angel Investor Leader Association in Beijing, Angel Investor Club in Shanghai, Grassroots Angel Committee in Shenzhen, Angel Club in Guangzhou, etc. However, organizations, companies and funds were different in organization management,

(Continued)

Case VIII: *(Continued)*

investment decision and the like. Chen said that investing would be better regulated in funds or companies, but public activities would attract more-diverse people if they were launched by NGOs; therefore, to support Boleyuma, we established Bole Commercial College, ran an entrepreneurial cafe, and operated two clubs "Bole Co-investment" and "Founder Club." The cafe was a public place for activities and the clubs were communication platforms for entrepreneurs and investors.

Bole Co-investment was the first online equity-based crowd funding platform in Ningbo. It selected 30 industrial leaders among 100 entrepreneurs. These leaders have investing capabilities, the willingness to invest, as well as rich experience and social resources. During the monthly road shows, all investors assessed and chose the start-ups together. Thus, they could avoid risks and grasp the opportunities that might be missed due to unfamiliarity. Moreover, more entrepreneurial ideas could get seed capital and business resources. These would greatly promote the healthy development of the angel investment ecosystem.

Bole Business School was a platform for exploiting commercial values and helping enterprises develop. The ecosystem embraced various people and promoted the communication and collaboration among them. Entrepreneurial starters with only ideas, seasoned entrepreneurs with years of experience, successful investors, law firms, clubs, banks and other services institutions could realize their missions on every Sunday during the four sessions: Bole Morning Jogging, Bole Entrepreneurial Lectures, Boleyuma Road Shows and Bole Dinners. With these sessions, entrepreneurs could get professional education about starting a business, investors could reach more fantastic projects and learn to be successful angels and the whole society could help people start businesses and make innovation, and assist micro enterprises to develop and fulfill social responsibilities.

Unlike VC or PE, angel investment was also about social responsibility. Chen emphasized that Boleyuma had established the Training Camp to build an ecosystem. The camp was open to two kinds of people. One category consisted of excellent graduates selected from 15 colleges and universities in Ningbo through competitions; they would be classified and trained accordingly, and then based on the specific industry, assistance would be given to help them start a business or develop the market. This was the solid basis for Boleyuma

(Continued)

Case VIII: (*Continued*)

to find start-ups and personnel. The other category of people that Boleyuma sought out consisted of young entrepreneurs with working experience. These people had worked for years and understood the industries, but did not know how to launch or run an enterprise, such as how to do commercial and industrial registration or manage financial affairs or strategies. Boleyuma would invite officials of local governments, successful businesspersons, industrial experts, among many other professions, to mentor entrepreneurs, and would assist entrepreneurs to expand social network and get resources through courses and docking activities. On the topic of earning profits, Boleyuma preferred offering angel services to making cash investment in exchange of micro shares. In other words, Boleyuma would get a few shares after offering resources needed by enterprises, and invest in cash when enterprises were successfully incubated. By doing so, Boleyuma not only increased the success rate of starting a business, but also reduced the risk of angel investment. Obviously, Boleyuma combined the operation of industries, commerce and services and connected all sectors of the angel investment.

Most people believed that building platforms was the hardest task, because sustainable development required continuous reformation and innovation. Chen said that many angel associations and clubs were formed out of traditions. These platforms were not companies, and thus lacked vitality and existed in name only. Therefore, Chen believed that it would be more efficient and sustainable to build a platform in a way that combined the methods to establish a company and an organization.

"To Increase the Success Rate of Angel Investment, We Need to Train both Entrepreneurs and Investors."

Why did angel investment or venture capital often fail? The cores of angel investment were entrepreneurs and investors. However, people usually blamed entrepreneurs only for failures, and thus paid great attention to incubating and educating entrepreneurs. Nevertheless, investors were also essential to successful investment. Chen pointed out that Chinese investors were less professional and therefore, training for future investors was necessary as well. He believed that in Ningbo, second-generation entrepreneurs were different from first-generation ones. Most of the second-generation entrepreneurs had stud-

Case VIII: (*Continued*)

ied abroad and learned new things, so they preferred novel ideas to traditional industries. They even inherited their parents' business with cultural innovative ideas. The second generation was willing to operate the enterprises with methods of financial investment, but lacked professional knowledge. As a result, investment training is in need. Boleyuma was one of founders of China Young Angel Investor Leader Association. It would use the rich resources of the association and invite famous members to mentor entrepreneurs or investors, such as Xu Xiaoping (the investor of Jumei), Mai Gang (the investor of Huangtaiji), Wang Tong (the investor of Tuniu), and Liu Dongqiu (the investor of Kogou). Boleyuma would even invite lead-investors to provide more-dedicated guidance for start-ups.

Regional Differences: Angel Investors in Ningbo Were Relatively Conservative; Assistance based on Local Conditions Should Be Provided to Help Them Find Proper Projects

China is of vast territory and abundant resources. Different regions are featured with different geographical conditions, cultures, resources, economic conditions and policies, which have led to diverse economic conditions, cultural concepts and industrial features, including entrepreneurial characteristics and investment cultures. Chen said that the older investors in Ningbo were relatively conservative. When they invested in a start-up, they would require the majority of shares and insist on controlling this company. However, angel investors would not request a lot of shares because they were only investors, not entrepreneurs. Entrepreneurs and investors had different goals. The former wanted to sell products, while the latter wanted to invest and participate in various projects. Nevertheless, as investors' energy was limited, it was appropriate not to take the majority of shares. More importantly, holding major shares would demotivate or discourage entrepreneurs and thus reduce the success rate. Therefore, taking fewer shares would encourage entrepreneurs because they were working for themselves instead of others. On the other hand, conservative investors in Ningbo would also make entrepreneurs here conservative. As a result, the most profitable start-ups usually chose to collect funds by themselves or loans from others, and would not ask investors for

(*Continued*)

Case VIII: (*Continued*)

help. Chen mentioned that because Ningbo investors were conservative, they tended to invest in less risky companies, like innovative modern services.

Great Support for Angel Investment from the Government of Ningbo

The government of Ningbo had done better than other local governments in terms of public policies. According to Chen, the government of Ningbo had greatly supported angel investment since 2012. At the end of 2012, an angel investment fund of RMB 500 million was established to cooperate with 500 individual and institutional angel investors through co-investment over a period of five years. The fund would mainly invest in high-tech companies, overseas students' projects and promising local start-ups. For companies that have received angel investment, the government would also match the angel capital raised. The government would take no shares, which reflected how great governmental support was. Meanwhile, the government also offered support such as offices, personnel training and technological allowance.

Case IX: State-Owned Angel Investment Institution — Angel Investment Fund of Chengdu Hi-tech Industrial Development Zone

Huang Guangyao: "Government Should Take the Lead in Creating a Better Environment for Angel Investment and Market Should Increase Efficiency"

Time/ Site: October 20, 2013/Chengdu, China

Mr. Huang Guangyao is General Manager of CDHT Investment Venture Capital Co., Ltd. and was Chief of the Finance Section of Chengdu Hi-tech Industrial Development Zone, deputy director of the Finance Office of the zone, member of China Venture Capital Association and Secretary-General of Chengdu Equity Investment Association. For many years, Huang has researched on financing and practiced a lot. He is one of the founders of

(*Continued*)

Case IX: (*Continued*)

"trapezoid financing model" of the development zone, and has rich experience and experienced success in SME financing, equity financing and reorganization for IPO. He led the establishment of the largest guidance fund of venture capital in West China — Chengdu Yinke Venture Capital Co., Ltd., participated in the reorganization of Guibao Technology, the first enterprise of Sichuan listed in Growth Enterprises Market, built the largest value-added service platform for enterprise financing, Winpower, in West China and introduced Shenzhen Stock Exchange and established the first road show center for IPO in Midwest China.

According to Huang, CDHT Investment Venture Capital Co., Ltd. was established in 2004. It is the wholly owned subsidiary of CDHT Investment Group, a state-owned sole corporation under the jurisdiction of the Management Committee of Chengdu Hi-tech Industrial Development Zone. The company mainly focused on managing the angel investment funds of the development zone to support seed enterprises and start-ups. It also invested in technology enterprises at early and growth stages. Meanwhile, the company launched and managed private equity investment funds such as some emerging venture capital funds, Winpower venture capital fund, and Chengdu Entrepreneurial Accelerator Fund.

Angel Investing Should Be Professionalized

Considering the history of private equity investment, Huang pointed out that Chinese PE Industry had developed rapidly from 2008 to 2010. It could be explained through three reasons: the amendment of Partnership Enterprise Law in 2006, the recession of dollar fund and the rising of Renminbi due to 2008 financial crisis and the launching of Growth Enterprises Market in 2009. Due to the obstacles to IPO and the reformation of share issuance mechanism in the latest 2 years, it became difficult for PE investors to scramble for Pre-IPO projects and most of the PE and VC institutions started to invest in early-stage projects. Elaborating on this, Huang said that Chinese PE/VC institutions were shortsighted and thus preferred mature projects. However, to get these deals, those institutional investors needed more money and channels than professional abilities. Early-stage investment, on the contrary, demanded professional skills. Huang further emphasized that angel investment demanded

(*Continued*)

Case IX: (*Continued*)

a lot of professional skills and knowledge, buyouts instead of IPO, might be the main exit strategy, and in the era of economic restructure, China would witness more cases of buyout.

Efficiency Government Should Take the Lead in Creating a Better Environment for Angel Investment and Market Should Increase Efficiency

What role should the authorities play in developing angel investment? Huang believes that at this stage, instead of merely guiding, the government should lead in relevant people and institutions in a certain direction. In other words, the government should provide financial support and establish an environment for boosting investment. Huang also introduced that in 2012, Chengdu Hi-tech Industrial Development Zone implemented "Tianfu Star", a plan for nurturing innovative & entrepreneurial enterprises with advantageous resources of the authorities, enterprises and institutions. Meanwhile, the zone established its angel investment fund of RMB 80 million in the first round and entrusted CDHT Hi-tech Entrepreneurial Investment Co., Ltd. with all the company's fiscal funds to make equity investments. Most of the start-ups were from the database of "Tianfu Star" which was founded under the leading of CDHT Investment Winpower and in which under the coordination of the Economic and Trade Development Bureau of Chengdu Hi-tech Industrial Development Zone, the Bureau of Science and Technology of Hi-tech Industrial Development Zone, the Innovation Center, the Software Promotion Office and the Office of Pharmaceutical Industry Promotion also participated. Angel investment fund focuses on the field of mobile network, biological medicine, electronic information and new materials. Mr. Huang pointed out that fiscal expenditure was not direct or voluntary any longer. It became indirect and compensable. As a result, the exploitation of money would be more efficient. The word "indirect" meant that although the government offered money, professional used the funds efficiently and operated according to market rules. The word "compensable" meant that moral hazards, illegal practices or misdistribution of resources could be effectively prevented and the risks became controllable.

(*Continued*)

Case IX: (*Continued*)

Angel Investment Needs to Reach Grassroots Enterprises and Governmental Supervision Should Be Moderate

Huang said that the zone included many industrial parks so that the early-stage investment was really for grassroots enterprises. CDHT Investment also boasted natural advantages of gathering local resources. The first round of the fund added up to RMB 80 million and the second, third and more rounds would be launched in the future. As a result, the leveraging function of fiscal funds would become greater and greater.

However, Huang also mentioned that state-owned institutional investors also faced structural and systematic obstacles and he himself encountered such obstacles. He thought that although proper supervision helped to regulate industries, excessive supervision might reduce the efficiency of management; for example, when they assessed the start-ups or decided to exit the start-ups, the state-owned institutions of angel investment might suffer overwhelming interference from the supervising departments.

Case X: Active Angel Investment Group — China Young Angel Investor Leader Association

Yang Ning: "Co-investment and Win-win Cooperation — Bringing the Organization Out of Beijing and to the World"

Interview Time/site: February 24, 2014/Beijing, China

Time/site of Public Activity: May 24, 2014/Shenzhen, China

Mr. Yang Ning is the founding partner of LeBox Capital, the founder of ChinaRen.com and Honorary Chairman of China Young Angel Investor Leader Association (CYAILA). He was also President and CTO of KongZhong Corporation.

CYAILA was established in January 2013, with the aim of helping angel investors communicate with each other about methods for project assessment,

(*Continued*)

Case X: (*Continued*)

trade practice, regulations, etc., so that angels could get more experience and more investments would take place. Another Honorary Chairman of CYAILA was Xu Xiaoping, a well-known angel inventor and the co-founder of ZhenFund, Chairman was Mai Gang, a celebrated angel investor and the founder of Ventures Lab, and Secretary-General was NiuWenwen, President of the periodical office of The Founder. There were over 100 members in the association at the time of the interview.

Expanding beyond China: From Point Systems and Regions, to the Rest of the World

Yang pointed out that CYAILA would launch services such as angel investment salons, venture capital salons and a point system. He also said that both the policies and the market could boost economy by encouraging innovation and entrepreneurial activities, which was an unprecedented opportunity for angel investors. Beside the headquarters in Beijing, CYAILA's activities also stretched to other regions. For example, CYAILA established its Shanghai branch in April 2014, with Mr. Zhang Min, the founder of Empower Investment, as Chairman, and Mr. Wang Lijie, the founder of Preangel, as Vice Chairman. To fulfill the goal of CYAILA, the Shanghai Branch would greatly support the development of angel investment, recommend fantastic projects found in Shanghai to angels in other regions, and assist local government to attract excellent projects into Shanghai. In May 2014, the Guangdong branch was established, with Mr. Mai Gang, being Chairman of this branch. This branch aimed to unite good angel investors in the Pearl River Delta, incubate and stimulate the venture capital industry in Guangdong (Pearl Delta) area, bridge entrepreneurs and inventors and encourage them to collaborate with each other. The final goal was to create a bright future for investors in the area. Beside these two branches, preparations were also being made to establish its Zhejiang branch, with Mr. Wu Bing, the angel investor of Vipshop, as the leader of the preparation team, and Mr. Liu Qiudong, CEO of Zhejiang Zheshang Venture Capital Co., Ltd., as the team's Vice Chairman.

(*Continued*)

Case X: (*Continued*)

In the afternoon of May 24, 2014, many celebrities attended the opening ceremony of the Guangdong branch held in Shenzhen. The ceremony was the largest feast for angel investors held in South China. The authors of this book, attended the ceremony with Mr. John May, Co-chairman of World Business Angels Association and Honorary Chairman of Angel Capital Associate. Mr. ZengLiqing (a famous angel investor and the co-founder of Tecent), Mr. Liu Xiaosong (a long-time angel investor), Mr. Yang Ning (Chairman of CYAILA), Mr. Mai Gang (Vice Chairman of CYAILA), and some CYAILA members and representatives of over 30 well-known VC institutions also attended the ceremony.

Building a Harmonious and Win-Win Ecosystem of Venture Capital

In 2014, CYAILA promoted international communication and cooperation, and stimulated various professional investors (including Microsoft Ventures Accelerator, SV Entrepreneurs, Entrepreneurial Industrial Park for Graduates of the Ministry of Education, and Virtue Inno Valley) to collaborate with governments of Qingdao, Tianjin, Changsha, and other regions. CYAILA brought abundant factors for entrepreneurial activities. Based on the existing angel investment and venture capital salons, Salon of Venture Capital Date was launched for the majority of entrepreneurs in order to expand the influence of the organization to the entrepreneurs; in the future, CYAILA would go on to establish Angel Investment College to popularize angel investment and nurturing more angels, so as to promote the rapid development of angel investment in China. By enriching and integrating the factors, CYAILA would strive to build a harmonious and win-win ecosystem of venture capital.

Source: Information compiled based on the authors' interview of Chairman Yang Ning, communication at the opening ceremony of Guangdong branch and data from the Secretariat of CYAILA.

Case XI:　Angel Investment Association — Zhongguancun Angels 100

Qiao Qian: Wisdom of a Hundred Persons; Realized Entrepreneurial Dream

Time/site: May 20, 2013/Beijing, China

Mr. Qiao Qian is Chairman of Angels100 of Zhongguancun Private Equity & Venture Capital Association (ZVCA) and has 25-year experience related to the science & technology industry. In 2010, Qiao founded Beijing YinheJinqiao Investment Co., Ltd. and started to focus on investing in innovative and early-stage enterprises, helping those with entrepreneurial dreams to realize their dreams.

Angels100 has been the secondary branch of ZVCA and was founded in the early 2013. The civil affairs department registered it separately and presently, the group developed into an excellent organization with around 100 angels.

Angels 100: "A Non-Professional Angel Investor"

Qiao has worked in the industrial section for nearly 25 years, but he lacks experience in making investment. According to Qiao, angel investment would go to an enterprise that might lack a sustainable profit stream but has a unique idea, a business pattern and a basic entrepreneurial team;VC investment, however, usually went to enterprises with relatively mature operation systems and needing external funds for further expansion; and the more mature an enterprise was, the more resources it would need.

Qiao believes that a strong heart is necessary for an angel investor. Although entrepreneurs have fantastic ideas, the earlier the investment is made, the riskier the investment is. Therefore, an angel really needs a strong heart to bear the risks. Secondly, angels should bring more resources to entrepreneurs. After several tries, Qiao found that many people had experience or opinions similar to his. Then, a question rose in his mind: when one person's resources were limited, was it possible to integrate resources and wisdom of more people? The answer was absolutely yes. Thirdly, angels should "mentor" entrepreneurs by sharing their experience.

(*Continued*)

Case XI: (*Continued*)

When he realized that entrepreneurs needed more resources, Qiao came up with the idea to unite more people to make investment. He believed that if there were more angels, then entrepreneurs could get more help. As a result, he promoted the concept of "the 100 Angels Association", i.e., the idea was to collect a hundred people's wisdom to help entrepreneurs realize their dreams. Which qualities are the investor has to be the member of Angels100? Qiao said one should have three qualities. One was that he or she should get prepared mentally that all his/her money might go for nothing. In other words, he or she should be able to bear the risks. Another one was that he or she should have the willing and motive to make angel investment. The last one was that he or she should have worked in some industry for at least ten years, because this guaranteed that he or she probably had started business or been a senior manager and thus boasted deep insight into the development and future of the industry. In other words, Angels100 was an organization covering many industries. Its members had different industrial backgrounds and the number of members from a same industry should not exceed five. In this way, people could share diverse experience. In fact, these qualities alone would be greatly helpful for entrepreneurs.

Qiao also emphasized that based on its qualities as well as its intention to help entrepreneurs, "Angels 100" was positioned principally as a "non-professional angel investor". That was to say that each member had his/her full-time job and making investment was just a hobby. With the group, the members got a chance to make investment together. Therefore, angels without experience would also get the courage to make investment and entrepreneurs could get better assistance from this angel group.

Method to Gather Members: Themed Meals, Entrepreneurial Forums, Visits to Enterprises, and Meetings with Professional Investors

Based on his experience home and abroad, group investing is difficult: The issue is how could members be gathered effectively? Qiao says he plans to launch 100 activities annually to nurture the cohesive power among members. There would be four kinds of activities in general. The first is the themed meals on each Friday (about 40 times a year). The themed meals are principally open to the members of the association. On each Friday, a member

(Continued)

Case XI: (*Continued*)

would invite 10 to 12 people to the meal and these people may communicate with each other about a project or an industry in a fixed duration. For example, thanks to a themed meal, some members recently made the decision to collaborate on a project. The second is the entrepreneurial forums on Saturdays (about 40 forums per year). These forums are organized with Peking University Alumni Venture Association. Participants are mostly entrepreneurs. At these forums, investors would be invited to give speeches or review entrepreneurial companies. At the forums, entrepreneurs and investors could have face-to-face communication. Qiao also mentions that one of the most important tasks is creating "1898 Cafe" — another place for entrepreneurs and investors to communicate. The third is visiting enterprises (about 10 visits per year). The members of the Angles100 would recommend which start-ups to visit. During each visit, 10 to 15 members would be invited to the enterprises and could discuss about the development of the enterprises at the discussion sessions. The fourth is meetings with famous investors (about 10 meetings per year). Since all its members are non-professional, they need to learn from professional investors and famous institutional investors about their experiences of successful investments. In other words, the activities double as training courses for the members.

This group is a loose organization. To guarantee sustainable development, it has a strict management system in place, which reflects the characteristics of the association. Firstly, the members fulfill "decent enrollment" by sharing their failures with other members. When someone wants to join the association, he/she should share with others a failed investment because failures are valued much. Also, they could quit decently if they couldn't fulfill the requirement of minimum participating time. The group organizes about 100 activities a year and each member was required to participate in at one out of 10 of these activities. If a member failed to attend 10 activities at least, he/she would be dismissed. Meanwhile, each one could make an "intellectual order". This meant that each year, when he/she encountered some difficulty, a member could make such an order and the association would require certain member to solve the problem. Lastly, the association introduced an innovative mode of "personnel investment". In other words, the group promoted the change from investing in "companies" to "people", i.e. from investing in "entrepreneurial enterprises" to "leading entrepreneurs". The group also advocated a transformation from short-term cooperation to long-term investment contracts. At the time of the interview, the group was studying on the legal implications of this type of contract.

Case XII: Online Platform for Angel Investment — VC.CN

Li Xiaoning: "Sticking to Grassroots Entrepreneurial Culture and Improving Domestic Entrepreneurial Environment"

Time/site: May 20, 2013/Beijing, China

Mr. Li Xiaoning is the founder and CEO of VC.CN (https://www.vc.cn/). He received a master's degree of business administration in The Wharton School of the University of Pennsylvania and a master's degree in the University of Delaware. He has also worked in the fields of technology and finance for over 10 years in the USA and thus understands the advanced technology and industrial trend home and abroad. Before returning to China, he was Vice President of Merrill Lynch. Li has already communicated, helped or mentored over 100 start-ups on VC.CN. Thus, he boasted firsthand resources and experience about investment in start-ups and the corresponding risks.

VC.CN is similar to AngelList and Fundersclub in the USA. It is a social network focusing on services for investors, entrepreneurs and services related to financing. It is a platform that gathers the best investors in China, and aims to provide a novel financing & communication platform for numerous entrepreneurs in China and to provide these entrepreneurs with essential services for "people, funds and ideas exploration".

Online Platform: Quality of Start-ups is the Priority

Several yeas ago, Li decided to quit his job in the USA and come back China for his own business. He planned to build an online platform similar to AngelList, to promote information exchange between angel investors and entrepreneurs. In June 2011, he founded "VC.CN" with the help from the Angel Association and the Innovation Works. When he was talking about the current conditions and outlook of online platforms for angel investment in China, Li said this mode was still at its infancy and it needed nurturing because there were limited angel investors and communities in China and thus offline activities were needed as supplements. He also pointed out that the online services of VC.CN were amazing and the website attracted most

(*Continued*)

Case XII: (*Continued*)

of the hits in China, since the super angels in China were also the investors of the website, endowing VC.CN with great influence. However, it could not launch too many online promotional activities as the market was immature. It could also not afford to ignore the trend of development, in particular, the mode of co-investing. A key to angel investment was to share risks. In this way, crowd funding was possible and an investor could make less contribution to each project while he/she got some better projects. Therefore, joint investment would not only help investors share risks, but also help the projects get more resources.

About how to "assess start-ups", Mr. Li said many start-ups on the platform were recommended by angel investors and thus are of better quality. Some of these companies had won investment before, but they were eager for more investment. In practice, some online platforms would work in an opposite way. In other words, they would complete offline negotiation first and then put the project on the online platforms. However, this way of operation might undermine the rules of online markets. Mr. Li also said frankly that many start-ups were less mature and many other start-ups were not open to co-investment. Besides, law systems in China were not perfect and most transactions were completed offline.

Li mentioned that VC.CN has wide deal flow, such as offline platforms and angel investors. During the activity of "120-Second Challenge", we would select valuable and unique ideas from more than 500 business plans for a road show. For example, several BPs were selected and won the co-investment during the latest activity. The investors and the entrepreneurs could choose the time of further negotiation on their own. VC.CN was only a platform for bridging them.

Generally speaking, Chinese investors needed more time to make up their decisions, because they selected teams and made outlook more prudently. However, some Chinese institutions were also promoting the mode of "fast investment" recently. About this, Mr. Li remarked that the agencies could not determine how long an inventor would make up his/her mind, especially in China, since the investment-demanding projects greatly outnumbered the active investors here. Therefore, it would take a lot of time to truly realize "fast investment".

(*Continued*)

Case XII: *(Continued)*

Features of VC.CN: Help from Elites to Grassroots, as well as Simultaneous Online and Offline Activities

The biggest difference between the angel market in China and US was that angel investors in China were more inadequate. Li believed that there were probably 300,000 angels in the US and they were rich, took little shares and invested actively. In China, there were many rich people, and they were potential angel investors. But they did not understand the rules or had little experience investing in early-stage companies. As a result, they could not become angel investors shortly. If there were more angel investors in China, the online platforms would be more effective.

Another question was whether there would be enough quality projects for Chinese angels in a long term. Li's answer was "yes". He pointed out that based on the pyramidal structure of the financial system, the scales of latter-stage investment (A, B, C and D rounds) were equal in China and the US. However, the scales of the base of this pyramid differed greatly. Start-ups could get angel investment in the US but rarely in China. In China, start-ups should fight for attention of venture investment institutions, which caused the grassroots entrepreneurs being diminished by elite entrepreneurs. Meanwhile, Chinese angel investors also rarely get the opportunities to make a try and be wrong. All these undermined the entrepreneurial environment in China. Therefore, VC.CN was established mainly to enhance the entrepreneurial environment in China with online and offline activities at the time. Among these activities, "co-investment" was a way to nurture grassroots angel investors by introducing super angels to small angels and letting elites help grassroots.

About the differences between VC.CN and online platforms like AngelCrunch and 36Kr, Li answered from three aspects: (1) VC.CN shared the same understanding about angel investment, which reflected the genetics and expertise of the entrepreneurial team, with professional VC institutions, so it was capable of recommending good projects; (2) angel investors of VC.CN were the best in China, holding numerous start-ups and great influence; and (3) while optimizing its online platform, VC.CN also launched offline featured activities, such as "120-second challenge" activities targeting on entrepreneurial road shows, "face-to-face dinners" for entrepreneurs and investors, and "duty days of investors" for solving entrepreneurs' problems.

(Continued)

Case XII: (*Continued*)

Currently, VC.CN provides free matching services for investors and entrepreneurs. Li said that his platform has enormous social value at this stage. So all he cares is to provide better services and it is not the time to think about the profits that could be earned in the future. Moreover, Li has paid a lot of attention and effort in contacting Chinese and American markets. He had contacted several venture capital institutions in the Silicon Valley to help foreign institution introduce their projects to China.

On the issue of governmental policies, Li said that financial support was the most convenient method, and, based on the industrial structure, financial support was also the trend of the development, so the government should issue more policies of financial support. He mentioned that China needed an angel certification system, like the Securities Law and JOBS of the USA, since investors in China were mostly judged by their acts.

Case XIII: Non-Profit Angel Investment Organization — ANGELSCANTON

Yu Wenhui: "Angel Investment Funds Should Feature the Humanity of Angel Investment and Rationality of VC Investment"

Time/site: July 9, 2013/Guangdong, China

Mr. Yu Wenhui is the partner of Thunderstorm Capital and the initiator of ANGELSCANTON. He used to be Investment Director of TeamTop, Deputy Chairman of South China Angel Investors Club, and the core researcher of Venture Capital Research Center of South China University of Technology.

Yu says that ANGELSCANTON aims to boost the development of angel investment in Guangdong, and is an organization working on education services, training courses, industrial researches and investment consultation services. ANGELSCANTON has launched both online and offline activities, bridged projects and capital so as to offer early-stage entrepreneurial teams timely financial and managerial support, to direct investment, to discover and nurture entrepreneurs, to increase the success rate of investment and business starting, and to foster a sound entrepreneurial environment.

(*Continued*)

Case XIII: (*Continued*)

Angel Investment Funds Include the Humanity of Angel Investment and Rationality of VC Investment

Guangdong is always favored by entrepreneurs. In recent years, local science and technology enterprises have witnessed rapid development, especially the TMT enterprises. This has encouraged the inter-transformation between angel investors and entrepreneurs in Guangdong. The insiders even named the year 2012 as the first year of the angel investment era: numerous angel investment organizations and institutions were established around China. Guangdong also witnessed the founding of many such organizations and institutions. Mr. Yu emphasized that these local venture capitalists and institutions were lucky enough to ride this tide to form ANGELSCANTON. The year 2013 was a year seeing the painstaking efforts of angel investors. Many angel investment institutions were established between the end of 2012 and the beginning of 2013.

Yu also remarked that angel investment funds were the combination of angel investment and venture capital. Although the institutions made investment for profits, they were still angels; in fact, any entity that invested in start-ups with money or resources could be called "an angel". According to Yu, one should first see the purpose of the fund to judge if a fund was more about venture capital or more about angel investment. "Angel investment fund" was derived during the institutionalization of angel investment in China. The funds met some people's needs, and could help enterprises as well as investors. Thus, as the old saying goes "anything exists for a reason", such funds were valuable. Moreover, angel investment funds needed the sensitivity and foresight. It needs both the flexibility and humanity of angel investing and the regulations and rationality of VC. A better combination could achieve the purpose of angel investment funds.

Better Entrepreneurial Teams and Founders: Five Keys & Five Abilities

Investors should have passion and rationality at the same time. Yu personally felt so. He said that he had started his own business before and had his own dream, but one could only learn from but not copy other people's success. However, investors had a complicated mind: they wanted to bind their dreams

(*Continued*)

Case XIII: (*Continued*)

with the entrepreneurs' and fulfill their dreams and profits at the same time. They started to talk about dreams when they could ensure their profits, but there was a switch between reality and dreams.

Yu also had his own indicators for choosing projects: (1) Teams, (2) industrial trend and (3) favorable resources of the teams. He also summarized a standard to recognize excellent teams and founders — "five keys and five abilities". He believed that a good team/founder should has (1) an outstanding sense of business, (2) love for his business, (3) professional abilities earned from rich experience, (4) the managerial capacity grown with the development of business and (5) strong ambition and patience for the career. Besides, the team/founder should also feature five abilities: (1) to determine the value; (2) to make a decision at the right time; (3) to turn ideas, commercial and profit modes into cash; (4) to learn continuously and (5) to lead the company. Yu said that the society now was anti-humanity. A humane society would provide people with more choices. Teams and founders should not only have the ability to make judgment but also the ability to make a decision to seize the opportunity at the right time. They should also keep learning new knowledge to ensure the ability to turn modes into money. Success was the result of luck and unswerving efforts. A good example is TCL, a company which succeeded by making right choices successively. Commercial sense was subjective, while professional abilities and managerial capacity were more objective. One's career was the combination of subjective and objective abilities. The ability to determine the value was subjective and objective while the ability to make a decision at the right time was more subjective. The abilities to profit from modes and to learn were subjective while the ability to lead people was subjective and objective. All in all, green start-ups were rigid but learned to be flexible as time went by. At the end of the day, success can only be guaranteed with less rigidity and more flexibility.

Regional Difference: East China Valued Long-Term Development while South China Preferred "Quick Cash"

In terms of the features of entrepreneurs and angel investors in Guangdong, Yu said people there were down-to-earth but relatively shortsighted. But people in

(Continued)

Case XIII: (*Continued*)

Shenzhen were different and there were many major enterprises there, probably because over 90% of people at Shenzhen were from other cities and Shenzhen was a special administration region with open-minded leaders and policies. Besides, the industry of online games was relatively developed at Guangzhou and this industry stimulates customers eager to purchase things, which enabled quick cashing and ensured stable cash flow. However, compared with Beijing and Shenzhen, Guangzhou lacked the internet flow resources. In east China, many angel investors have internet background. According to Yu, those investors succeeded in starting up businesses as they had certain experience and resources. Their angel investing was down-to-earth. The angels are more open, and love to share with others.

Angels in North China were successful entrepreneurs or senior managers before and have rich experience, resources and influence. They had great dreams and ambitions and turn their backs on quick cash. On the contrary, living at the city of food, angels in South China were business persons or rich people with enough money for angel investment and strong capacity of cashing, but they lacked ambitions or foresight.

Notes

1. Liu Manhong, 'Venture Capital,' Lecture Notes, Renmin University of China, 2009.
2. The Zhongguancun Angel Investment Report 2013, published by Zero2IPO Group in January, 2014, indicates that the number of active angel investors in *Zhongguancun* was about 500, and 76 angel investment funds were established between 2008 and 2013.
3. By looking at the Internet, and related books and reports, we have learned that the number of angel institutions and organizations has reached 50.
4. By the end of 2013, investors registered in Angelcrunch, the eminent online platform of angel investment, have reached more than 900.
5. Scott Shane, *Fool's Gold? The Truth Behind Angel Investing in America* (*First Edition*), Oxford University Press, 2008.
6. The research team has made investigations in nine areas: Beijing, Shanghai, Suzhou, Guangzhou, Shenzhen, Ningbo, Wuhan, Chengdu, Hong Kong between April and August 2013. The team looked for angel investors

through joining the angel investment industrial activities and "Snowball effects," i.e. recommendations made by acquaintances, and the subsequent giving out of out questionnaires and one-to-one interviews, and finally retrieving 70 valid questionnaires and 50 interview notes.

7. We find that foreign countries put emphasis on individual investment behavior when discussing "angel investment". The concept of angel investors are mostly quoted from the concept definition of "business angel" made by Mason and Harrison (2000), that is, the investor invests in non-listed start-up enterprise individually or cooperatively; there is no tie of consanguinity between investor and the enterprise invested, and the investor participates in management work after investment to make financial return. However, in China, the industry stresses the behavior of angel investment, that is to say, the subject shall consist of individual, organization, institution or government. Recent reports emphasize the systematic and institutional development tendency of angel investment.

8. Lucinda Linde and Alok Prasad, 'Venture Support Systems Project: Angel Investors,' MIT Entrepreneurship Center, 2000.

9. Research conducted by *Zhongguancun* Management Committee shows that, more than half of the approximate 100 influential angel investors in *Zhongguancun* possesses entrepreneurial experience.

10. The data was collected from the secretariat of CYAILA and the authors attended the third salon in 2013. For details, refer to Case V in Chapter 7.

11. The authors interviewed Mr. Qiao Qian, Chairman of Angel Chapter in May 2013. Mr. Qiao said that the chapter would be built into a fantastic organization of a hundred people — an organization "gathering wisdom of a hundred people and helping entrepreneurs." For details, please refer to Case Six, which can be found at the end of this chapter.

12. The data was collected from AngelCrunch.com. Since the data is updated daily, the number here is an approximate number.

13. Refer to stefg.org (website of Shanghai Technology Entrepreneurship Foundation for Graduates). The information above is from CBAA's internal data.

14. Refer to AngelsCanton.com.

15. Further interviews were conducted on telephone on August 22, 2014.

Chapter 9

The Ecological Environment for Angel Investment in China

The interactions between start-up, innovation and angel investment are not isolated, but coexist in the same ecological environment. Figure 9.1 indicates that the interaction of every part of start-up eco-network, start-up activities are sources of start-up education, every kind of start-up services effectively put forward the start-up activities, the start-ups both in school and in society create innovative enterprises, talents, technology and other marketing factors through the effects of external relationship network. On the whole, a good entrepreneurship atmosphere in China, a large number of entrepreneurship activities and the diversification of the entrepreneurship services contribute much to the excellent external environment of the entrepreneurs and angel investors.

Market Conditions for Angel Investing in China

Market conditions for angel investment refer to the external environment factors that affect the development of angel investment. The market environment of the angel investment development tends to be good but something more still remains to be done.

I. The Market Environment for Angel Investment Development Has to be Ripe

With the development of China's economy, the market environment of angel investment development tends to be good. This chapter will talk about the environment from three aspects: market demand environment, macro-economy environment and capital market environment.

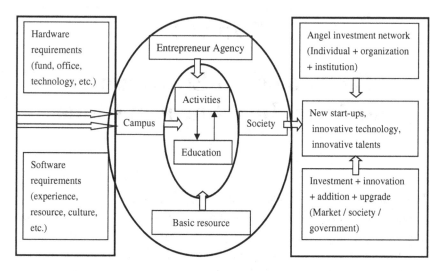

Fig. 9.1   Ecological Environment for Angel Investment.

1. Market demand environment

Small and medium-sized enterprises play a major role in the state technology innovation. However, capital shortage and difficulty in financing still influence their existence and development, and restrict their abilities for technology innovation. According to the a survey conducted by the authors, 50% of small and medium-sized enterprises will choose self-owned funds to finance the enterprise's development as the preferred manner of financing; 35% of them said they would choose bank loans to expand their scale of production; and less than 15% of them would choose other kinds of financing. We can conclude that although many measures have improved the financing environment of the small and medium-sized enterprises, the actual result is not optimistic. Still, local financing is the first choice of small and medium-sized enterprises.

There exists high risk in the research and development of small and medium-sized enterprises which are still in their seed and start-up stages. Their futures are uncertain. Angel investment and government funds are main sources of external funds for these enterprises. In the system of small and medium-sized enterprises funding, the government funds can actively support and guide the development of small and medium-sized enterprises in their seed and start-up stages. However, due to the limited resources, it is far from being able to satisfy the enterprises' demand for funds.

In the current economic environment, small and medium-sized enterprises have become main market players with independent management and self-dependent innovation that banks on the future to earn profits. The business activities of those enterprises are characterized by high marketization, with their technology innovation and technology standards rising rapidly. The People's Bank of China-led construction of the business and personal credit information database has made progress at breakneck speed, which constantly improves enterprises' credit consciousness and credit level. Because of the market environment in which enterprises are playing the main role in innovation and in raising credit awareness of the whole society, the capital demand of the small and medium-sized enterprises, especially those in their seed and starting-up stages, are far from sufficient. Therefore, angel investment will fill the gap between capital supply and demand for the small and medium-sized enterprises to develop their technology during their early stages of development.

2. Macro-economic environment

According to a survey conducted by China's commerce ministry, the actual direct investment in 2014 is US$119.56 billion, with an annual rate increasing 1.68%. With the increase of investment attraction, more and more capital will be introduced, and what's more, many more high level management staffs and excellent overseas Chinese of foreign-owned enterprises will come to China; these individuals are most likely to be the angel investors in China at the present stage.

At the same time, the deposits of the urban and rural residents have increased quickly in those years. In 2014, the deposits surpass RMB 48 trillion, with an average annual growth rate of 11.34% from 1978 to 2014, which means that non-governmental capital now exists in abundance. According to China High Net Worth Individuals' Asset Allocation Report conducted by Hurun Research Institute and Haiyin Wealth, till May of 2015, the millionaires (including the billionaires and the richer) were up to 1.21 million in 31 provinces, municipalities and autonomous regions. This category includes private entrepreneurs and they have formed the wealthy class of a certain size. After the preliminary perfection of the regulation and law system, and with the increase of the angel investment awareness of those wealthy people, the mass affluent class in China will have the largest potential and inclination to engage in angel investment. This will make angel investment one of the most efficient financing methods in the near future. More importantly, present funding methods will remain as important sources of capital and source of guidance to the early phase development of angel investment.

3. Capital markets environment

A standard and smooth exit channel is a necessary condition as an outcome of angel investment. The main exit channels include: through the IPO to sell out shares; through the acquisition and reorganization of a company to sell out shares; through share repurchase by other enterprises; through the liquidation of the enterprise. The main board of the stock market and SME-board market in Shanghai and Shenzhen provide the IPO channels. At present, the reform of equity division has made great progress, which fundamentally solves non-tradable share problem in China's share market and paves the way of IPO withdrawing of the initial capital contributed by angel investment. However, it is rare to see the small and medium-sized high-tech enterprises to get initial public offering. In order to solve the small and medium-sized high-tech enterprises' problem of getting initial public offering, and to promote the circulation of their funds, many technology equity markets have been established since 1999 in many cities, such as Shanghai, Beijing, Tianjin, Shenzhen and Wuhan. Those technology equity markets provide vital platform for the technology equity trading and initial capital withdrawing. With the completion of the equity division reform and the implementation of the new Securities Act, the structure of the capital market will be further completed. Therefore, the capital market of China will face a stage of development and it may be possible that the venture capital, such as the angel investment, is listed and withdrew in China and the equity is traded with standard process.

II. *The Market Environment for Angel Investing still Needs Perfecting*

1. Promote academic research on angel investment

Due to the differences in both development stage and environment in angel investment between China and foreign countries, scholars in China should conduct research on angel investment in a detailed and systematic way, particularly in light of the rich research already available in those countries. They should discuss the origin and process of angel investment abroad; analyze the industry development situation, basic operation mode and relevant policies, laws and regulations of angel investment abroad; analyze the investment motivation, basic channels and forms of the overseas angel investment; analyze the function and effect of angel investment for promoting economic development and industry structure adjustment, both in theory and in practice. Indeed, China have a lot to learn from its foreign counterparts in the area of angel investment.

2. Perfecting the environment for angel investment policies and regulations

Placed at the forefront of equity investment, angel investment has a great effect on supporting the development of seed enterprises. At the same time, it also is significant in supporting technology innovation. However, compared with the preferential policies gained by private equity investment, venture investment is far from enough. Therefore, in order to promote the enthusiasm of angel investors, one should offer reduction and exemption of individual income tax to the invested funds. Taking the UK as an example, the UK government released the "Promotion Plan of Venture Investment Co., Ltd." in 1995, through which tax could be mortgaged or deducted if the venture investors put 80% of their funds into company with a net capital of less than £10 million pound. In the 1990s, 80% of the venture capital was invested in big merger and acquisition deals and only a small portion was put into companies that really needed capital. Moreover, the high risk of angel investing may decrease the likelihood of private capital to participate in the investment. So the government should guide private capital to investment through risk subsidy, or invest in quality projects in a certain proportion to the private capital.

Entrepreneurial Environment of Angel Investment

China's economy has developed rapidly in the past 10 years, which has generated a lot of entrepreneurial opportunities. With entrepreneurial activities increasing every day, the entrepreneurial motivation changes from "survival type" to opportunity-orientated. The entrepreneurial activities gap of different regions is widening while the overall entrepreneurial environment is improving. "The Global Entrepreneurship Monitor Report in China 2013" pointed out that China's ranking of entrepreneurship jumped to 2nd place from 11th in 2002, which made China one of the most active places for entrepreneurship. Although most of China's entrepreneurship is opportunity-orientated, the overall quality is not high, with only a small group of the entrepreneurs having received higher education and most industries focusing on low technology areas. What's more, most of the companies only try to take advantage of lower labor cost and contribute little to the economic growth and export. This chapter will look at China's entrepreneurship environment through the country's entrepreneurial groups, its entrepreneurial education and training and its entrepreneurial competitions (and conferences), and also through examining incubators of tech-enterprises and innovation.

I. *Entrepreneurial Groups in China*

More and more experienced employees in China are becoming self-employed, hoping for further career development. Besides, two "special" groups of people are also following the trend.

One is the group of young college students. According to the statistics, the proportion of self-employed college graduates has been on the rise in recent five years (1% from 2008, which doubled when it comes to 2012). However, the success rate for those college students in China who try to start their own businesses stands only at 1%, whereas the average success rate worldwide is 10%.[1]

The other is the group of returnees that have worked and studied overseas. Drawn by the opportunities for domestic development and family reunion, more and more returnees have started their own business in China. Since the formation of "One Thousand Talent" plan in 2008, more than 3,300 overseas experts have come to work in China, among whom ethnic Chinese account for 90%. According to a survey, the business of returnees' companies mainly concentrates on the high-tech intensive industries, such as the new electronics and information technology industry (39.7%) and new bio-tech and pharmaceutical industry (18.2%). In the enterprises started by returnees, locals play an important role in sale, production and operation, financial affairs and human resources, but in R&D, the returnees play a more prominent role. As far as capital is concerned, most comes from personal deposits. Finally, the "dual" cultures embodied by the returnees contribute to the development of those companies.[2]

Judging from the hottest industry for entrepreneurs, the Internet, 68% of the entrepreneurs were born after 1980; 72% of them started their business because of interest; 62% of them chose areas in which vertical segmentation marketing dominates, with interactive entertainment, lifestyle products and services, and IT ranked top three; 85% of them depend on their own money to start a business; most of their teams are small, fewer than five usually. More than half of them clearly said that they wanted to get an investment by selling the share. However, 67% of them were worried about the lack of communication channels with the investors.[3]

II. *Entrepreneurial Education and Training*

After 2002, under the guidance of the government, entrepreneurship education for college students in China entered into a phase of diversified development, which has been promoted through introducing pilot projects and related policies. First, nine universities, including Tsinghua University and Renmin University, became the first "pilot" universities for entrepreneurship education in 2002; in 2008, the Ministry of Education set up an additional 30 new pilot areas for innovation and entrepreneurship education. Second, the entrepreneurship education projects led by the government, like SIYB and KAB, were introduced into China during

2004–2005. Third, the Ministry of Education reiterated the importance of entrepreneurship education in a number of important directives. According the regulation issued by Ministry of Education, each college and university should have its own required course of "Basis of Entrepreneurship". In the vocational education, entrepreneurial training was rather abundant. Some schools establish courses like MBA, and some schools have all kinds of activities offered by entrepreneur service agency, like entrepreneurship open class, entrepreneurial training, themed salon, etc. Those activities provide a platform for the green hands to share experience and communicate with each other. Compared with the mature and sounder entrepreneurship education system abroad, China's has a lot of deficiencies, such as the imperfect entrepreneurship education system, the lack of good teachers, and lack of combination involving production, teaching and research. In our opinion, entrepreneurship education is the weaker part in China's entrepreneurial ecosystem, which should be an area of focus for the government.

III. *Entrepreneurship Competitions and Conferences*

Innovation and entrepreneurship competition in campus is regarded as an important way to practice entrepreneurship education. Looking at the key events in the development history of entrepreneurship education, the real implementation of undergraduates' entrepreneurship education practice in China can be traced back to the first undergraduate entrepreneurship plan competition at Tsinghua University in May 1998. It was the first undergraduate entrepreneurship plan competition in China and a variety of lecture trainings and entrepreneurial salons, which exerted positive effects on popularizing entrepreneurial knowledge, were also organized as part of competition.

Apart from the services mentioned above, the government, the media and some private institutions have, in recent year, been organizing various large-scale activities such as innovation and entrepreneurship competition and conference. They aim to create effective project displays and information exchange platform for technology-based SMEs, and to actively guide more and more social resources to support innovative entrepreneurship and promote the development of innovative SMEs. One of the most influential activities is the "Dark Horse Contest" organized by *The Founder* magazine. Since June 2011, this contest has been held in more than 20 cities, attracting more than 5,000 enterprises and 700 investors, with 200 million investment made to 200 enterprises each season, and a total investment fund of RMB 1 billion. Besides, there are other activities, like "Innovation China (2006–13)" by magazine, *CYzone*, "China's Innovation Entrepreneurship Competition (2012–3)" by the Ministry of Science and Technology. All those activities have also been to many cities and attracted many angel investors to put money into good projects.

IV. *High-tech Enterprises Incubator*

The technology business incubator provides office facilities, management consulting, business counseling, and incubation services to seed enterprises for helping early business growth and increasing business survival rates. Such institutions have not only to promote an entrepreneurial business growth, but also contribute to technological innovation and industrial upgrading, and promote the economic development through employment generating. Al-Mubaraki and Busler analyzed the incubators in developing countries, such as China, Bahrain, Jordan, Morocco and Syrian Arab.[4] The results showed that the high-tech business incubator could promote the success rate of establishment and the development of regional economy.

In 1986, Dr. Song Jina, former minister of science and technology, initiated the plan of constructing the "Technology Innovation Center in China" — the prototype of the China science and technology business incubator. After that, the first technology business incubator was established in China in 1987, the Wuhan Donghu Business Incubation Center. It was the milestone of China's science and technology business incubator development. After more than 20 years of development, the science and technology business incubator in China has made great progress, not only in quantity but also quality. According to a survey by The Torch Center of China, by the end of 2013, there were 1468 science and technology business incubators in China (see Figure 9.2), with 77,677 million enterprises in incubation and 1.58 million workers in entrepreneurship teams.

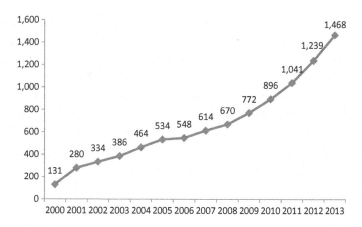

Fig. 9.2   The Scale of China's Science and Technology Business Incubators (2000–2013).
Source: The Chinese Torch Statistical Handbook 2013.

Recently, a rather perfect incubation system has been made across the country through the utilization of market economy rules with a new aim at the promoting of innovation and combining the venture capital market, intermediary service institutions and other innovation resources. The development of all kinds of incubators contributes much to the regional innovation and entrepreneurship, the foster of strategic emerging industry, the adjustment of regional industry structure and the transformation of economic development mode. Taking Beijing as an example, by the end of 2012, there were 101 science and technology business incubators, 6,182 enterprises in incubation and 26 university science parks, providing 103,000 employment opportunities. Depending on the local science and education resources and the industrial developing advantages, those incubation institutions involved almost all fields of strategic emerging industries, like electronic information industry, new material industry, biological medicine industry, energy and environment industry, etc.

V. *Innovative Incubators*

A number of innovation incubators are established because of the insufficiency of the traditional science and technology incubators. Among those incubators, some combine the early phase investment and the deep incubation service together, like the Innovation Works or Legend Star; some, in order to satisfy the professional needs of enterprises, become more and more specialized and provide differentiated service, like Ivy high-end talent agglomeration areas, the garage cafe society, *CYzone*, *Magazine Chuangyejia* and 36kr.com. After the energetically exploration, Zhongguancun has set up a leading incubation system across the country through the incubation mechanism of "Project incubation, early-made enterprise incubation and industrial chain incubation". The aim of Zhongguancun is to synchronize the innovation mode of incubation with that of the Silicon Valley in US. The incubation mode of Zhongguancun has been copied by other places quickly, becoming the weather vane of China's incubation development and leading the innovation of incubation development (Table 9.1). See details in Section 4.

Table 9.1   Innovation Incubators in Zhongguancun, Beijing.

Incubator	Character of Institution	Incubation Mode
Innovation Works and Legend Star.	Social financing	Comprehensive incubation in early phase
The garage cafe, 3 w cafe, hdcxg.com	Social financing	Open office
36kr.com, *CYzone*, *Magazine Chuangyejia*	Social financing	Entrepreneurship Media
Huilongsen.com, balc.com.cn	Social financing	Technology platform incubation
Microsoft's cloud accelerator, NEIC, Gamewave.net/, Cloud Valley incubator	Platform oriented enterprise	Industry incubation
Ivy high-end talent agglomeration areas	Private unprofitable firm	Top-level talents incubation
AAMA (Asia America Multi-technology Association)	Society and organization	Tutorial instruction + students interaction

Source: "Creating a Center for Entrepreneurship with Greatest Global Attraction in Zhongguancun 2013" by Zhongguangcun Administrative Committee.

Policy Environment of Angel Investment

Since the 1990s, China's central government and local policies have been giving high priority to innovation and entrepreneurship, formulating a great number of policies to support SMEs, innovation and entrepreneurship, science-and-technology enterprise incubators etc., all of which have helped to create a sound external environment for angel investment to an extent. In recent years, relevant policies were issued especially for angel investment by some provincial and municipal governments. Examples of these policies include "Opinions of Encouraging and Guiding the Angel Investment to Support the Development of S&T SMEs" (2012) and "Interim Measures of Jiangsu Province for the Management of Angel Investment Guidance Funds" (2013) by Jiangsu Provincial Government, "Business Angel Investment Fund" (2012) established in Chengdu High-tech District, and policy-type "Angel Investment Guidance Fund" (2012) with a funding scale of RMB 500 million established in Ningbo; "Technology and Business Angel Investment Fund and Seed Fund" (2013) was officially launched in Wuhan, and in Yangzhou and Qingdao in 2013, the "Interim Measures of Yangzhou City for the Management of Angel Investment Guidance Funds" and "Interim Measures of Qingdao Municipal Finance Bureau for the Management of Angel Investment Guidance Funds" were published.

I. *The Relevant Policies Supporting SMEs, Innovation and Entrepreneurship*

The Chinese government has created a sound external environment to develop angel investment through a series of policies that have supported SMEs, innovation and entrepreneurship, incubators, etc.

1. Innovation fund for technology-based SMEs

For a long time, China's Ministry of Science and Technology has been attaching great importance to innovation and entrepreneurship development of SMEs, especially technology-based ones. The innovation fund for technology-based SMEs, established in 1999 by the central government, is the first special fund aiming to meet the needs of the development of

SMEs. In 2007, the Ministry of Science and Technology and the Ministry of Finance issued the "Interim Measures for the Management of Innovation and Entrepreneurship Guidance Funds for Technology-based SMEs", setting up innovation and entrepreneurship guidance funds for these firms, and adopting two major free support methods: risk subsidies and investment guarantee. Moreover, central financial fund has adopted the staged participation way of "equity investment" to aim to fix "market failure", guiding and driving mass social capital to support innovation and entrepreneurship of SMEs through a more marketable and flexible way. According to the *IFTF Annual Report*, up to the end of 2013, the accumulative total amount of technological innovation fund has exceeded RMB 26 billion, supporting more than 40,000 technology-based SMEs and effectively strengthening their presence.

2. National development fund for SMEs

SME is a vital part of national economy. In 2012, SMEs' operating pressure increased and profitability decreased in some regions and industries affected by soaring labor cost, raw materials cost and other factors. To solve these problems, the Ministry of Finance seriously considered and implemented the "State Council's Opinion on Further Supporting the Healthy Development of SMEs", issuing and carrying out a series of policies and measures to uphold the healthy development of SMEs, especially small and micro-enterprises. Among them, financial support channels were created. Since 2012, the central finance ministry has planned to spend RMB15 billion setting up a national development fund for SMEs over the course of five years. The fund will adopt market-oriented operation and unify all sorts of social funds to support the development of SMEs.

3. Support policies of local governments regarding innovation and entrepreneurship

Besides policy of central government to support the development of SMEs, local governments have massive policies to support innovation and entrepreneurship. For instance, the "1 + 6" policy of Zhongguancun

Science Park is to build a Zhongguancun innovation platform and uphold the further implementation of six pilot reform policies. These include:

- Pilot policy for reforming scientific and technological achievements' disposal and benefits right of central public institutions
- Tax preference pilot policy
- Stock option incentive pilot policy
- Pilot policy for reforming allocation and management of scientific research funds
- Pilot policy for identifying new high-tech enterprise
- Pilot policy of building a national over-the-counter market

The other policy deals with the state of the business incubators: In 2013, Hubei Province spent RMB 20 million to support undergraduate business incubator demonstration base; Shanxi Province provides subsidy of site rental fees for those enterprises which are moving towards in-business incubator; Hunan (Xiangtan) Undergraduates Technology and Entrepreneurship Park will withdraw 30% from business base fund in advance to use as subsidy of operational fees for advantageous projects and free financial aid no more than RMB 200,000 for some internal projects which meet requirements, and so on.

The government also offers great support to college students who have plans to start a business: in the province of Shandong, self-employed undergraduates with low-profit projects can apply for guaranteed small-sum loans of no more than RMB 100,000; in Henan, the Zhengzhou municipal government will provide one-off business subsidy of RMB 5,000 for enterprises in the initial start-up period; in Nanjing, Jiangsu Province college students can rent the site for free and have the opportunity to win an award of RMB 50,000 if they start a business in Jiangning District; the city of Xuzhou has set up a RMB 30 million guidance fund for undergraduates' entrepreneurship; in Sichuan, the Chengdu municipal government provides an annual entrepreneurship training subsidy of RMB 900 per person for local college students; and last but not least, the Tianjin municipal government provides residential rental subsidy for graduates who start a business.[5]

II. Relevant Policies Boosting the Development of Angel Investment

Since 2013, some local governments have boosted the development of angel investment directly through establishment of guidance fund, risk premiums, and network formation.

1. Qualification threshold

The Securities Act of the United States has specifically stipulated who can be "accredited investor(s)", yet China does not have any relevant laws regarding who should be qualified as angel investors. Only some local governments have formulated special access threshold system for angel investment in order to meet the requirements of policies that can support the development of angel investment. In 2009, the Bureau of Technology and Information of Shenzhen set up a registration system for angel investors: the investor's personal assets shall exceed RMB 5 million, s/he should have actual cases or project source channels of angel investment and social resources, and should be recommended by industry associations; the angel investment institution's registered capital shall not be lower than RMB 30 million and it should have actual cases or project source channels of angel investment and social resources, possess relatively high reputation, powerful economic strength and risk tolerance, have senior managers with over two years' experience in investing or relevant business operation experience in charge, and should be recommended by industry associations. In 2013, Ningbo City formulated regulations regarding the registration system of angel investment: the angel investor shall possess the investment capital (deposit in a bank) of more than RMB 1million, and be intended to or have already conducted angel investment; while for angel investment institution, its single investment amount shall not be lower than RMB 1 million, have at least three senior managers with over two years' experience in investing or relevant business operation experience in charge, and should plan to or have already conducted angel investment.

2. Guidance funds

The benefit of guidance funds lies in giving full play to the leverage effect of innovation funds, thus attracting more social capital to support the development of newly-established enterprises. Many local governments have attached great importance to innovation and entrepreneurship in recent years. Therefore, "Seed Funding", "Innovation Funds", "Angel Funds", etc. were founded by public finance. On the amount of capital involved, Chongqing Municipal Science & Technology Commission and Youth League Committee established Innovation and Entrepreneurship Angel Funds for Chongqing youth with an initial capital of RMB 100 million in 2012; in the same year, Chengdu Hi-tech District set up a Angel Funds of RMB 80 million; in 2013, the initial amount of Angel Funds of Beijing Software Exchange reached RMB 80 million; while the total amount of Angel Investment Capital of Wuhan municipal government in 2013 also reached RMB 300 million, with the initial scale counted to RMB 100 million. On operation modes, zhongguancun resorted to joint stock (no more than 30% of the total capital) and contract (joint investment with partners) in 2011; Chengdu Hi-tech District carried out direct investment by entrusting Chengdu Gaotou Venture Capital Co. Ltd. With more funding in 2012. Ningbo municipality adopted follow-up investment to develop its angel investment and the Qingdao municipality applied differential investment to angel investment guidance funds in accordance with the scale and developing stage of different enterprises, steering methods include stage investment, follow-up investment, risk allowance, etc., but excluded the participation of ordinary enterprise operational management. The investment field, however, shall generally meet certain standards and development demands of local industries. For example, funds in Chengdu Hi-tech District are mainly used to support excellent enterprises of Tianfu Star; angel investment in Wuhan is mainly applied to develop such fields as photoelectron, new generation of information and technology, new material, advanced equipment manufacturing, high-tech service industry, biological medicine, new energy, new energy automobile, energy conservation and environmental protection, modern agriculture, as well as traditional industries that employ high- and new-tech; while the program of Nanjing Wenchuang Angel Investment is primarily used to invest leading cultural industry and newly established cultural and scientific enterprises. Overall, these funds exert positive roles in bringing in talents, encouraging innovation and entrepreneurship, as well as promoting the development of regional industries (Table 9.2).

3. Risk premiums

Risk premium is another method for the government to support Angel investment beside angel investment guidance funds. Chengdu High-tech District has introduced the code of practice for specialized angel investment risk premium, namely that if investment institutions invest more than 500,000 yuan to entrepreneurship enterprises in high-tech district, the invested enterprise will be subsidized with 20% of the investment amount, while subsidy ceiling for each enterprise is 400,000 yuan. Jiangsu Province established the Angel Investment Guidance Funds as compensate funds for offsetting loss caused by angel investment. It mainly provides loan loss provision which shall be no more than 30% of the initial investment amount for angel investment institutions that have invested small- and micro-sized science and technology enterprises in seed stage or start-up stage, and 20% of the initial investment amount shall be given according to the regulations set up in different districts. If any loss is incurred within three years, the angel investment institutions can be compensated with 50% of the actual amount of loss from the provision. Angel Guidance Funds established by Yangzhou City will provide loan loss provisions no more than 20% of actual investment that the Angel investment institutions invest to small- and micro-sized science and technology enterprises in seed stage or star-up stage. It's worth mentioning that Z-park made a new policy to incentivize college teachers to be angels and invest in their students' start-ups. If a teacher supports investing in his/her students' company, the investee can then apply for subsidy, with the maximum amount worth half of the invested capital.

4. Set up angel investment network

Problems like poor information communication and lack of norms and regulations are common in the angel investment industry. Therefore, it is

Table 9.2   Angel Investment Policies Based on Government Guidance Funds (Partial).

Type	Funds	Content
To support seed funds, entrepreneurship guidance funds in the initial period of entrepreneurship	Entrepreneurship guidance funds in Suzhou Industrial Park (2008)	To limit share capital in investment stage, or introduce policies to encourage investment at seed stage or early stage of entrepreneurship. For example, regulate venture capital enterprises that apply guidance funds to follow up investment when investing in pioneering enterprises in the Industrial Park. Follow-up investment provided by guidance funds, in principle, shall be no more than 30% of the recent amount of investment of venture capital enterprises. However, for seed funds filed in the Park, the ratio between guidance funds and follow-up investment can be increased to 100%.
	Interim Procedures for Venture Capital Guidance Funds Management of Beijing Municipality Cultural Creative Industry (2009)	Has made it clear that Beijing municipality will arrange RMB 300 million as Seed Funds to directly support the development of Beijing's cultural creative industry. And this amount of capital is expected to activate about RMB 100 million of social investment.
	Government Guidance Funds for Wenzhou's Scientific and Technological Innovation (2010)	The initial amount is RMB 200 million, funded by Wenzhou municipal public finance, and it will attract RMB 600 million of venture capital, specialized to provide funds for nurturing early (seed stage) scientific and technological innovative enterprises, achieving innovation in profit model, operation model,as well as management mechanism. This guidance funds will adopt the operation method of compensation fund for finance of science and technology to resolve the problem of difficult loan without mortgage of enterprises in the seed stage of entrepreneurship period, and encourage banks to provide credit support for enterprises. To decrease risks that endanger banks thatoffer loans to enterprises in seed stage, compensation fund for finance of science and technology will provide risk compensation for them. And compensation for every project shall not be higher that 25% of the loan value.

Angel investment capital funded by government finances	Interim Procedures for Venture Capital Guidance Funds Management of Hubei Province (2011)	It regulates that profit rewards of guidance funds are limited to invest strategic emerging industries and small-and median-sized scientific and technological enterprises at seed stage, initial stage and early to mid-stage in Hubei Province, and is restricted to occur in the year when some programs drop out, and it shall be determined to be no more than 10% of the net profit after agreed investment projects compensate any loss.
	Entrepreneurship Angel Investment Fund in Chengdu High-tech District (2012)	Fully invested by the government, Entrepreneurship Angel Investment Fund in Chengdu Hi-tech District which features the operation mode of marketization and professionalization is officially launched. As China's first entrepreneurship investment fund fully invested by the government at present (whose initial raise amount reaches 80 million yuan), it aims to promote the development of Chengdu High-tech District, further cultivate and incubate high-quality and potential entrepreneurship projects, encourage and accelerate the pace of high-caliber talents to settle in Chengdu High-tech District.
	Innovation and Entrepreneurship Angel Funds for Chongqing youth (2012)	Chongqing Municipal Science and Technology Commission and Youth League Committee will, by the joint implementation of Angel Plan, set up Innovation and Entrepreneurship Angel Funds for Chongqing youth with an initial amount of money about 100 million yuan, establish an Angel Service Station and Youth Innovation and Entrepreneurship Base in Chongqing Municipality, and provide all-around help and support for Chongqing youth to engage in Innovation and Entrepreneurship. The Angel Plan will, within threeyears, complete its service to 10,000 small- and micro-sized scientific and technological enterprises. Among which 5,000 enterprises have gained Angel guaranteed credit support, 1,000 enterprises have received angel investment, 200 enterprises have grown into high-growth star enterprises that are able to raise funds by IPO or multi-level capital market.

(Continued)

Table 9.2 *(Continued)*

Type	Funds	Content
	Luoyang Municipality Youth Entrepreneurship Funds (2012)	The funds raised an initial amount of money about 21 million yuan, which is used to help realize entrepreneurship dreams of Luoyang's youth. The youth entrepreneurship fund was set up by Municipal Young Entrepreneur Council, Municipal Junior Chamber of Commerce, Luoyang Hengsheng Science Park Property Ltd., Defeng Micro Loans ltd. that invested 10 million yuan respectively, and Luoyang Tiansheng Industry and Trade CO., LTD RMB 1 million. The fund is mainly used in three aspects as follows: First, it is used as insurance fund to guarantee entrepreneurship youth who apply finance discount loans. Second, it is directly used to provide finance support and reward for entrepreneurship youth who have succeeded in getting into Youth Business Incubators. Third, it is invested in the Municipal Micro Loan Guarantee Center for the unemployed to directly provide micro discount loans for entrepreneurship youth.
	Ningbo City Angel Investment Guidance Funds	The fund is a non-profitable policy fund set up by Ningbo municipal government, whose total amount is RMB 500 million of investment in five years, RMB 200 million among which is municipal level financial funds. Its principle is to encourage Angel investment institutions (people) to invest innovative newly established enterprises by follow-up investment of guidance funds.

Source: Collated by the authors from sources available on the Internet.

a program strongly supported by the government to set up Angel Investment Network, thus to form industry self-discipline organizations. In the document Opinions of Encouraging and Guiding the Angel Investment to Support the Development of S&T SMEs, which is introduced by Jiangsu provincial government in 2012, it is clearly highlighted that the role of angel investment industry institutions shall be fully tapped, and establishment of angel investment associations, alliances and other social organizations shall be encouraged. In 2012, Ningbo City's paper, "Some Proposals Concerning Accelerating the Development of Angel Investment", also indicated that it is necessary to build exchange platform for angel investment, set up angel investment clubs and launch programs exchange and information exchange. Since 2014, most Chinese cities have set up angel investment network such as clubs, alliances and association one after another. For example, Ningbo Angel Investment Club, Wuhan Guanggu Angel Investment Club, Tianjin Angel Investment Association, Jiangsu Angel Investment Alliance, and Zhongguancun Angel Investment Association. All of them are established under the joint support of government and non-government organizations. China Business Angel Association is the only member of World Business Angels Association form China. Attached to China Technology Venture Association of China's Ministry of Science and Technology, and supported by the Torch Center of China's Ministry of Science and Technology, the association, through the form of council, as well as individuals, absorbs investors, entrepreneurs, experts, academics, policy-makers, investment institutions, enterprises and intermediaries, colleges and universities, industrial parks, associations and other social organizations to carry out work like website information, research and publicity, forum salon, project exchange, training and certification, entrepreneurship services, etc. It provides a multi-level communication platform features information sharing, resources exchanging, cooperation and progress.

Case XIV: Entrepreneurial Service Institution — Wuhan Optics Valley Start-up Cafe

Xuan Jie: "Nurturing an Ecological Environment for Angel Investment in Wuhan"

Time/site: August 2, 2013 Wuhan, China

At the time of this interview, Ms. Xuan Jie was the Standing Vice General Manager of Optics Valley Start-up Cafe (OVSC).

She first introduced the idea of setting up a "café": as a novel model for entrepreneurs and venture capitalists, it was different from traditional entrepreneurial models which were based on fixed offices, such as incubators and accelerators. The cafe was built as an open platform for business and communication. Entrepreneurs could not only attend salons or lectures here, but also consult professionals about industrial and commercial registration, legal problems or accounting affairs, free of charge. These would help them solve problems encountered when they started their own businesses.

Developing a Leading VC Platform in China

Since the birth of "Garage Cafe" at Haidian Book City in Beijing in 2011, entrepreneur service platforms based on cafes had been a hot topic among insiders. Garage Cafe was even entitled "Innovative Incubator" by the Management Committee of Zhongguancun Science Park. In the recent two years, approximately 100 entrepreneurial cafes had been founded around the country, including 3W Cafe, Beta Cafe, IC Cafe, DEMO Cafe and C&IN COFFEE. Supported by the Management Committee of Wuhan East Lake High-tech Development Zone, Lei Jun, the founder of Xiaomi Technology, and Li Ruxiong, General Manager of Optical Valley Soft Co., Ltd., co-founded OVSC at the beginning of 2013.

Xuan pointed out that OVSC was special because it stood at a high point from the very beginning: as an open office and communication zone, it broke through the old pattern such as incubators and accelerators where fixed large offices were needed. One could order a cup of coffee and work all day here with no more further charge. What it was promoting was the concept of "one coffee, one chance". It was a place where entrepreneurs, angel investors,

(Continued)

Case XIV: (*Continued*)

headhunters, etc. gathered, where free consultation about commercial and industrial registration, legal problems and accounting affairs were provided, and where professional consultation activities including salons and lectures for entrepreneurs and investors were regularly held. It would be built into a platform where people might start up a company, work or exchange ideas in a better place at lower costs. Moreover, the cafe offered a cloud server, an environment for R&D and testing, guidance about interfacing, training on development, etc. The outsourced platforms included the flagship store and development platform of Xiaomi Fans Club, as well as other platforms in China (built by TABLE, the five first-class internet enterprises).

Xuan also mentioned that the tasks of OVSC in 2013 included: (1) building a large platform for venture capital investment both online and offline; (2) establishing two funds, namely Wuhan Shunwei Angel Fund and Wuhan Optical Valley Angel Fund for Entrepreneurs; (3) founding an entrepreneur club and a management club on the basis of Optical Valley Angel Investment Club; (4) launching four kinds of events, including road shows of entrepreneurial projects, training courses about angel investment, entrepreneur public classes (e.g. "Optical Valley Night School" co-launched with colleges and universities) and innovation/entrepreneurship competition of university students (e.g. Cultural Innovation Competition of Hubei Province); (5) besides the established cafe in Optics Valley Capital Tower, developing new chain stores at Financial Harbor, Future Science & Technology Park, Biochemical Park and Optics Valley Creative Industry Base; and (6) nurturing 200 local angel investors in the following two years so as to cover surrounding cities in Mid China, such as Hunan, Jiangxi and Anhui.

Nurturing an Ecological Environment for Angel Investment in Wuhan

Established later than other cafes in China, OVSC boasted the merits of most of the famous entrepreneurial cafes. By 2013, entrepreneurial cafes could be found everywhere around China. Among them, Garage Cafe in Beijing and Beta Cafe in Hangzhou were relatively well known. In fact, cafes were always connected to entrepreneurship. This was a pattern that was first identified in Silicon Valley. By hanging out in cafes, investors, entrepreneurs and

Case XIV: *(Continued)*

headhunters could look for potential cooperators. As a matter of fact, cafes cradled a lot of Internet tycoons.

When positioning OVSC, Xuan emphasized that by analyzing the merits of other entrepreneurship cafes, OVSC not only acted as a micro incubator, a platform for communication, but also made angel investment. Xuan and her colleagues hoped to build a leading platform for entrepreneurs and venture capitalists in Mid-China and to nurture a sound environment for angel investment, because only by doing so could they provide entrepreneurs and investors with better services and promote local angel investment more efficiently.

Apart from all these, OVSC also had its own advantages such as Xiaomi Fans Club, Investors Club and Angel 200 Program. It was estimated that an entrepreneur fund of Optical Valley could be established to promote culture of angel investment. It was possible that such a fund could only make small investment in the beginning; however, as it grew up, it would accelerate the development of many industries. According to Ms. Xuan, Mr. Lei Jun and Mr. Li Ruxiong, the founders of OVSC, would seek breakthroughs from industries with which they were familiar, and then expand the influence of OVSC to peripheral fields including new energy, biological medicine and new materials. Thus, they might better assist start-ups to find routes for future development. On the other hand, entrepreneurs also wished to develop with teams as they might offer entrepreneurs resources needed in the future, such as PE.

Attracting More Professional Personnel to Stay In or Return to Wuhan

Environment is of great importance for angel investment, which is a key factor to attract and nurture talents. Though compared with many other cities in China, Wuhan boasts relatively leading education resources and R&D powers, locals, especially those in high-tech industries, tend to choose to work in other places, because its development of regional industries, environment for entrepreneurs and public policies, and so on are less favorable.

Xuan knew this condition well and shared a case: an entrepreneur once wanted to start up a business back in Wuhan, but failed since he could found no platform, no proper cooperator, no sound entrepreneurial team, which made it extremely difficult to develop any program. This was why OVSC

(Continued)

Case XIV: *(Continued)*

wanted to optimize the environment for entrepreneurs and investors in Wuhan. By bettering the environment and attracting professional personnel, OVSC wanted to invite people to start business in Wuhan and accelerate the development of local economy.

Therefore, it was obvious that OVSC wanted to build a favorable entrepreneurial environment and was clear about its own position. For example, in terms of Internet enterprises, there was Alibaba in Hangzhou, Tencent in Shenzhen and Zhongguancun in Beijing, but there existed no leading enterprise in Wuhan, which made it hard to boost the industry chain. Xuan pointed out that the city wanted its own Internet enterprises, wanted a better environment for entrepreneurs and angel investors, and wanted follow-up support, angel investment, venture capital, private equity and listed companies; the city needed a chain that connected every element and ensured that capital ran smoothly. With a platform and a team serving as the chain, entrepreneurs would have greater enthusiasm and could start business easier. OVSC wanted to nurture more seeds to increase the chance of getting a fantastic seed. With even one successful seed, entrepreneurs would develop similar projects in the region, which would change the region and make it a better place for angel investors and start-ups. As a micro incubator, OVSC would work with entrepreneurs and help them to discover and solve problems.

Case XV: Entrepreneurial Service Institution — UTOU Incubator

Dai Ruihong: "What to Expect from the Formation of Angel Investment Culture"

Time/site: June 4, 2013/Beijing, China

At the time of this interview, Ms. Dai Ruihong was CEO of UTOU. UTOU was a professional online social platform for investors and the invested, and a place where entrepreneurial teams, businesspersons, institutional investors, angel investors and financial institutions gathered. UTOU was dedicated to supporting entrepreneurs and innovators. It was a platform for investors and

(Continued)

Case XV: (*Continued*)

the invested to communicate and cooperate with each other online and offline. For example, UTOU regularly held the offline road show "UTOU DEMO".

The Culture of Angel Investment Yet to Be Formed

When OTOU was first established, angel investment was relatively new in China, there were not many active angel investors. So-called "big angels" often remarked that China only had a vague definition and idea about angel investors and angel investment. These insiders generally believed that angels must be super famous people with lots of money and experience. When talking about angel investors, most people had only famous investors in their minds, for example Xu Xiaoping, Xu Biqun and Lei Jun. Dai believed that Internet and computing information tycoons had the biggest potential of becoming angel investors due to their their professional background. In other words, because these two industries boasted great space for innovation and light assets, entrepreneurial projects were abundant. In fact, angel investors provided entrepreneurial teams with not only financial support but also professional guidance. However, people other than well-known businesspersons could also join the game. For example, professional personnel such as attorneys, accountants, doctors and other people with high-income could also become angel investors as long as they met certain requirements and were willing to make early-stage investment. Nevertheless, in order to attract these people into the game, we not only need to show them models like those famous angel investors, but also need to help them understand the nature of angel investment and nurture their willingness.

Dai also mentioned that some friends of her were interested in angel investment, but did not know how to get into it. Therefore, only a few of them really became angel investors. She thought there might be three reasons. Firstly, angel investment was highly risky and ordinary people could not bear such risk. They were unfamiliar with different industries and thus lacked the ability to properly determine the value and potential of projects. Instead of angel investment, Chinese people tended to invest in real estate, financial products of banks or other stable investment schemes. Secondly, the period

(*Continued*)

Case XV: (*Continued*)

of return of angel investment was long. Over the past few years, private equity was popular among investors due to its high payback. However, projects for angel investors were in their early stages and the invested companies needed a long time before they were listed. Thus, their stock equities were unlikely to be transferred, the period of return was relatively long, and the cashability was relatively poor. Thirdly, there lacked professionals that guided or organized angel investors. Meanwhile, problems existed in terms of channels for getting projects, methods to make judgment and ways to manage projects.

Needs of Investment Unmatched for Early-stage Projects

When talking about the environment for start-ups in China, Dai pointed out that: (1) first-tier cities such as Beijing and Shanghai boasted better entrepreneurial environments, and entrepreneurial competitions and shows were growing vigorously as undergraduates faced big pressure of getting jobs and the government encouraged them to start up their own businesses; (2) in terms of the entrepreneurial concept, Chinese entrepreneurs were those who owned the projects, but they might not be good operators of sound mechanism to enable the transfer of projects across countries. With this mechanism, people could put their projects in a database so that the projects might be transferred to better teams or enterprises; (3) many entrepreneurs still worked alone and faced many problems about team building and fund raising. Financing, in particular, was a key element that limited the development of projects.

Also, Dai believed that it was necessary to combine online investment services with offline communication and docking. She mentioned that an online platform solved the problem of information asymmetry and offered a tool for displaying project information and exchanging simple messages. However, unlike commodity transaction, investment was more complicated and face-to-face communication was necessary. Therefore, offline activities were supplementary to online platforms. By taking part in road shows, entrepreneurs got the opportunity to be shown in media, to be mentored by investors, or to have their business plans reviewed. It would be hard for entrepreneurs to make progress if they locked themselves in offices and did

(*Continued*)

Case XV: (*Continued*)

not make contact with people outside. Road shows offered people opportunities to exchange ideas about investment, to meet interesting people or potential partners pursuing a common goal, or to find support for expanding markets. In other words, road shows were assemblies where entrepreneurs and investors could communicate with each other more effectively.

When organizing UTOU DEMO and communicating with project proponents, Dai noticed that needs for investment were not fully satisfied. On the one hand, there was only little investment and angel investors available for projects at early stage. On the other hand, Chinese proponents required too much investment at early stage. Most start-ups wanted at least RMB 1 million, which prevented many people from becoming angel investors. Ms. Dai thought this was because project operation by Chinese entrepreneurs was defective. Firstly, in terms of operation concept, small firms wanted to run in an ideal way like big companies, and wanted too much in terms of offices, premises, personal allocation, marketing, etc. Secondly, when making financial estimations, they wanted to get all the money needed for years of operation at one shot. However, early-stage investment should only be the money needed for a short period. Further financing would be done after a period of sound operation. Thirdly, Chinese start-ups tended to dream that outside investors would give them all the money needed for launching and developing their projects. However, if proponents did not invest in their own projects, they could not start their projects, which made it hard to get any investment.

Seeking "Brilliant Projects" Across Cities with the Assistance of Entrepreneurial Parks

In China in the early 2000s, most of the institutional investors were located in major cities like Beijing and Shanghai. However, start-ups in second- and third-tier cities also wished to get investment. The problem was that local authorities' capacities were limited when it came to providing financing services to enterprises. Therefore, professional service agencies were needed for docking projects and capital across regions. Dai said that UTOU wished to allocate capital for good projects. Parks were different from each other, which

(*Continued*)

Case XV: (*Continued*)

made it possible to dig up good projects in different cities. UTOU also held road shows in cities other than Beijing. Considering how familiar local governments were with SMEs in parks, the company had established strategic partnership with some local authorities. The authorities would recommend projects, and the company could invite institutional investors to different parks to take part in road shows and docking activities. For example, in 2013, UTOU visited eight enterprises in two days in Shijiazhuang. Thus, UTOU and local authorities could supplement each with their own advantages, and, jointly, help start-ups get investment.

UTOU cooperated mostly with VC institutions, but Dai expressed the intention to expand the database of angel investors in the future, so as to improve services targeting early-stage projects.

More Support for Service Platforms from Local Governments Needed

Policies favorable to entrepreneurial service platforms were insufficient. In fact, most of such policies were for service entities like incubators. These incubators had gotten policy assistance. Nevertheless, there were many "virtual incubator-type platforms" in the market. Without premises, these platforms were not real incubators but provided start-ups with similar services. Dai expected local governments to issue relevant policies to motivate and support these platforms. She believed that since entrepreneurial and innovative environments formed one system. Due to information asymmetry, entrepreneurs and angel investors could not reach each other easily by themselves. In fact, for some projects in their early stages, premises or even incubators were not necessary. These projects could be done at home and still needed the services from other sources. This was why agent platforms were needed. When governments could not provide assistance, other institutions would naturally offer the start-ups the services needed. The governments could certificate other kinds of service platforms, virtual incubators for example, as they certificated real incubators and could offer them some financial support. She also suggested that governments should give more support early-stage projects with guidance funds, or reduce/exempt tax for angel investors so as to boost the industry.

Case XVI: Innovative Incubator — Inno Valley

Yu Bo: "Learning from International Incubators and Increasing the Success Rate of Early-Stage Projects"

Time/site: July 10, 2013/Shenzhen, China

At the time of the interview, Yu was Vice President of Inno Valley. He had worked in the world of Internet, gaming and media for years and boasted rich experience of product R&D, content operation and market promotion. Before joining Inno Valley, Yu had been Vice President of Rekoo and was responsible for creating and managing Rekoo's teams of mobile games. Prior to that, he had been one of the first product managers of SinaWeibo Team, responsible for clients on smart phones first and then open-platforms on smart phones. He had also worked for CCW MEDIA as Director of Internet value added services and General Manager of CNW.

Inno Valley was both an incubator and an accelerator focusing on supporting entrepreneurs in the fields of TMT and mobile network. Inno Valley aimed at increasing the success rate of early-stage projects. Compared to traditional incubators in China, Inno Valley borrowed the merits of incubators and accelerators in Silicon Valley. That was getting commercial return completely by sharing the successes of entrepreneurs. Therefore, Inno Valley had the biggest motive to make entrepreneurs successful. The founders, shareholders and strategic partners of Inno Valley included famous Internet enterprises in China such as Tencent, 360, UCweb and Renren. Well-known venture investors like China Renaissance and Tigercub Funds also invested Inno Valley. In other words, Inno Valley boasted resources from both upstream and downstream industrial chains. The company believed that empty talk by the government harmed the country while hard work rejuvenated it, and thus, it kept doing its best to serve entrepreneurs and create more value for them.

"Angel Investment" Devalued in China

Since 2011, with the rapid development of IT, Internet and E-commerce, the elites in these fields started their own businesses one after another. As more and more people became entrepreneurs, "angel investment" became more and more popular in China. However, when assessing Chinese people's

(Continued)

Case XVI: (*Continued*)

understanding of angel investment, Yu believed that the phrase had lost its value. In fact, not everyone investing in early-stage projects was an "angel investor". Judging from the development of angel investment around the world, the first angel investors were generally leaders in their fields, having considerable entrepreneurial experience or great industrial background, or having been senior managers of some listed companies. However, many angel investors in China were fake ones who always reviewed projects but never made investment. He also marked that Inno Valley wanted to be a "real angel" and would provide all-round services regarding to funds, premises and experience so as to incubate start-ups, helping them grow fast and increasing their survival rates.

Being an Angel Investor and an Incubator: Doing Everything to Find Good Projects and Help Start-ups

Like traditional incubators, Inno Valley provided start-ups with office areas (stations), IT infrastructure and cloud services, as well as services regarding to accounting affairs, industrial and commercial registration, tax, legal problems or other matters related to launching and running a company. Besides all these, Inno Valley offered services about human resources, entrepreneurial training, business development and financial support. So, what was the position of Inno Valley? Yu answered that it was an institutional investor, and it did everything to find more and better projects. In fact, being an angel investor was demanding, both technically and financially. So was being the operator or manager of an incubator. This was because an incredibly high proportion of angel investment at early-stage projects went bust. Inno Valley was a commercial institution eager to invest in good projects as soon as possible. The only differences between Inno Valley and other investors were that incubation was introduced, and the core of services was catered for invested enterprises.

Apart from these, Inno Valley had something special to help start-ups to develop. Mr. Yu emphasized that Inno Valley would collect, invest in and mentor as many good projects as possible in all ways which included the following four modes of incubation. The first mode was the magic cube program targeting projects at "idea" stage: Inno Valley would screen out projects according

(*Continued*)

Case XVI: (*Continued*)

to standards, incubate these projects for three months and give each of them RMB 150,000 as seed funds. The second mode was the magic stick program, targeting projects and teams that had their ideas transferred into products: any project passing the screening would get 6-month special incubation and seed funds of RMB 500,000–1,000,000. Products under the magic stick program would be recognized by the market for their executive force and vitality. After the magic stick program, there was the magic power program targeting projects of which products were marketed and sent to customers. Projects at this stage would get 12-month incubation, opportunities to dock with the best promotion platforms, as well as seed funds of RMB 1–5 million. Then, it was the magic program. The goal at this stage was to find proper investors and Inno Valley would make a slow exit. Incubated projects would be covered under the magic program and Inno Valley would find the most suitable investor to finance projects.

Inno Valley did not just to find excellent projects; it focused on converting more projects and held many offline activities accordingly. Yu also further introduced four special activities: "18 Strikes against Dragons" — where 18 top leaders of different industries would be invited to share their successes and lessons strategically; "Entrepreneurial Tactics" — where experts and the public would be invited to discuss about exploiting opportunities for entrepreneurs in certain fields; "Napa Wine Club" — where industrial leaders of Internet platforms and entrepreneurs would sip wine and talk face to face in this semi-open salon; "Open Day of Inno Valley" — a day where all entrepreneurial teams were welcomed to review and assess the services and functions of Inno Valley during site visits.

Regional Differences in Angel Investment: The Internet Industry's Geographical Advantages in Shenzhen

When being asked about the differences between angel investment in Shenzhen and in Beijing, Shanghai and other places, Yu said that every place was different. For example, angel investors of the Internet were absent in Shanghai, while Shenzhen had unique advantages for these investors due to its close proximity to Hong Kong.

(*Continued*)

Case XVI: (*Continued*)

Yu also mentioned that the four partners of Inno Valley had started up their own businesses or worked in the world of IT or the Internet, and had seen numerous successes and failures. Thus, they founded Inno Valley in order to find and nurture promising projects in the familiar world of Internet, projects that were undervalued. Angel investment was a business without admittance. Every one could call him or herself an angel inventor, but real angels were those who really helped start-ups, who invested in undervalued projects and who made these projects blooming. However, nowadays, fake "angels" were out in the market but real angels were rare. Yu said that Inno Valley wanted to be acknowledged by its shareholders, so it did everything that was worthwhile; Inno Valley did not make profits like other incubators, namely by charging administrative fees, but it did receive high returns mainly by exiting.

Case XVII: Innovative Incubator — Garage Cafe

Su Di: "Willingness Brought People Success and Desire-Free State Made People Strong"

Time/site: May 27, 2013 / Beijing, China

Mr. Su Di was the co-founder of Garage Cafe and had been Investment Director of China Cache, a company listed in NASDAQ. Garage Cafe was dedicated to lowering costs to start a business, increasing the success rate and improving the environment for start-ups.

"Helping Start-ups Lower the Cost to Start a Business"

Opened in April 2011, Garage Cafe had an operation principle of "helping start-ups lower the cost to start up a business" — an entrepreneur could use the open office area with no more charge other than that for a coffee. The open environment in the entrepreneurial circle at Garage Cafe enhanced the communication among investors, entrepreneurs, enterprise service institutions and media. According to Su, Garage Cafe was the permanent office for over ten

(*Continued*)

Case XVII: (*Continued*)

entrepreneurial teams and some new teams worked in the cafe from time to time; during the two years or more after its establishment, the cafe had served over 300 entrepreneurial teams, 40 to 50 of which had got angel investment. In December 2011, the Management Committee of Zhongguancun Science Park granted Garage Cafe the title of "Innovative Incubator" and planned to rebuild the place where the cafe stood into a street for entrepreneurs and investors.

When talking about the future of this kind of cafes in China, Su summarized the answer with two words "Public Welfare". Actually, Entrepreneurial cafes were founded preliminary for helping start-ups and created a place where entrepreneurs and investors gathered. Insiders were also worried about how these cafes made profits or developed in a sustainable way. About that, Su said that there were many ways to make profits, for example, by selling peripheral products, filming entrepreneurial stories or launching social apps on mobiles during later periods. About the development of the cafe, Su said that there were no specific plans, no chain stores or funds, and the cafe would develop in the way it did. Most importantly, it would help start-ups save money. He truly believed that Garage Cafe was under a good team, and everyone would do his or her best to serve more entrepreneurs.

Not to Select the Best, But to Help the Disadvantaged

About specific entrepreneurial services, Mr. Su introduced Yin Jiatan to answer the question. She was the head of Entrepreneurial Service Department of Garage café during the interview, and had worked in the world of TMT for 10 years and served many Internet companies by incubating new projects.

Entrepreneurial Service Department was a core department at Garage Cafe. Yin pointed out that department was established because Chinese entrepreneurs experienced tough conditions at early stage, and venture capitalists only made investment when the start-ups reached certain stages. However, venture capitalists only invested in elite entrepreneurial teams, while grassroots entrepreneurs could do nothing but wait to be knocked out. Yin said frankly that platforms like Garage Cafe mainly served entrepreneurs at early

(*Continued*)

Case XVII: (*Continued*)

stage. Many of these entrepreneurs could not develop their projects further only because they lacked experience or resources. Some of these people grew fast when they could communicate with other people on platforms like Garage Cafe and thus they could progress their projects. She explained her view with an example of a team working at the cafe permanently: a founder, with no companion at all, brought his project scheme to the cafe for negotiation before his team was formed; although the cafe doubted if he was well prepared, it did not turn him down; later, as the founder got support from the cafe's entrepreneurial service system and made friends in the cafe, he grew very fast, formed a team of five and progressed his project steadily; all in all, the team was solid after months of incubation.

Yin also remarked that, initially, Garage Cafe was not founded to screen out the best early-stage projects, but to lower the cost to start up a business, to increase the success rate and to improve the environment for entrepreneurs in China; Garage Cafe aimed more at helping entrepreneurs who were unlikely to success originally to improve themselves, support themselves and their teams, earn some money, and be responsible to themselves, their teams and their families. This was what Garage Cafe wanted most. In some way, Garage Cafe made investment out of its sense of social responsibility and thus played an important role in the development of angel investment in China.

Entrepreneurial Services: Lower the Cost and Increase the Success Rate

About the basic content of the entrepreneurial services of the cafe, Yin said there were two ways to assist enterprises. One was to lower the cost of development. For facilities essential for TMT industries like bandwidth and servers, the cafe would help entrepreneurs to negotiate with the suppliers, and to get some fundamental facilities without any charge. Entrepreneurs might also test the speed of network without any payment at the early stage, which increased the working efficiency; by deploying and improving all these hardware facilities, the cafe helped entrepreneurs save a lot of money. The other one was to increase the success rate. In fact, lowering the cost also helped to increase the

(*Continued*)

Case XVII: (*Continued*)

success rate. Garage Cafe created a friend circle for entrepreneurs. It regularly launched some themed forums or parties to allow people sharing experience about starting up a business. For example, the cafe recently arranged people to watch American Dreams in China, and organize a QQ chat group so that anybody could timely call out for help or support from friends when he or she met problems. In other words, apart from saving hardware resources, building friend circle was also important. Ms. Yin pointed out that entrepreneurs felt lonely too: nobody was a superman, and people needed to improve themselves through group communication.

Entrepreneur Certification: Gathering More Information through Face-to-Face Communication

These days, the industry is full of entrepreneurial service platforms like online platforms, scientific incubators and themed cafes where people could display their projects and get opportunities for incubation. Yin emphasized that a team must be certified by Garage Cafe before it can join the cafe's entrepreneurial service system. Nevertheless, pure online certification was not reliable. The team must be "interviewed" by the Entrepreneurial Service Department, and must have started up some real business, at least into the "DEMO" stage. Any team at the stage of "IDEA" would be recognized as ill-prepared and be turned down or asked to share the ideas with friends in the cafe and perfect the idea first.

Yin said that many projects would be displayed on multiple platforms, which was okay as long as these entrepreneurial service platforms could really help entrepreneurs; Garage Cafe also recommended the certified teams to join other incubators, because it hoped that these teams could develop better in different environments. Besides, the cafe encouraged the certified teams to go out of the garage at some certain stage, to rent their premises and run their businesses alone, which was the sign of maturity. She mentioned that Garage Cafe was cooperating with other entrepreneurial service institutions. For example, the cafe had signed a strategic cooperation agreement with ATCAFE in Xiamen and thus might tailor some services for specific investors in the future.

Case XVIII: Innovative Incubator — Virtue Inno Valley

Deng Yongqiang: "Innovative Incubation Service Helped Enterprises Grow"

Time/site: June 4, 2013/Beijing, China

At the time of the interview, Mr. Deng Yongqiang was Executive General Manager of Virtue Inno Valley (VIV) and Secretary General of Tsinghua Alumni Association of TMT.

Over the span of 20 years after graduating from the Department of Computer Science at Tsinghua University in 1992, Deng started up businesses with his alumni many times, including firms related to software manufacturing, the Internet and mobile network. He had actively promoted the communication and cooperation among enterprises, schools, institutions and investors, and supported his alumni to start up businesses or make investment relating to TMT. In May 2013, he was hired as the "Representative of Young Entrepreneurial Mentors of Beijing".

Deng first said that VIV was a professional incubator focused on mobile network and cultural creativity and could provide all-round entrepreneurial services and full-course financial support to accelerate the development of start-ups. VIV was capable of these because it was supported by Tsinghua University that boasted strong technical force and industrial resources and of which alumni featured rich experience and international resources related to starting up, running or investing in businesses, and because TUSPARK was able to incubate and nurture enterprises in an efficient and professional way. As a result, the Management Committee of Zhongguancun Science Park granted VIV the title of "Innovative Incubator".

VIV Features: Four-Wheel Drive and Open Services

Deng said that the unique services of VIV were shown in its name. VIV was different from traditional incubators in many aspects, particularly, in its innovative and special "four-wheel drive" incubation services. The four wheels included: (1) traditional property management and value-added services, such as those regarding to offices, commercial and industrial registration, HR, agents for financial, tax-related or legal problems, IP agents, etc.; (2) dependable

---

(Continued)

Case XVIII: (*Continued*)

entrepreneurial mentors who had either successfully started their own businesses or made good investment, or taken middle-class jobs relating to products, technology or operation in major enterprises like Baidu, Tencent or Alibaba; (3) affiliated fund support, including seed funds (RMB 60,000 to 200,000), angel funds and co-investment funds, which formed material and multilevel financial supports for start-ups throughout all stages; (4) industrial docking, which helped entrepreneurial teams get promotional and marketing sources from Tencent, Baidu, online stores or international sources, so that entrepreneurial projects were put online preferentially.

Most importantly, VIV was open. It was an incubator open to all partners and all media; it built an open platform with providers of technology, application as well as capital, and incubators; and the open docking procedure lowered the costs of communication and trust building.

"Do Not Follow the Commercial Models of Foreign Countries Completely"

There was a big gap between China and other countries in terms of entrepreneurial concepts, commercial culture and external environments. Therefore, it was not wise for China to completely follow the commercial pattern of the US. Deng believes that Chinese legal system still needs further improvement, Chinese education, technology and markets are lagging behind, and more importantly, American people emphasize the rule of law as well as the spirit of contract which are not the case in China, so being angels or mentors is more demanding in China. Chinese angels or mentors need to have the abilities to recognize promising people and projects.

What could enterprises do with seed funds? Deng answered that seed funds were for product R&D and for helping a team get through the early stage. Seed funds were start-up capital. To be specific, seed funds were used to solve problems of premises, make prototypes and conduct simple launch. With large online platforms like Baidu and Tencent, investors were able to determine the potential of the project. This was the function of VIV mentors, incubators and funds. People could accurately determine the product operation of the team.

With regard to whether VIV owned any equity of the incubated enterprise, Deng said that VIV adopted the mode of Y-Combinator and started a "sailing

(*Continued*)

Case XVIII: (*Continued*)

program". In other words, VIV set up seed funds for exceptional teams to launch their projects and invested RMB 60,000 to 200,000 in different enterprises. In return, the incubator, mentors and funds jointly owned 6–10% of the company shares and separately held certain proportions. Each of them played different roles to support start-ups. About cooperation with mentors, VIV not only gave mentors "dry shares" but also encouraged mentors to made investment on their own, so that the incubator and the mentors were closely bonded. Mentors should guide entrepreneurial teams in different ways and VIV stood out because it tended to let mentors recommend projects, a method learned from other countries.

On the topic of affiliated funds, VIV had invested more than 10 projects in China: 80% of these projects were related to mobile network, and some of the projects were under the negotiation for A round financing. Since June 2013, VIV started to invest in 10 seed projects every month. These projects did not have to move into VIV, and might settle in affiliated incubators (cooperators), or at their own premises while VIV made direct financial investment. Deng also marked that VIV would try its best to invest in 120 small projects every year, help 20 projects or so to start A round financing in 2 or 3 years, and then successfully incubate 100 companies within seven years so that they could enter A round financing. The incubator would open to all angel and institutional investors home and abroad.

Incubation Services for Undergraduates: Seeking Dependable, Seasoned, Outgoing and Adaptable Undergraduates

When talking about his opinion about entrepreneurial projects done by undergraduates, Deng said that the incubator would offer funds to "reliable" undergraduates who were not introverted or bookworms, such as those who had graduated from universities under Project 211, or those who had done projects with their mentors before and boasted strong commercial background and skills of adaptability. The incubator would provide these promising students with resources to develop their projects. Recently, VIV focused on the entrepreneurial team formed by senior students of Beihang University. In 2012, the team won the champion of the entrepreneurial competition held by Microsoft in China. VIV was planning to finance the team. Deng also said that it required

(*Continued*)

Case XVIII: *(Continued)*

insight to find good projects from those carried out by undergraduates. Mr. Deng mentioned that he had been in the business of computers since 1980s, and then started his own business related to Internet, and made some investment. As a result, he had earned extensive experience of starting business and making investment, and had a unique view on spotting good projects.

Case XIX: Public Policies of Angel Investment — Support from Suzhou Government

Yu Hongye: "Platforms of Angel Investment Services Needed to Find Proper Models and Positions"

Time/site: September 11, 2013/Suzhou, China

Ms. Yu Hongye is the founder of Suzhou Xingyebang Investment Management Co., Ltd. and Deputy Secretary General and Financial Adviser of Suzhou SND Association for International Personnel. She obtained a PhD in finance at Sorbonne University in France and has dedicated herself to studying the development of venture capital around the world. She was also General Manager of Department of Investment Bank and Vice General Manager of the Treasury Department of the Bank of China's Suzhou Branch.

According to Yu, Xingyebang is specialized in providing financial services, and its core business is venture capital, primary investment services and research.

Most Angel Investors in Suzhou Connected to the Government

In the 2013 List of Chinese Cities on Innovative and Entrepreneurial Environments released in September 2013, statistics of eight Level One indicators from 173 cities at prefecture level and above (excluding municipalities directly under the jurisdiction of the central government) with GDP over RMB 100 billion were collected. These indicators included "governmental support", "industrial develop", "personnel environment", "R&D environment", "financial

(Continued)

Case XIX: (*Continued*)

support", "agent services", "market environment" and "innovative reputation". The Top 100 cities were assessed systematically. In this list, Suzhou ranked fourth, after Shenzhen, Guangzhou and Hangzhou. In other words, Suzhou boasted unique advantages for entrepreneurs and innovators.

When talking about angel investors, entrepreneurs and innovators in Suzhou, Ms. Yu said that angel investors in Suzhou were mainly state-owned entities, which could offer some functions or services regarding to incubation or early-stage investment. For example, "Suzhou Technology Venture Capital Co., Ltd." under direct management of Suzhou Bureau of Science and Technology, "Suzhou Yuandian Venture Capital Co., Ltd." under Oriza Holdings (originally China-Singapore Suzhou Industrial Park Venture Capital Co., Ltd.) in China-Singapore Suzhou Industrial Park, "SND Technology Venture Capital Co., Ltd." and "Suzhou Technology City Venture Capital Co., Ltd." under SND Ventures Group (originally Jiangsu SND Ventures Co., Ltd.) in Suzhou National Hi-Tech District (SND), the seed funds under Suzhou International Development Venture Capital Holding Co., Ltd., the funds established by Wuzhong District for incubation under Interim Methods to Manage Special Funds for Supporting the Development of Scientific SMEs in Wuzhong and incubators founded by the authorities of districts and development districts in Suzhou. Among these, the larger ones included BioBay in Suzhou Industrial Park. A few private funds for early-stage projects existed in Suzhou, but there was no private funds especially founded for making angel investment. Private angel investment was mainly direct cooperation between owners of private companies and entrepreneurs of scientific projects. However, some professional angel investors were emerging in Suzhou.

Yu thought that the entrepreneurial environment in Suzhou was unique because in a way, business people in Suzhou controlled traditional industries and most of the major private enterprises. These enterprises were transferred from village- or town-owned enterprises, so transformation was necessary. However, these business people did not accept innovative or high-tech projects easily. Although they had money, they preferred to invest in real estate and pre-IPO. On the other hand, since the implementation of "The Recruitment Program of Global Youth Experts" of China, Suzhou Government launched favorable policies, and introduced the venture capital platform of the

(*Continued*)

Case XIX: (*Continued*)

Recruitment Program, held brand activity of "Winning at Suzhou", or even hosted talents attracting activities directly in Europe and America, and actively introduced the projects under the Recruitment Program and other talents programs. Some of these projects were brilliant and thus welcomed by venture capitalists. However, there were no proper financing channels in Suzhou for projects at earlier stages, riskier projects, local entrepreneurial projects, or undergraduates' projects. For the purpose of docking these projects, special angel investment funds might be a proper answer.

Platforms of Angel Investment Services Need Proper Models and Positioning

The booming innovative and entrepreneurial activities as well as early-stage investment created great space for the development of an "angel investment and entrepreneurial service industry". Service platforms like virtual incubators and investor clubs were springing up around the country, but these platforms were not all good, providing different services and making profits in unclear patterns. Therefore, sustainable development became a problem. Yu said that there were no platforms exclusively built for angel investors in Suzhou, and entrepreneurial service platforms were mainly state-owned ones, offering mostly entrepreneurial services to the "SME service centers" founded by development park. In the first half of 2013, some proactive local practitioners in the field of venture capital planned to found a "Union of Angel Investors" with the support from Suzhou Bureau of Science and Technology, but the plan suspended because of lacking proper models or positioning. Since 2013, activities related to angel investment services have been held. For example, the first salon for angel investors in Suzhou on the afternoon of March 16, 2013 was jointly organized by the SME center of the Park, Scientific Financing Department of Suzhou Branch of Bank of Communications, Property Rights Transaction Center of Suzhou and Banx Angel. Mr. Tang Tao, a pioneering angel investor, was invited to make a themed speech, and approximately 100 entrepreneurs and entrepreneurial teams attended the salon. The salon was held to find the angel investors recognized by entrepreneurs most, to create an atmosphere for angel investment and to make road show of the most promising projects. Thus, entrepreneurs and angel investors could have a chance to deepen communication.

(*Continued*)

Case XIX: (*Continued*)

Policy Support for Angel Investors Should be Enhanced

Angel investment boomed over the last three years; developing from a single pattern industry of personal investment to an industry where multiple patterns coexisted, including group investment, institutional investment and incubation investment. In Suzhou, angels were mostly institutional investors, represented by SND Ventures Group and Yuandian Venture Capital Co., Ltd. (an enterprise located in the industrial park), both of which were founded by the government and both of which provided start-ups with special seed funds and angel investment. What were the advantages and obstacles of institutionalization? Should angel investors in China institutionalize themselves? To these two questions, Yu answered that for any novel financial investment, personal investment always came first in the private market. Then, group and institutional investors started to flourish. The industry of angel investment also followed this pattern. According to her, major angel investors were state-owned institutions, which was the feature of Suzhou. However, these institutions did not reflect the institutionalization of angel investors in Suzhou. Enjoying advantages like other state-owned enterprises, state-owned angel investors also faced some obstacles, for example, how to determine the loss or over-administration of state-owned assets.

In addition, policy support from the government was essential to angel investors. Yu pointed out that the provincial government of Jiangsu had released Opinions about Encouraging and Guiding Angel Investors to Support Sci-tech SMEs and Interim Methods for Managing Guidance Funds of Angel Investment of Jiangsu Province in August 2012 and February 2013 respectively, so as to encourage and guide angel investors to support sci-tech SMEs and regulate the management of guidance funds of provincial angel investment; moreover, Suzhou government issued Regulations about Guidance Funds of Venture Capital for Sci-tech Start-ups of Suzhou (Trial), according to which venture capitalists could apply for risk allowance after investing in sci-tech start-ups. She said that angel investment was very risky, but also boosted innovation, entrepreneurship and scientific development; considering the booming economy of the US in 1960s and the "entrepreneurial nation" of Israel, one could understand that although culture was a key factor, early-stage venture capital and angel investment were also financially essential. Therefore, to boost the market of angel investment, Chinese government needed to issue some more powerful and committed policies to assist angel investors.

(*Continued*)

Case XX: Public Policies of Angel Investment —
Encouraging Researchers to Become Angels

New Policies of Zhongguancun Encouraged Teachers
to Support Students to Start Business

In the beginning of 1980s, some researchers quit their jobs, and started their businesses. Currently, the structure of entrepreneurs in Zhongguancun was changing materially. Students were encouraged to start businesses, and groups of college students became the main entrepreneurs and innovators. At the 2014 Summit of Young Entrepreneurs and Innovators held in Beijing, the Beijing Committee of China Communist Youth League officially issued "The Investigation Report about Young Entrepreneurs in Beijing". The investigation team scientifically sampled 570,000 teams formed by the young entrepreneurs and registered at the industrial and commercial departments. Then, the team reviewed these teams from the aspects of demography, economics, sociology, etc. According to the investigation, graduates without a fixed job became the mainstream of entrepreneurs. People who completed junior college or further education accounted for more than two thirds of the total young entrepreneurs. Nowadays, many graduates do not choose "stable jobs" anymore. A total of 5.7% of these young entrepreneurs had studied overseas, a proportion much higher than other cities in China. Meanwhile, the report showed that 22.9% of the young entrepreneurs did not understand the favorable policies of Beijing, and 30.8% of them never enjoyed such policies.

However, the fact was that the central and local governments all attached great importance to entrepreneurs and innovators, and Beijing boasted excellent geographical advantages and entrepreneurial human resources. To further assist researchers and college students to start sci-tech companies, the Administrative Committee of Zhongguancun Technology Park issued The Method for Managing Special Funds for Researchers and College Students to Start Sci-tech Companies (Trial) in November 2014. Compared to other policies, this was the first policy that encouraged teachers to invest in start-ups of students. The policy encouraged college and university teachers became angel investors of students (including those who were still studying or had graduated within two years). According to this policy, if a teacher had invested in the scientific project of a student and the student found a scientific enterprise as the legal person, the enterprise could get a special fund equal to

(Continued)

Case XX: (*Continued*)

50% of the teacher's cash investment at most. For example, if the teacher had invested RMB 500,000 and got no more than 30% of the shares of the student's company, then the company could get financial support of no more than RMB 250,000.

Innovation, entrepreneurship or angel investment was more about the atmosphere than money. The biggest purpose to encourage teachers to make such investment was to form a bond, a culture and an ecosystem for entrepreneurs. Only when they became the students' investors could the teachers know the front-line entrepreneurs and stay at the front line of scientific research, grasping the development directions of science and new industries.

Source: Collated from publicly available governmental documents and the Internet.

Notes

1. See the *Employment Report of Chinese Graduate 2013*.
2. Wang Yaohui and Lu Jiangyong, *Annual Report on Chinese Returnee Entrepreneurship (2012)*, Beijing: Social Sciences Academic Press, 2012. (in Chinese)
3. *Internet Entrepreneurs' Survival and Development Report 2012*.
4. Hanadi Mubarak Al-Mubaraki and Michael Busler. 'Business Incubators: Findings from a Worldwide Survey, and Guidance for the G.C.C States,' *Global Business Review*, 2010, 1(11):1–20.
5. This information has been collated according to relevant policies implemented in Shenzhen, Ningbo, Chongqing, Chengdu, Wuhan, Yangzhou, Qingdao and other local governments. For more details, please see Appendix 4.

Chapter 10

How China Can Learn from the Development of Angel Investment around the World

Compared with the mature market in the West, angel investment in China is still in its infancy. Thus, China still has a long way to go in nurturing the concept of investors, regulating the development and formulating proper policies. Our research shows that there are three major obstacles to the development of angel investment in China, namely a shortage of professional personnel, limited professional knowledge and insufficient policy support. Therefore, it is suggested that China should proactively learn from developed countries so as to accelerate the development of angel investment and support the development of innovative economy.

Trend of International Angel Investment

Angel investment plays an important role in boosting macroeconomy. As shown in the statistics in the US, every investment yields 4.1 jobs on average. In 2012 alone, angel investment created 274,800 new jobs in the US. As the biggest market for angel investors in the world, the US boasts about 350 active angel groups, with 67% of their transactions ranging from USD 150,000 to 500,000 and the average investment at USD 340,000 for each transaction. Although the failure rate is 56%, approximately 9% of the projects boast return rates of 1,000%. Unlike other types of investors, angel investors are more interested in fulfilling personal interests, giving back to society, and supporting entrepreneurs and innovators, over achieving economic returns. Foreign governments issue powerful policies that are more powerful to support angel investment, mainly with methods such as tax incentives, co-investment, voluntary donation and assistance to incubator.

During recent investigations, the authors noticed seven trends about the development of international angel investment: 1) angel investment has prospered not only in the US but also in many countries and regions; 2) relations between angel investment and venture capital and between angel investment and crowd funding attract more attention, especially in this era when potential crowd funding around the world has become popular; 3) micro-VCs, a new kind of fund supporting entrepreneurs of early-stage projects, are emerging at the Silicon Valley and spreading across the US, and the secondary market of angel investment — a new exit strategy that improved liquidity — is also emerging; 4) more and more angel investors conduct transactions with convertible notes, a financial instrument that has made exiting more convenient; 5) female angels and social investment are rising in the international market; 6) angel groups have become more mature; and 7) sandboxes, incubators and accelerators are internationalizing and playing greater roles in the market of angel investment.

Unique Features of Angel Investment in China

In China, many people are offering services related to angel investment, but they are not always familiar with the concept of angel investment or have strong connection with other angel investors. Angel investors in China share some common features with their counterparts in many other countries. For instance, most of them are successful entrepreneurs, investors, bankers and other professional personnel; they invest in start-ups for high returns and to help these entrepreneurs. These professionals all pay great importance to the "people" of those invested projects. However, Chinese angel investors are unique in some aspects.

Firstly, angel investment in China is smaller and thus there is potential of investment to be released. According to experience and statistics, investment in seed and early-stage projects accounts for 36.7% of the total equity investment of unlisted enterprises in America, but only 4.6% in China. In America, sci-tech enterprises are divided into early-stage, middle-stage and listed enterprises, corresponding to angel investment, venture capital and PE investment. Angel investment at the bottom of this stable, upright pyramid outnumbers other kinds of investment in quantity, and keeps incubating good innovative enterprises and feeding them to markets. However, in China, as not every competent person or institution becomes an angel investor, the pyramid is upside down. Most of the funds go to mature enterprises at the latter two stages, while many early-stage enterprises find it difficult to develop or innovate due to fund shortage.

Secondly, many returnees and "silver-spoon kids" become angel investors, making investment models more diverse. Angel investors in China include not only local successful people but also two special groups — returnees and silver-spoon generation. Some of these people have worked or studied overseas before, and successfully start businesses or became angel investors after returning to China. Some other investors are young, ambitious silver-spoon kids with dreams; these people are also entrepreneurs and help promising entrepreneurial teams with angel investment. This has helped investment models become more diverse, and people have more angels to take after; such as entrepreneurial angels like Lei Jun, financial angels like He Boquan, and angels involved with few management duties after investment like Xu Xiaoping.

Thirdly, development is more systematized and institutionalized. Apart from angel investment institutions that have been founded in recent years, some venture capital institutions have started to pay attention to early-stage projects, and the authorities and private institutions have also created special angel guiding funds, which in turn have led to many private institutions providing angel investment services. China lacks a complete system of angel investment, and the systematization and institutionalization of the industry have just begun. These organizations and institutions generally face two common challenges, namely, how to ensure stable operation and sustainable development. Therefore, exploration and improvements are necessary in terms of personnel nurturing, scientific management and effective operation.

Fourthly, the ecosystem and environment for entrepreneurs and investors need to be further improved. Most Chinese investors lack understanding about angel investment and a lot of funds tend to be channeled toward stock and real estate markets. Government guidance funds for early-stage projects are not strong and efficient enough, and public policies for angel investment, tax incentives for investors in particular, are insufficient. Entrepreneurship education system is incomplete and the ecosystem and environment for entrepreneurs and investors need to be further improved.

Generally speaking, angel investment in China is still in its infancy and more support should be given to entrepreneurs and innovators. There are two reasons to this situation. One is that incentives for angel investors are insufficient. Rich Chinese represented mainly by business people rarely make angel investments and lack deep understanding about the market. From the points of assets allocation in Chinese financial market, angel investment is not an investment product commonly chosen by people with high neat value, such as senior managers of enterprises. Meanwhile, due to the high housing price and poor welfare in China, high-income professionals such as lawyers, senior managers and doctors do not have a lot of spare money and thus tend to choose less risky financial products. As a result, not many of them have committed to angel investment. Moreover, as there is no preferential tax policy for angel investors in China, it is hard for angel investors to win high return from their highly risky investment. This is because on the one hand, angel investors bear an astonishing risk of failure that is higher than 90%, and on the other hand, they have to pay exorbitant individual income tax for the rest 10% of successful cases. The other reason is that exit channels for angel investors are incomplete. Angel investment features long periods of return, poor liquidity, etc., and could not be cashed quickly like real estate and stocks. According to statistics, individual angel investors of nearly 60% of the entrepreneurial projects at Zhongguancun have not exited from the projects, and only less than 30% of those who have exited through buyout. However, American angel investors exit from the projects mainly through buyout and the proportion is over 50%. The reason why China is lagging behind is the underdevelopment of its capital market: leveraged buyouts are possible in the US, but not in China.

Suggestions to Further Develop Angel Investment in China

Considering the weakness of the current policy system, it is believed that the authorities need to make the following three improvements.

1. The authorities should enact laws and regulations to regulate the development of angel investment and establish a system for nurturing and managing angel investors.

Angel investment is a relatively blurry idea in China. Both the authorities and the academic circles have no accurate idea about the definition, development and current conditions of angel investment. Moreover, there are almost no policies or laws about angel investment in China. Unlike Chinese government, American government issued the Securities Law to strictly regulate the qualification of angel investors. According to this law, only the person or the family with net assets worth over USD 1 million, or a person earning over USD 200,000 annually, or a couple earning over USD 300,000 annually could qualify to be "competent" angel investors. Laws like the Securities Law help national governments manage angel investors, and keep disqualified people from the risky market of angel investment so that these people wouldn't lose so much that they couldn't afford the daily necessities. Meanwhile, these laws are also the legal foundation for authorities to make decisions. Nowadays, China lacks a national system to promote the development of angel investment. In China, the support mainly comes from local authorities. It is suggested that a registration system be formed to cover angel investors around the country and to administrate these investors on the basis of their local investment records. Those with sound records can get financial support and training, while those with bad records will be blacklisted. Thus, risks should be managed, and greater financial support and training should be given to specific investors so as to establish a system for nurturing and managing angel investors.

2. **Environment for angel investors should be improved and relevant incentive policies such as preferential tax policies should be implemented.**

Angel investors face high risks and long return periods, and thus it is difficult for them to survive independently under the market mechanism. In other words, governmental guidance is essential. In western countries like Canada, the government would encourage angel investors by means of co-investment, pledge of equity guarantee, etc. However, it's important to mention that the government is usually the co-investor of angel groups, instead of individual angels.

For example, when a certified angel institution invests RMB 100,000 in a start-up, the government would also invest RMB 60,000 in it, and the researchers and personnel of the invested could apply to the government for reimbursement in a certain proportion. Apart from these, western countries also vigorously support angel investors with tax preferential policies. For instance, local authorities of the states of Hawaii, Kansas, Wisconsin and Kentucky in the US have implemented policies of tax credit or tax exemption. In Hawaii, particularly, the amount of tax credit/example could equal that of the investment. In the UK, the Enterprise Investment Scheme of Britain also covers regulations about the deduction and exemption of income tax, the deduction, exemption and deferral of capital gains tax, the tax deduction for losses, the exemption of inheritance tax for angel investors.[1] But in China, tax preferential policies mainly target SMEs. Tax incentives for angel investors are inadequate. The "double taxation" faced by investors of stock rights should be solved with policies. Therefore, the writer suggests that tax preferential policies be issued to promote the development of angel investors.

3. **The national government should take the initiative to set up angel investment funds and provide more guidance to angels.**

Although some provincial governments are financing early-stage angel investors, only local investors get such funds. Thus, this kind of government support is limited. Most of angels intend to invest in projects around the country, but if the angels invested by a local government make no investment in the region and thus do not accelerate the development of local economy, the government would lose the willingness to support angels as the time goes by. On the other hand, funds and projects are poorly matched or managed in some regions. Therefore, it is suggested that the national government should establish a unified guidance fund to promote healthy and rapid development of private angel investment.

Outlook for Angel Investment in China

In the next 5 to 10 years, plenty of opportunities will arise for entrepreneurs and investors during China's transitional period. The market is promising in China and angel investment will progress with each passing day.

Outlook 1: Angel investment is moving from its infancy to the period of expansion.

With the development of angel investment, investors who prefer stocks, real estate and products with constant returns will know more about early-stage investment. As a result, more and more people and organizations will become angels. Moreover, entrepreneurs who have been supported by angels or VC investors will also become angels and help more start-ups when these entrepreneurs succeed. Angels in China will therefore be keener on pursuing something other than profits. They will begin to seek the sense of self-fulfillment that they will get when they help entrepreneurs succeed. More and more angel investors do not require majority shares after investment, but might instead insist on owning part of the shares or even no shares. Also, the institutionalization of angel investors will be accelerated. Online financial platforms will break the traditional pattern of operation and hasten the birth of new commercial activities. As a result, investors and the invested will communicate more efficiently and the cost of transaction will decrease, promoting the development of angel investment industry.

Outlook 2: Owning to continual exploration and strategic improvement, entities like angel investors, entrepreneurs and agents will become more professional and regulated, and the environment for entrepreneurs and investors will develop in a healthy way.

Internal and external environments for angel investors are key to the development of the industry, and the environments combine into an ecosystem that covers both entrepreneurs and investors. This ecosystem needs the services and support of the authorities, and demands external collaboration related to personnel, technology and markets. Since 2014, entrepreneurial and innovative activities have increased sharply and early-stage investment has generated enormous space for industries of angel investment and entrepreneurial services to develop. Besides parks and incubators run by the authorities, private service providers such as entrepreneurial cafes, virtual incubators and financing platforms were springing up. However, there is no mature commercial model in these fields. But with continual exploration and strategic improvement, it is certain that these institutions will abandon the primitive model of development and will properly position themselves. They will flourish in a more professional, efficient, regulated way, and the environment for entrepreneurs and investors will develop healthily.

Outlook 3: To further support the development of the real economy, the authorities will enhance the support for entrepreneurs, innovators and angels.

High rent and personnel cost of first-tier cities will drive entrepreneurs to second-tier cities such as Tianjin, Nanjing, Suzhou, Hangzhou and Wuhan, where talent pools and government policies are obviously more desirable.[2] As mentioned above, most of the policies about angel investment were issued successively in the past two years. A large number of excellent entrepreneurial enterprises have won the guidance funds and risk premiums from the government, but these funds or premiums are inadequate to satisfy the financial needs of numerous SMEs, particularly grassroots enterprises, in China. Meanwhile, local governments are still seeking ways to issue effective public policies. They cannot simply imitate or copy foreign policies. Therefore, the applicability and effectiveness of current policies are uncertain and proactive exploration is required to find proper tax incentives for angel investors. The authors hereby predict that in the future, the general trend, namely the real economy being supported by the financial world, will remain unchanged, and Chinese government will increase its support for entrepreneurs, innovators and angels.

Notes

1. See *2012 Research Report of Angel Investment and Angel Incubation in China.*
2. According to the "2013 Ranking of Chinese Cities Based on the Environment for Entrepreneurship and Innovation", cities in East China were still far ahead, but cities in Midwest China were catching up rapidly.

Part IV
Special Research

Chapter 11

Angel Investment in Hong Kong SAR, China

In July 2013, we went to Hong Kong for an investigation and interviewed Mr. Allen Yeung, Chairman of Hong Kong Business Angel Network,[1] Mr. John Y. Lo, Partner of Edwards Wildman Palmer, Dr. Dominic Chan from Dark Horse Investment and other senior experts.

1. Independent angel investors dominant in Hong Kong

In regard to the institutionalization and systemization of angel capital in Hong Kong SAR, China, Dr. Chan expressed how independent angel investors dominated the angel investment scene in Hong Kong while less institutions engaged in angel capital in the form of funds or groups. Among the reasons, he further pointed out: first, it was related to the development background of angel capital in Hong Kong. Before 2008, investors in Hong Kong had no clear idea about angel capital and invested mainly in the two fields of real estate and stocks, in which they gained rich investment experience; angel capital required higher professional quality from the investors as it was mainly involved in investment in emerging industries and technology start-ups, and therefore it was not popular. Second, judging from the switch from setting up local angel clubs in Hong Kong to establishing partnership direct investment companies, the group mode required a more effective and carefully designed management system. For example, before establishing Dark Horse Investment, Dr. Chan also set up a membership club called Asian Angel Alliance with over 20 members.[2] The bottlenecks of management and constraint on the club members resulted in less participation in project evaluations and disagreements among some members. Finally, six members who were more active contributed individually to form a corporate direct investment institution.

317

2. Angels differed sharply in Hong Kong and in mainland China

With the development of angel capital, angel investors in different places communicated more frequently. Through communication with angel investors in mainland China, Mr. Allen Yeung pointed out two differences between angel investors in mainland China and angel investors in Hong Kong. First, they had different scopes of investment, i.e., angel investment projects in mainland China were focused on domestic market while investment projects of Hong Kong featured internationalization, with investor's capital invested in some emerging countries in Southeast Asia. Second, they had different perspectives of project evaluation, i.e., angel investors in Hong Kong tended to review the projects from the perspective of PE or VC, with emphasis on the analysis of the investment return based on operation data, and thus angels in Hong Kong tended to invest grown companies. Angel investors in mainland China in contrast, paid attention to the seed-stage projects in addition to the investment in start-ups, and thus impulsive decision-making occurred now and then. Mr. Yeung thought, based on the second difference, angel investors in mainland China were more consistent with the basic concept of angel capital and were more true angel investors.

3. Hong Kong Business Angel Network was a non-profit organization with government background

As the demand side of capital, start-ups often face many difficulties in financing process while angel investors as the supply side of capital often have trouble finding suitable projects. Hong Kong Business Angel Network emerged in order to bridge an investment and financing platform for the start-ups and angel investors. In 2010, Hong Kong Business Angel Network was established jointly by Hong Kong Science & Technology Parks Corporation (HKSTPC), Hong Kong Venture Capital and Private Equity Association (HKVCA), Chinese University of Hong Kong (CUHK), Hong Kong University of Science and Technology (HKUST), University of Hong Kong (HKU) and Hong Kong Polytechnic University (POLYU), and was officially registered as a non-profit organization in July 2011.

As of March 31, 2013, Hong Kong Business Angel Network had 67 Angel members and 12 institution partners. Over the three years since its establishment, a total of 20 angel investors successfully invested for 13 start-ups with the amount up to USD 64.72 million, through the investment platform of Investment Matching Gathering of Hong Kong Business Angel Network. Mr. Yeung also said: in the future, Hong Kong Business Angel Network would unite the well-known universities and research institutions in Hong Kong and mainland to develop a more advanced and convenient investment platform for better intermediary services for investment and financing, thus providing facilitation for start-ups.

On the other hand, Hong Kong incubators made an outstanding contribution on supporting innovation and entrepreneurship. As one of the mature incubators in the Greater China, HKSTP provided three different incubation modes for start-ups: Incu-App, Incu-Tech and Incu-Bio, which are respectively telephone and network application incubator, technology incubator and biotechnology incubator. It aims to provide necessary software and hardware support for start-ups of different types. Compared to traditional incubators, which only provide office space, HKSTP also provided technical and management support, marketing support, business support, financial support, etc., for start-ups. As of March 31, 2013, HKSTP had incubated a total of 285 start-ups, with the survival rate up to 74%. In addition, some innovative incubators gradually caught public attention, like such co-working places as Good Lab, Cocoon, Hive in Hong Kong. These institutions not only have office space, facility and other hardware service functions as traditional incubators but also provide start-ups with investment and financing agency, entrepreneurship counseling and other value-added services, which is similar to the famous "garage café" in mainland China. These innovative incubators bridge a cooperation and exchange platform for both capital supply and capital demand sides to improve the transaction efficiency of investment and financing in a unique way.

4. Policy suggestion: Restrictions on angel investors outside the mainland should be loosened

On August 29, 2012, the NDRC, Ministry of Finance, seven other departments and Beijing Municipal Government jointly issued the first guidance document on science and technology, and finance, "Opinions of Constructing National Innovation Center for Science & Technology and Finance in Zhongguancun National Innovation Demonstration Zone", with particular attention given to angel investment. The report proposed to strongly cultivate angel investors, study and issue policies that support the development of angel investment, foster the groups of angel investors, guide and encourage individuals at home and abroad to carry out angel investment business; build a project library of innovation and entrepreneurship, and guide and encourage the development of the system of intermediary organizations that provided services for angel investment; encourage the construction of accumulation areas and platforms that promote the development of angel investment, extend publicity efforts and create an environment conducive to the development of angel investment.

As a lawyer and angel investor, Mr. John Y. Lo felt deeply the imperfection of some aspects of the legal system in mainland China. Its corporate law set limits on residents outside the mainland and requirements for the identity of shareholders, which, to some extent, blocked the financing channel between angel investors in Hong Kong and entrepreneurs in the mainland. Based on this, he suggested that when new policies for angel capital were to be issued, the investment demand from angel investors beyond the borders should be fully considered, and policy restrictions on angel investors outside the mainland, especially in Hong Kong, Macao and Taiwan, should be properly loosened.

Note

1. Mr. Yeung had stepped down as Chairman of HKBAN. He has been serving as HK Government CIO since July 2015.
2. Global angel capital non-profit organizations are formed in clubs, networks, associations, alliances, etc. "香港天使投资脉络" (Hong Kong Business Angel Network) is the official Chinese name of the organization.

Chapter 12

Centers of Angel Investment: Zhongguancun Science Park, Beijing

According to the "2012 China Angel Investment Report" released by CYzone, angel investment projects have increased to 747 in total in China since 2011, most of which are based in Beijing, Guangdong, Shanghai, Zhejiang and Jiangsu. 224 among such projects are in Beijing, accounting for nearly 30% and mainly located in Zhongguancun Science Park where the number of Angel Investment projects ranks No. 1 nationwide. Since 2009, angel investors within Zhongguancun Demonstration Zone have increased over 60% to be approximately 200 active. By 2012, there were about 33 angel investment funds established in Zhongguancun Demonstration Zone, including 10 established in 2011 and 14 established in 2012.

1. Two types of angel investors in Zhongguancun

(1) **Individual angel investors**. Entrepreneurs or enterprise senior managers are important sources of individual angel investors, a few investment bankers, lawyers, university professors, engineers, financial industry practitioners and industry experts have also engaged in angel investment.

(2) **Zhongguancun angel investment funds**. Angel investment funds in Zhongguancun can be divided into following three groups based on different background of fund managers: 1) a total of 23 regular angel investment funds with industry or investment background, which are the backbone of angel investment funds; 2) three seed funds set up by incubators or science parks (Legend Star, Innovation Works and

Virtue Inno Valley); 3) seven angel investment funds under platform companies (Qihoo 360, Tencent, Microsoft, Sina, Netease, Lenovo and UC) (see Table 12.1).

2. Characteristics of Zhongguancun angel investment

Angel investment in Zhongguancun features diverse fundraising channels and interpersonal relationship-based project sources; new-generated IT-oriented investment; single investment amount below RMB 5 million without equity holding; short investment decision-making cycles and great attention to teams, technology or business model and focus on added-value services after investment. Such investment brings about some outstanding start-ups including listed companies such as SOHU, Sumavision and Jiayuan.com, and industry leaders such as Lakala, Lightinthebox, Xiaomi Tech and Jumei.com.

3. Development trend of Zhongguancun angel investment

(1) Zhongguancun angel investment has grown more and more active with a noticeable trend of systematization and institutionalization. On the one hand, Zhongguancun angel investment is on a fast track growth in terms of number and scale of funds. According to incomplete statistics of Zero2IPO Research, angel investment institutions active in Zhongguancun in 2013 have completed fund-raising for eight new angle funds with a total amount of RMB 494 million. As to the scale of newly invested funds, most funds have a total amount of capital less than RMB 100 million and only two have raised more than RMB 100 million. Compared with the average fund raising scale of RMB 220 million by VC funds in 2013, Angel Investment funds are rather small. On the other hand, various associations have been established in Zhongguancun, including our major initiators such as Zhongguancun Angel Investment Association, Angel 100 and Association of China Angle Investment of Youth, which are founded only recently. Besides, funds set up by joining of individual angel investors also flourished in 2013.

Table 12.1   List of Angel Investment Funds Active in Zhongguancun (23).

Name	Time of Establishment	Total Amount of Fund	Investment Projects	Major Founders
Shangdi Angel Investment Fund	2008	RMB 20 million	WWW Win, Taohui Pottery Club, ConMISE	Gong Shanbin
Taishan Angel Investment Fund	2009	USD 10 million	XISHIWANG, Lashou.com, JIAPIN	Yang Lei, Chen Liang, Bei Kangning
Legend Star	2008	RMB 400 million	Nano Think, Eedoo, CidTech	Legend Holdings
Lumipath Angel Venture Fund	Phase I in 2009 and Phase II in 2010	RMB 21 million in total	Apothecary, Zitengqiao Themed Restaurant, Fulushouxi Gyeonggi Cuisine	Su Yulie, Huang Letian
FUHO Angel	2010	RMB 250 million	MoneyHub, Juwo Technology, Sanroad Biological, Recomgen Biotech	Zeng Jun, Lin Haiyin
ZhenFund	2012	RMB 100 million and USD 30 million	Idapted, Jiayuan.com, Lightinthebox, Jumei.com, Hantones	Xu Xiaoping, Shen Nanpeng
Shunwei Fund	2011	USD 200 million	Xiaomi Tech, Letao.com, Yek Mobile	Lei Jun, Xu Dalai
LeBox Angel Fund	End of 2011	RMB 100 billion	Kingdowin, Rekoo, 1ting.com, FPI	Yang Ning, Zhang Hui
Unity Ventures	2011	RMB 100 million	Estrongs, Xiachufang App, EoeMobile	Wang Xiao
Qidi Yinxing Angle Investment Center	2011	RMB 150 million	ECOMAN, Xunguangda Communications, Honghuowang.com	Lv Dalong, Luo Jianbei, Luo Zhuo
China Renaissance K2 Ventures	2011	RMB 100 million	Jumei.com, Moweather	Bao Fan, Chen Keyi

(Continued)

Table 12.1 *(Continued)*

Name	Time of Establishment	Total Amount of Fund	Investment Projects	Major Founders
Innovation Works	2011	USD 180 million	More than 50 projects including Diandian.com, Wandoujia App Store, DianXin OS, Zhihu, Xing Cloud and AppChina	Kaifu Lee, Liu Yuhuan, Wang Zhaohui, Wang Hua
	2011	RMB 300 million		
	2012	USD 275 million		
Asia America Angel Fund	2012	RMB 30 million	BabySpace, ToPay	Li Hansheng, Zeng Zhijie, Yang Dong
Haiyin Entrepreneurship Technological Incubator Fund	2012	About RMB 200 million	VINUX, Haoyoumeishi App, EntDigital, Yinbei.com	Wang Yuquan, Charles Xue
Cloud Angel Fund	2012	USD 10 million	None	Tian Suning, Deng Feng, Shen Nanpeng, Qin Jie
Zhongyun Ronghui	2012	RMB 100 million		
Big data App	2012	RMB 10 million		
Tianze Investment	2012	RMB 10.8 million	None	Xu Qian
Gobi Oasis Angle Investment Center	End of 2012	RMB 600 billion	None	Xu Chen. Dong Weiliang
Qidi Yinxing Angle Phase II	End of 2012	RMB 40 million	None	Lv Dalong, Luo Jianbei, Luo Zhuo
Tsinghua Science Park Angle Fund	End of 2012	RMB 30 million	None	Mei Meng, Tai Zhiqiang

Source: Authors' compilation of reports by Zhongguancun Administrative Committee (2013) and Zero2IPO Research (2014).

(2) Deep integration of angle investment and incubator. A new form of "angel investment + incubator" with marketized operation emerges in Zhongguancun in recent years, such as Innovation Works and Legend Star. It is similar to new combination of angel investment and incubator in the US. This is a new pattern of angel investment worth promotion since it usually focuses on investment to some specific industries and provides more standardized and perfect value-added services than regular patterns.

(3) Emerging of crowd funding in angle investment. In 2013, typical models of Internet finance became very popular. In such context, angel investment came up with a model of crowd funding for financing by quick group purchase of high-quality enterprise shares, which has gradually evolved into a financing platform.

(4) Continuous improvement in service system of Zhongguancun angel investment. There are currently a wide range of entrepreneur service agencies in Zhongguancun, such as new service agencies represented by Garage Café and 3W Coffee mainly with offline activities and network service; platform agencies represented by AngelCrunch, 36kr, the Founder and CYzone with mainly online activities and complementally offline exchange meetings and project docking meetings. Such agencies offer platforms for communication between angle investors and entrepreneurs to enable entrepreneurs to quickly position investors, and for investors to quickly identify projects with good investment value, thus promoting development of angel investment. In terms of government support, Zhongguancun Administrative Committee set up pilot programs of angle investment guidance funds in 2012 to operate in manners of capital contribution and contracting. Such funds use fiscal capital to attract social capital to support development of small and micro businesses in incubation stage and start-up stage, further improving investment industry chain in Zhongguancun.

(5) Platform companies in Zhongguancun play an important part in supporting the establishment of new businesses. In pursuit of development, platform companies use platform resources to attract entrepreneurs to set up new businesses based on its platforms. They also establish industry development funds or investment funds for investment in entrepreneurship projects and thus become a new source of angle investment.

4. Problems in Zhongguancun angel investment

(1) Conditions for promoting participation of social capital in angel investment are inadequate due to the difficult business registration and complicated procedures in place, insufficient preferential tax policies, poor credit environment, lack of intellectual property protection and unreasonable investment culture and preference.

(2) Angel investment industry organizations that have just started have limited influence and angel investors are inexperienced. Some angel investment organizations have not been set up for long and suffer a lack of funds and full-time staff. Their members have little communication and no effect has been obtained. Compared with those in America, angel investors in Zhongguancun are inexperienced in the following three aspects: 1) there is no specialized information platform to tell entrepreneurs where to find angel investment; 2) angel investors usually have good knowledge of certain industry but are not specialized in investment with difficulty in industry technology development trend and understanding of entrepreneur teams; 3) in an age full of entrepreneurship opportunities, the number of angel investors fall far behind passion of entrepreneurship in China and angel investors have little access to professional trainings.

(3) Compared with mature market in western countries, Zhongguancun has only a small number of angel investors and funds. According to surveys and statistics, there were only 23 angel investment funds active in Zhongguancun in 2012 with less than 500 individual angel investors and there are only 224 cases of investment of angel funds since 2011 with a total investment amount of RMB 1.12 billion; while at the same period, Silicon Valley had about 60,000 individual angel investors with investment cases of 13,000 and investment amount of USD 3.74 billion (seed stage and early stage). There is a big gap between angel investment in Zhongguancun and Silicon Valley in terms of the number of investors and investment scale. Moreover, the capital invested in start-ups, seed stage and early stage in America accounts for 36.7% of the entire equity investment market of unlisted enterprises, while the figure is only 4.6% in China and 7% in Zhongguancun. We can safely conclude that angel investment

Table 12.2   Comparison of Angel Investment in Zhongguancun and Silicon Valley.

Indicator	Zhongguancun, China (as of 2012)	Silicon Valley, America (as of 2011)
Number of angel investors	Individual angel investors: <500 (available for statistics) Funds: 33 (by 2012)	Individual angel investors: 60,000 (not including VC)
Cases of angel investment	About 224 (subject to statistics in reports of CYzone)	>7,000
Amount of angel investment	About RMB 1.12 billion	USD 3.74 billion

Source: Zhongguancun Administrative Committee (2013).

only claims for a very small part in investment market. Unlike Silicon Valley, Zhongguancun has poor number of angel investors and funds and the reasons are a low degree of involvement of the wealthy, and preference of high-income groups in purchasing financial products with low investment risk and their lack of enthusiasm in angel investment (see Table 12.2).

(4) Zhongguancun angel investment has limited exit channels and exits cases by acquisition are rare. Currently, individual angel investors in Zhongguancun have nearly 60% projects yet to be exited and mergers and acquisitions account for less than 30% for project exits. Annual Angel Investment Report by UNH shows that acquisition is a major approach for exit of angel investment projects, which accounts for over 50%. While among successful exits from angel investment in Zhongguancun, exit by acquisition is not prevailing. As to reasons, on the one hand, leveraged buyout which is common in America cannot work in China due to its capital market conditions. On the other hand, enterprises in Zhongguancun are usually of small size and only large enterprises prefer acquisition due to profit-driven nature of capital. Besides, large enterprises tend to compete with start-ups in low-cost manners including copying and poaching core staff with higher salaries as a result of a market culture of little respect for other people's work and lack in legal protection.

Chapter 13

Survey Report of Innovative Incubators in Zhongguancun, Beijing

1. Development history of incubators in Zhongguancun[1]

(1) Construction period of hi-tech industry development pilot area (1988–1999). An incubator for scientific researchers to venture into business was taking shape. The policy of reform of scientific and technological system by "allowing [the] setting up of scientific research or technical service organizations", introduced by the State, encouraged a large number of teachers from universities and scientific researchers to start new businesses. In consideration of lack of administrative services especially for private enterprises during transition period, governments in Haidian District and Fengtai District set up business incubation centers as competent authority for businesses established by scientific researchers. As a prototype of Zhongguancun incubator, business incubation centers offered office space and basic administrative services for start-ups and served as the only channel for governmental departments to provide services for private technology enterprises.

(2) Construction period of Zhongguancun Science Park (1999–2009). Development of the incubator accelerated to attract overseas students to return and start new businesses. To accommodate requirements of overseas students returning to start new businesses, Zhongguancun introduced policies and services for this purpose and gave support in setting up some entrepreneurship incubation vehicles such as science parks, specialized incubators and pioneer parks for overseas students, which not only provided office space and basic services for enterprises, but also helped explore modes of value-added services such as public technology platforms and early stage investing, becoming an importing service platform for overseas students.

(3) Construction period of National Independent Innovation Demonstration Zone in Zhongguancun (since 2009). In March 2009, the State Council approved the proposal to establish a National Independent Innovation Demonstration Zone in Zhongguancun in an official reply and asked to build Zhongguancun into a technological innovation center with global influence. Since then, Zhongguancun has vigorously promoted strategic new industries and a number of innovative incubators emerged. Social capital owners such as platform companies, angel investors and successful entrepreneurs begin to invest and set up incubators and use investment and improved service to promote founding and fast development of enterprises. A group of innovative incubators with new operation mode and strong innovation capability represented by Innovation Works, Garage Coffee and Makerspace become the most energetic new blood in Zhongguancun business incubator system and thus a new development pattern of business incubation in service industry with participation of state-owned capital, private capital, industry associations and private non-enterprise organizations and marketized operation is taking shape.

2. Economic benefits of incubators in Zhongguancun

Over the last 20 years, incubators in Zhongguancun have maintained a leading position in service innovation entrepreneurship and made remarkable achievements in attracting top talents for starting new businesses, cultivating successful entrepreneurs and strategic new industries, promoting transformation of scientific and technological achievements and carrying forward the culture of innovation and entrepreneurship, becoming core driving force of Zhongguancun development.

(1) Incubate a number of listed companies and enterprises. Incubators integrate such resources as capital, talents and technology based on needs of start-ups to accelerate their fast growth and give birth to a number of successful enterprises. So far, 55 incubators have incubated 48 listed companies including Venustech, ORG, Sumavision, Highlander and iREAL, accounting for 22% in Zhongguancun and 18% in Beijing. A total of 55 incubators have incubated 1,523 successful graduate enterprises with a graduate rate of 25%, among which 3 innovative incubators including Innovation Works have a graduate rate of 60%. Among all graduate enterprises, 561 get venture capital, accounting for 25% of all graduate enterprises and 36% of all enterprises in Beijing; 127 have been merged and acquired, accounting for 14% in Beijing; 787 have increased capital and shares; 57 have been named "Gold Seed Enterprises".

(2) Cultivate a number of entrepreneurs. Incubators take initiatives in establishing mechanism and platform for spotting, selecting and coaching outstanding talents for starting new businesses and helping in their transformation into successful entrepreneurs. Altogether, 55 incubators account for 15.7% talents in "1,000 Talents Plan", 35.7% talents in Overseas Talents Agglomeration Program and 77.4% talents in Top Talents Agglomeration Program. AAMA Cradle Plan includes enterprise tutors such as Lei Jun, Deng Feng and Zhou Hongyi and has coached 146 entrepreneurs including Chi Yufeng, Shen Wanqiu, Chen Ou and Guo Quji.

(3) Promote transformation and industrialization of a number of scientific and technological achievements. Incubators use accumulated resources in professional fields to integrate industry chain resources and provide professional technology platform and market expansion services to promote transformation and industrialization of a number of scientific and technological achievements. From January 2011 to June 2012, 55 incubators transformed 386 scientific and technological achievements of incubating enterprises and undertook 183 national and provincial science and technology programs in which high-temperature superconducting filter technology of HTS, high-speed low-power memory design technology of GigaDevice and two-photon fluorescence imaging technology and simplified microarray gene chip technology of Femtosecond are of international leading levels.

(4) Carry forward innovation and entrepreneurship culture in Zhongguancun. Incubators set up via varied channels and form a platform for new starters to interact and exchange with successful entrepreneurs, venture capitalists, experts and scholars. Zhongguancun entrepreneurship lecture has been held for over 80 times with attendance over 30,000; entrepreneurial CEO special training session held by Legend Star has trained 210 trainees; over 3,500 enterprises took part in entrepreneurship competitions organized by CYzone and the Founder; 3W Coffee has held over 300 Internet industry salon activities. A developed entrepreneurship atmosphere in Zhongguancun will ignite passion toward entrepreneurship of excellent talents. It is becoming very popular to resign and start new businesses. As serial entrepreneurship becomes a new manner of working, a virtuous cycle of "new business — success — more new business", similar to that in the Silicon Valley, will then be formed in Zhongguancun.

3. Innovative development of incubators in Zhongguancun

Zhongguancun has entered a new stage of innovative development by providing new starters with personalized business incubation services and becomes the weather vane of incubator development in China, leading Chinese incubator industry toward innovative development.

(1) Entrepreneurial entities become more diversified. In following the global trend of diversification, open innovation and entrepreneurship, social capital owners such as successful entrepreneurs, angel investors and platform companies become new force in driving development of incubators in Zhongguancun and promoting incubator development with innovation elements including industrial resources, venture capital and top talents to promote diversification of incubating entities and services similar to those in the Silicon Valley.

(2) The its operation mode of incubators becomes market-oriented. As angel investment in Zhongguancun develops quickly, entrepreneurs will demand better services and a trend of separation between property and service, and integration of investment and incubation will grow. Some innovative incubators combining early stage investing and deeper incubator services have already emerged, pushing the rents-dominated profit model of incubators toward that which relies more on capital and incubation services.

(3) Incubation services extend to early stage of entrepreneurship.
Constantly improving innovation and entrepreneurship environment and
urgent needs of leading enterprises for original technology and of angel
investors for excellent new projects in early stage attract outstanding
teams gathering in Zhongguancun. Some business incubation service
institutions devoted to serving entrepreneurs and early projects arise to
further improve entrepreneurship service chain in Zhongguancun.
Incubators in Zhongguancun are in a path of virtuous cycle of spotting,
gathering and graduating of potential start-ups. At present, 34 among
55 major incubators have established a mechanism of project selection,
incubation service, graduation, assessment and exit and a turnover rate of
incubating enterprises of 31% was achieved in 2011.

(4) Professional services grow more diversified. To meet growing specialized needs of start-ups, incubators in Zhongguancun starts to proceed
on the track of specialized incubation and differential services to establish
entrepreneurial education, entrepreneurial community, venture capital,
entrepreneurship coaching, technical development platform, technical
service platform and entrepreneurship media services. A typical example
of entrepreneurial education is the Ivy Pioneer Park; for entrepreneurial
community, there are Garage Coffee and Makerspace; for venture capital,
there are AngelCrunch and Chuantouquan; for entrepreneurship coaching,
there are Cradle Plan and Legend Star; for technical development platform, there are Sina Weibo Open Platform, Cloud Valley, UC open mobile
gaming platform and 360 freeware takeoff plan; for technical service
platform, there are 94 public technical platforms founded by 27 professional incubators including Zhongguancun Life Science Park; for entrepreneurship media, there are 36kr, the Founder and CYzone.

**(5) Incubating service is exported and expanded to the whole coun-
try.** Incubators in Zhongguancun expand their service scope through the
whole country via branding and service exporting. 60% of 55 major incubators export service externally. Innovation Works have set up branches
in Shanghai and Taiwan; 3W Coffee has established incubation base in
Shenzhen; Fengtai Business Incubation Center has founded 19 offices
in Fengtai District.

(6) Allocation of resources is going global. In pursuit of the development goal of establishing an innovation center for science and technology in Zhongguancun with global influence and in order to follow the trend of accelerated flow of global resources, incubators seek for and gather top projects within global range and link international technology, capital, market and talent resources by introducing branches of well-established foreign incubators, holding international exchange activities, sharing international enterprise tutor resources and setting up foreign incubators. Zhongguancun Zpark has introduced China–Finland Golden Bridge (Beijing) Innovation Center to provide services for Finnish enterprises settled in *Zhongguncun*; Tuspark has set up innovation incubator in Silicon Valley to establish a service platform for top overseas entrepreneurs to transfer to China.

4. Case study of various innovative incubators in Zhongguancun

(1) Comprehensive incubation model. Innovation Works is an investment institution dedicated to early-stage investment and providing all-round innovation fostering founded by Kaifu Lee in September 2009. As a comprehensive innovation platform, Innovation Works aims to foster innovative talents and high-tech enterprises of new generation. By providing a package of targeted services for capital, business, technology, market, manpower, legal affairs and training required by entrepreneurs in early stage, Innovation Works help start-ups in early stage to launch successfully and grow quickly. Meanwhile, it helps entrepreneurs to develop a number of products with greatest market value and commercial potentials. Innovation Works target its investment in the most popular fields in IT industry, including mobile Internet, consumer Internet, e-commerce and cloud computing.

Comprehensive incubation model as in Innovation Works features capital, office space, business and training services for start-ups in their seed stage as well as VC financing and even PE financing. Take Innovation Works as an example, it completed fund raising for its first dollar fund of USD 180 million on September 1, 2010 with participation of WI Harper Group, Foxconn Technology Group, New Oriental Group, SVB, Sequoia

Capital, IDG, Chunghwa Telecom, MTK, Qihoo 360, Canada Pension Plan Fund and Motorola. Such fund not only invests in seed enterprises, but also provides financing services for them after Series A.

(2) Open office model. Garage Café started business in April 2011 and entrepreneurs only need to pay for a coffee to enjoy free open office space for a whole day. Garage Café currently has 10 resident teams with irregular staying of new teams from time to time (after some time, some teams begin to have their own offices and leave). After operation for nearly two years, Garage Café has helped several teams to get angel investment. Garage Coffee comes up innovatively the concept of virtual incubation, namely Garage Entrepreneur Club to serve more entrepreneurs and help them to grow up faster and better. Every year, some teams will be selected for incubation from those registered by providing essential resources for starting new business, such as servers. What it mainly does is to help integrate resources, enhance internal communication and save resources. Open office space in Garage Coffee mainly features open office environment for entrepreneurs at low prices where they can open their minds and get into contact with other entrepreneurs and more investors. Innovative incubators of open office model only provide a platform for communication between entrepreneurs and investors rather than financial support.

(3) Technology media model. CYzone was jointly funded and established by IDG and Zero2IPO Group in January 2007. By 2010, CYzone had launched cyzone.cn, *CYzone Magazine* and various entrepreneurial activities. Cyzone.cn is a portal of information and interactions of Chinese entrepreneurs and strives to become an online home to Chinese entrepreneurs. *CYzone Magazine* is committed to being a paradise of ideas and a guide of action for entrepreneurs in China, providing solutions for various obstacles in development of growing small and medium-sized enterprises. Besides, CYzone holds regular entrepreneur salons, project demonstrations and other activities to promote offline interactions. Technology media represented by CYzone features its aim to provide latest information and practical handbooks about entrepreneurship for growing small and medium-sized enterprises in China, discuss relevant hot topics and solutions, hold offline and online activities including salons and project demonstrations, create platforms for offline and online communication, help entrepreneurs set up, accumulate and enrich business partner network and resources and in very rare cases invest directly.

In conclusion, innovative incubators bring forth new ideas mainly in service modes. Its advantages lie in providing more flexible space and services, more attentive infrastructure services and effective linking of all kinds of capital with incubators. Currently, incubators in Zhongguancun are in a good state of development and greatly promote development of angel investment.

Note

1. It is compiled based on *Creating a Center for Entrepreneurship with Greatest Global Attraction in Zhongguancun 2013* by Zhongguancun Administrative Committee.

Chapter 14

Development of Crowd Funding of Angel Investment in China

The idea of "crowd funding" has a long history which dates back to Germany in the 17th century when publishers came up with a business model called "Praenumeration". Under such a model, publishers collected advance payment for subscription fee at a discount and used such prepayment to support subsequent operations.

The development of Internet technology and acceleration of information exchanges have laid the foundation for the development of crowd funding. A typical early example of crowd funding is the tour of a British rock band "Marillion" in America, which was successful thanks to crowd funding.

With the success of crowd funding platforms such as Kickstarter and IndieGoGo and improvement in legal systems, global crowd funding market has prospered. According to a research report by Massolution, the total amount of global crowd funding rose sharply to USD 1.5 billion in 2011 from a mere USD 530 million in 2009; the number of global crowd financing platforms grew to over 450 in 2012 from less than 100 in 2007. As a supplement to traditional financing tools, crowd funding plays an increasingly important role in the context of booming "Internet Finance".

Schwienbacher and Larralde defined crowd funding as "a way of funding launched by a group of common individuals rather than professional teams for financing specific projects or starting new businesses".[1] Mollick pointed out that "crowd funding allows fundraisers of profitable projects, cultural projects or social projects to raise money from individual investors with promise of future products, shares or sense of identity".[2] As we can see, crowd funding has a few investment objects in common with angel investment but differs in investment subject and consideration payment. Current subjects of angel investment mainly include angel investors, angel investment groups, angel investment funds, incubators and professional investment platforms, while crowd funding tends to have the general public as subjects. Angel investments in narrow terms generally obtain subsequent profits allocated via equity, while crowd funding uses equity, creditor's right, material object or even non-physical element as a way of consideration payment.

In this section, we will discuss the opportunities and challenges faced by crowd funding patterns of angle investment in macro, industrial and legal aspects. We will also discuss this in the context of China's special economic environment and present local models proven to be feasible on the basis of existing practices.

1. Herald of a great era: Prospects from a macro perspective

(1) The gradual decline of "two bonuses". Since 2001, rapid economic development in China was driven by two bonuses: its population and its system. With the approach of the "Lewis turning-point" and increasing effects of the rule of decrease in marginal capital return, such two bonuses are phasing out in China. Thus it can be seen that innovation is an inevitable course to avoid falling into the "middle-income trap" in China. More importantly, innovation is a source of angel investment and a wave of innovations will bring unprecedented development opportunities for a variety of angel investment (including its innovative mode — crowd funding). In fact, we can already see an outline of "innovative age" from booming of culture and media and mobile Internet industries in recent year.

(2) The need for alternative financing channels. Alienation of "mainstream" financing system gives rise to a thirst for capital by start-ups. The difficulty in financing SMEs is a problem throughout the whole world, especially for start-ups. In the context of alienation of the "mainstream" financing system dominated by indirect financing in China, start-ups have a very strong need for alternative financing channels. Since crowd funding can take in social savings, such financing method is not only a supplement to but also a overturn of traditional financing channels.

(3) Integration of high net worth individuals may bring about abundant capital supply. High net worth individuals are an important source of angel investors. As the Chinese economy rapidly grew and increase in value of assets over recent years, a large number of high net worth individuals emerge in China with abundant capital for investment and high risk tolerance. As indicated in the Private Wealth Report of China Merchants Bank, China had 181,000 high net worth individuals in 2006 and the number has increased to 840,000 in 2013. High net worth individuals in China commanded per capita investable assets of RMB 28.72 million in 2006 and that amount had increased to RMB 31.8 million in 2013. According to the report of Bain & Company, most high net worth individuals in China prefer moderate and low risk for their personal investable assets (accounting for about 80% of interviewees). This may be an important reason as to why high net worth individuals have low participation in angel investment. However, as high net worth individuals become younger and knowledge of angel investment grows, entrepreneurs have a great chance of attracting their huge amount of capital with diversified sources via crowd funding.

(4) The flourishing of Internet finance accelerate transformation of ideas and systems. While Alipay's "YU E BAO" that comes out of nowhere helps create the historically first fund of over RMB 100 billion in China — "Tianhong Zengli Bao", it also shows the enormous potential of Internet finance in overturning traditional financing models. Although new to the business world, Internet finance represented by "YU E BAO", "Zhong An Online Insurance" and "Peer to Peer Lender" shows a surprising growth momentum. The coming new age of "Internet finance" will benefit crowd funding pattern of angel investment in three aspects: first, degree of recognition of the public of investment & financing via Internet platform will be increased to speed up transformation of ideas; second, improvement of relevant laws and building of basic information system by regulators will be promoted to benefit crowd funding platforms; third, savings of the pubic deposited in the bank system will be more effectively circulated and crowd funding platforms will benefit from such "capital overflow".

(5) Challenges of crowd funding in angle investment in macro perspective. Under the current macroeconomic environment, crowd funding pattern of angel investment faces a series of challenges, such as little support in taxes. *Notice of Tax Policies in Promoting Development of Venture Capital Enterprises by the Ministry of Finance and the State Administration of Taxation* introduces preferential tax policy for venture capital enterprises in investing in unlisted small and medium sized hi-tech enterprises. However, as the subject of angel investment in crowd funding pattern is the individual investor, such policies are not applicable. Of course, crowd funding requires standardization. Many governments are formulating relevant laws and regulations. On the one hand, if not properly managed, the outlaws may take advantage of crowd funding; on the other hand, excessive control may result in the destruction of such new financing modes.

2. "Dream Factory" for "grassroots angel investors": An industry-based analysis

In addition to the above macroeconomic effects, crowd funding pattern also helps to cure some defects in angel investment in China and therefore to provide an opportunity for healthy industrial development.

(1) Overcome geographic restrictions. Geographical concentration of investment is currently a major problem of angel investment in China. Angel investment mainly concentrates in economically developed regions due to costs of searching and investigation of projects, resulting in very limited access to capital for enterprises from interior regions which lack angel investment. However, there is no solid proof that developed regions are superior to others in innovation strength. Crowd funding based on Internet platforms may break such limitation to enable access to equal financing conditions for innovative projects nationwide. Kim and Hann, through a study of crowd funding projects and their geographic locations, found that small cities seemed to benefit more from crowd funding platforms, thus proving effects of crowd funding in breaking geographic restriction. If a nationwide angel investment crowd funding platform can be established, it can help open up a broader "innovation battlefield".[3]

(2) Make up for absence of protection for intellectual property rights in specific projects. Absence of protection for intellectual property rights is a key factor restricting development of innovation industry in China. Taking cultural industry as an example, low awareness of intellectual property rights of the public and lax regulatory oversight more often than not result in serious piracy of literature, music and film works. It prevents authors of such works to fully enjoy benefits of their labors, dampens their enthusiasm and leads to reduction in good works, forming a vicious cycle. However through crowd funding platforms, authors can get remunerations and subsidies in the way of "advance payment" before they complete their works, which will significantly reduce losses suffered due to piracy of works. However, since information of innovative projects needs to be disclosed on the Internet in the mode of crowd funding, ideas of some technology projects may be stolen. To address the problem of plagiarism of entrepreneurs' projects under the background of information disclosure is a major challenge that has emerged in crowd funding pattern of angel investment.

(3) Reduce the risk of information asymmetry between entrepreneurs and consumers. Market recognition for products remains a major risk of innovation projects. Even the most experienced angel investors are unable to accurately predict market sentiment and response. Ideas of entrepreneurs are often inconsistent with consumers' demands, which is a major cause of failure in starting new businesses. Crowd funding helps to minimize such information asymmetry between buyers and sellers. When financing goal of each project is achieved, it also means that consumers have endorsed for sales of products with their investment; if the goal is not achieved, it means the market disapprove of the project, leaving room for relevant projects to be canceled to avoid failures of high probability. Crowd funding combines investment with market survey to significantly avoid misallocation of resources and reduce risks of both investors and entrepreneurs.

(4) Contribute to integration and intensification of resources. Angel investors bring initial capital as well as help and support in terms of expertise, management and experience to entrepreneurs. Crowd funding platforms gather together investors with different resources to complement each other in order to integrate resources and maximize the probability of success of projects. Currently, many crowd funding platforms feature specific specialties, such as PetriDish, dedicated to fund raising for scientific research activities and MyC4, especially for charity projects in Africa. Specialized platforms help to gather investors of specific categories and intensify advantageous resources to enable investors to identify projects in a more purposeful manner.

While on the negative side, crowd funding is different inherently from angel investment in some aspects, which, if not properly dealt with, will result in challenges in their combination.

First, earning modes are inconsistent. Investors in crowd funding mode feature much more complex motives. A study by Greenberg, Hui and Gerber divided earnings of investors into six types: emotion, status, service, information, commodity and money, in which money is not the major return for investors.[4] For example, investors of Kickstarter mainly obtain goods and services; investors of IndieGoGo mainly obtain status and commodity; investors of RocketHub mainly obtain services. There may be legal explanations for it (remunerations in equity are subject to much supervision) and it also may have something to do with characteristics of crowd funding itself. Angel investment, for its sheer pursuit for financial benefits (or at least to a great extent), poses a potential challenge for possible successful operation in crowd funding platforms.

Second, difficulties for protecting medium and small investors further increase. Protection for medium and small investors remains a long-standing problem in the Chinese capital market and their interests are frequently hurt even in the Main Board Market where the supervision is relatively strict. Start-ups, on the one hand, cannot afford high cost of full information disclosure and on the other hand are concerned about leakage of intellectual properties due to excessive disclosure. Therefore, angel investment is inherently an industry of extremely high risk and insufficient information. If medium and small investors enter this industry, protection of their interests will be more challenging.

Third, crowding fund has negative effects on post-investment management. Angel investors can be divided into "cheque angel" (with only small investment), "added-value angel" (participated in operation of invested enterprises with large amount of investment) and "super angel" (providing unique support for invested enterprises with large amount of investment) based on the degree of their participation in post-investment management of invested enterprises. Under crowd funding pattern, most investors take part in post-investment management only as cheque angels, unable to provide substantial help for subsequent development of such enterprises. For those with large amount of investment, diluted rights to future earnings weaken their initiatives for post-investment management. As to invested enterprises, supports in strategies, brands and refinancing from investors are instrumental to forming long-term competitive capacity. Trying to minimize negative effects on post-investment management is an unavoidable challenge faced by crowd funding pattern of angel investment.

Fourth, communication cost increases. For fundraisers, their cost actually consists of two parts: 1. Direct cost of financing by angel investors; 2. Cost of necessary communication with investors. The total cost of fund-raisers fits into a U shape normal curve. As the number of investors increases, the cost of capital has a descending trend as the supply increases. However, communication cost shows an increasing trend as the number of investors increases. When the number of investors is too much, even cost of capital saved is not enough to cover communication cost increased.

3. Legal boundary of crowd funding in angle investment

Legal restraint is the most direct and real obstacle in promoting a crowd funding pattern of angel investment in China.

(1) Relevant laws and regulations in America. JOBS (Jumpstart Our Business Act) officially signed to law by President Barack Obama in April 2012 relaxed restraints on crowd funding of angel investment, providing it with a clear legal basis in America.

The Securities Act of 1933 stipulates that all securities issued or sold must be registered with the SEC unless they qualify for exemptions. Since the amount of crowd funding is usually not very large, it is impossible to afford the high cost of registration at SEC. The JOBS Act includes qualified crowd funding pattern into the scope of exempted transactions to avoid SEC registration, making crowd funding of angel investment in equity trading possible. The "JOBS Act" took full consideration of protection of investors' interests during rule making by controlling risk with a cap for investment amount on the one hand and imposing many requirements on fundraisers and intermediaries on the other hand (see Table 14.1.).

The introduction of the JOBS Act plays a decisive role in development of crowd funding pattern of angel investment in America. As calculated by Crowdsourcing.org, there are 536 crowd funding websites worldwide by December 2013 and 60% of them were founded in 2012 (after promulgation of JOBS Act).

(2) Changes in supervision in China. Compared to the US, China has no official laws or regulations on crowd funding yet and crowd funding of angel investment has not been clearly approved or prohibited by laws.

However, we can see some positive signals. It is reported that one bank, three commissions (People's Bank of China, China Securities Regulatory Commission, China Insurance Regulatory Commission and China Banking Regulatory Commission) and the Ministry of Industry and Information Technology are busy laying down methods for supervision of Internet finance to define supervision responsibilities, in which equity-based crowd funding will be under the charge of the China Securities Regulatory Commission. In March 2014, the China Securities Regulatory Commission spokesman pointed out in a press conference that the Commission was surveying on equity-based crowd funding and would introduce relevant guidelines. In June 2014, another official source indicated that the new revision of Securities Law was intended to provide some legal basis for equity-based crowd funding. In the end of October 2015, US Securities and Exchange Commission approved regulations in relation to Title III of the 2012 JOBS Act, which is good news for promoting the development of local crowd funding investment industry. On the whole, regulators have been brought to attention of legal basis for crowd funding of angel investment and are now seeking to make substantial breakthrough to put an end to the situation of lack in laws and regulations for crowd funding of angel investment.

Table 14.1   Articles of the JOBS Act.

Legal Entity	Articles
Investors	• Investors are not allowed to resell securities from crowd funding within a year. • If investors' earnings are less than USD 100,000 in the first 12 months, their investment amount shall not exceed USD 2000 or 5% of their annual earnings (the larger one). • If investors' earnings exceed USD 100,000 in the first 12 months, their investment amount shall not exceed 10% of their annual earnings with a upper limit of USD 100,000.
Fundraisers	• After filing at SEC, fundraisers shall disclose information as specified to investors and intermediaries (different requirements of information disclosure for different amount of fund raising). • Fundraisers are allowed to send notices to investors via network platforms of intermediaries, but advertising promotion is prohibited. • Restrictions are imposed on how fundraisers compensate promoting personnel and compensation plan shall be disclosed. • Fundraisers shall submit to SEC and investors annual reports about enterprise operations and financial status.
Intermediaries	• Intermediaries shall register at SEC as brokers or funding portals. • Intermediaries shall register at an approved self-regulation association. • Intermediaries shall explain risks of crowd funding to investors and educate them. • Intermediaries shall take actions to reduce frauds in crowd funding transactions. • When intended targets are not met, Intermediaries are not allowed to provide fund raised. • It shall be ensured that investors have not exceeded maximum investment amount. • Measures shall be taken to protect privacy of investors. • Restricts shall be imposed on compensations for promotion. • Intermediaries and fund raisers shall be prevented from forming any interest relationship.

Source: Authors' own compilation.

(3) Possible legal risks in China. Since equity trading is involved, crowd funding is faced with two legal risks: 1) Approval is required for "public offering" with more 200 shareholders as specified in Securities Law (2006) in China; 2) Plan design and operation of crowd funding must comply with relevant regulations in "Explanations to Several Issues in Specific Application of Laws in Hearing Illegal Fund-Raising Criminal Cases".

4. Localized practice of crowd funding angel investment

In recent years, some successful pioneers stood out in combining angel investment with crowd funding in China and most of them adopt the form of "equity-based crowd funding". In this section, a brief introduction will be given on two most representative projects: AngelCrunch and Chuantouquan.

(1) The "leading + following" pattern. The "leading + following" pattern of AngelCrunch went into operation (online) in November 2011. AngelCrunch is the pioneer company in China to provide platform of angel crowd funding for angel investors and start-ups. AngelCrunch adopts a "leading + following" pattern in its operations. As the name suggests, investors are divided into "leading investors" and "following investors". Leading investors have a higher threshold and take more responsibilities and obligations and therefore are returned with more rights and earnings. In fact, WeFunder, Angelist and other overseas equity-based crowd funding platforms in addition to AngelCrunch work in the same manner.

In October 2013, AngelCrunch together with other institutions and angel investors released "Rules of Leading Investment of Angel Crowd Funding in China" (Rules), providing outlines and guidelines for leading investors in crowd funding angel investment in China. According to the Rules, "leading investors" are different from "following investors" in rights and obligations, as outlined in Table 14.2.

Such a model is designed to ease to some extent problems of angel crowd funding in general sense. Firstly, one leading investor or two joint leading investors should be determined to avoid absence of post-investment management due to excessively scattered investment. Secondly, leading investors attend directors' meeting while following

Table 14.2   Rights and Obligations of "Leading Investors" and "Following Investors".

Investor	Rights and Obligations
Leading investors	<ul><li>Leading investors are authenticated investors in AngelCrunch.</li><li>They take precedence in viewing candidate projects and projects recommended by leading investors' Wechat group.</li><li>Leading investing projects have priority to quick combined investment service.</li><li>Leading investors participate in post-investment management of projects on behalf of following investors, attend directors' meetings, obtain 5–20% profit-sharing (the specific percentage is subject to joint decision of project owners and leading investors).</li><li>Performance and returns of leading investment in specific segments will become investment track records of relevant investors in such fields and an important reference in deciding whether to follow or not by other investors.</li></ul>
Following Investors	<ul><li>Following investors have the same investment terms with leading investors.</li><li>Following investors should confirm to pay 5–20% profit sharing to leading investors, but no overheads are required.</li><li>Entrepreneurs and leading investors have the final say in the selection of following investors and allocation of shares. If the subscribed amount exceeds the total amount, leading investors and entrepreneurs can choose trustworthy following investors capable of providing important added values to companies and if subscribed amount still exceeds the total amount, it is suggested to reduce contribution percentage of all investors.</li><li>If following investors can provide rare and significant values, entrepreneurs may consider offering additional options as compensation, but information disclosure is required.</li><li>If investment amount of following investors in certain round exceeds 50% or accounts for accumulatively over 20% of total shares of enterprises, an application can be made for an observation seat in directors' meeting and entrepreneurs and leading investors will decide whether to grant permission for such application.</li><li>Following investors may request for due diligence of projects, but it is up to entrepreneurs to decide whether to fully disclose all information.</li><li>Following investors may send inquiries via AngelCrunch platform if they have any doubt about information disclosure of projects and investment management by leading investors.</li><li>Following investors do not participate in major decision making of companies or investment management. If following investors ask to exit prematurely, they need to abide by arrangements by the board of directors and leading investors to automatically exit according to partnership agreements or apply to exit via AngelCrunch or assign at LP share assignment platform. Premature exits of following investors will be recorded and leading investors during selection will screen out following investors with a record of frequent premature exits.</li></ul>

investors do not participate in major decision making; leading investors serve as the only medium of communication between investors and investees to avoid "communication cost" that are too high due to the involvement of too many investors. Thirdly, high requirements for leading investors include certain professional competence and investment experience as well as relevant credit records and performance evaluation system help to reduce investment risks to some extent and avoid unwise investment of the public.

In addition to AngelCrunch, another crowd funding platform — "Dajiatou" adopts the same "leading + following" pattern with the only difference lies in that AngelCrunch is targeted to elites while Dajiatou is targeted to the general public. AngelCrunch is very particular about their leading and following investors and pick a team of investors of less than 1,000 from over 5,000 candidates. Those without risk resistance capacity and working experience can never pass the assessment or see projects of AngelCrunch. Therefore, AngelCrunch is more like a community open only for investors rather than an open platform for the general public. By contrast, Dajiatou has significantly low thresholds: leading investors should have some working experience while there is almost no restriction on following investors.

(2) Dynamic fund model of Chuantouquan. Established in June 2011, Chuantouquan was jointly funded by Tianshihui and Innovation Works and positioned itself as an "investment and financing platform of a new generation". It introduces a new service concept of "VC2.0: Dynamic Fund" on the basis of existing combined investment services.

Compared to "combined investment" in general, dynamic fund is more standardized. General combined investment is defective in ambiguous responsibilities and undefined returns, while dynamic fund combines traditional forms of fund with venture capital projects to clearly define rights and responsibilities of each interested party. Meanwhile, venture capital projects operated in the form of funds can be included into traditional legal framework to avoid many compliance risks. Compared with "combined investment" in general, dynamic funds have smaller scopes. A dynamic fund is only targeted to qualified investors with risk resistance capacity and usually limits the number of investors to less than 20. In short, a dynamic fund is a kind of more standardized combined investment and a way of crowd investment with participation of only a few qualified investors.

On a dynamic fund platform, there are two types of investors. They are general partners (GP) and limited partner (LP). GPs only need to provide a small amount of funds (such as 5%) for projects and the platform will contact other LP to provide the remaining funds. However, GPs are responsible for leading investment and management of investment projects, while LPs pay a proportion of investment income (such as 20%) to GPs as returns for their services. Small investors can choose to be GPs or LPs.

Such mode as dynamic fund combines traditional fund framework with venture capital projects to become a more standardized angel crowd funding mode, greatly reduce compliance risk of angel crowd funding.

5. Reflections on local models of angel investment crowd funding

The following three ways are more practical for developing angel investment crowd funding with less resistance in combination of macro-economic situation, industrial development level and legal environment.

(1) Limit the "crowd" in "crowd funding". By doing so, this helps to target specific investors rather than the general public. Such limitation has three advantages: firstly, limited number of investors helps to avoid legal risks of "public offering" and "illegal fund raising"; secondly, selection of experienced investors helps to avoid the risk of blindness in investment so as to indirectly protect interests of investors; thirdly, it helps to avoid excessive scattering of equity, reduce communication cost and address problems in post-investment management. AngelCrunch, which is a domestic angel investment project in crowd funding pattern with good performance, adopts such method.

(2) Establish investing platform for non-financial proceeds. For the general public who are not professional angel investors, financial proceeds are often not their only purpose for investment. Emotion, status, service, information and commodity are very important consideration during their investment and some of them even want to invest for charity purpose without asking for any return. If a platform of investors is focused on such group of investors, no equity transaction is involved and most legal risks can be avoided. Meanwhile, it can also adequately finance some small projects.

(3) Use crowd funding of angel investment funds to attract social capital. There is no doubt that absorbing idle funds from the society is the main purpose of angel investment activities via crowd funding platforms. Direct contact between investors and fundraisers is not necessarily required to achieve this purpose. Angel investment funds can be used to bridge investors and fund-raisers. Since funds are standard products, their legal risks are lower than crowd funding directly for projects. Meanwhile, specialized investment of fund managers and the law of large numbers also help to reduce high risk of single project in angel investment so as to protect small and medium investors.

Notes

1. Armin Schwienbacher and Benjamin Larralde. 'Crowdfunding of Small Entrepreneurial Ventures,' in Douglas Cumming (ed.), *The Oxford Handbook of Entrepreneurial Finance* (Oxford University Press, 2010), pp. 369–391.
2. Ethan R. Mollick, 'The Dynamics of Crowdfunding: An Exploratory Study,' SSRN Working Paper, June 26, 2013, available online at http://papers.ssrn.com/sol3/papers.cfm?abstract_id=2088298.
3. Keongtae Kim and Il-Horn Hann, 'Does Crowdfunding Democratize Access to Finance? A Geographical Analysis of Technology Projects,' SSRN Working Papers, October 13, 2015, available online at http://papers.ssrn.com/sol3/papers.cfm?abstract_id=2334590.
4. Michael Greenberg, Julie Hui and Elizabeth Gerber, 'Crowdfunding: A Resource Exchange Perspective,' Working Paper, 2013, available online at http://www.juliehui.org/wp-content/uploads/2013/09/greenberg_resource exchange.pdf.

Appendices

Appendix I: Selected Active Angels in China

Name	Background	Personal Style
XU Xiaoping	Founder of ZhenFund (2006 to date); co-founders of New Oriental Education and Technology Group.	• Known as the most popular angel investor among entrepreneurs, he never reads financial reports and makes off-the-cuff decisions. If a project does not interest him within 30 minutes, he will turn it down. • At the end of 2012, Gong Haiyan, founder of Jiayuan.com, which he invested in, left to set up 91 Waijiao.com and he provided financial support again without hesitation. He never quits a project halfway because he believes that one should never back off after he/she starts something.
LEI Jun	Founder, Chairman and CEO of Xiaomi Technology (2010 to date); CEO and President of Kingsoft.	• He often participates in the early stages of projects. Generally, he comes up with a good idea and finds a partner for investment. In this sense, he is more like an investor in entrepreneur's role. Those who have worked their ideas for a long time come to Lei Jun to work out plans together and then Lei Jun makes investment and bring them into operation. • He only invests for those he knows. • He makes investment decisions based on entrepreneurs and their teams. • He is not a full-time angel investor and angel investment is only his hobby.

ZENG Liqing	Executive Director of Decent Capital (2007 to date) and Co-founder of Tencent.

- He usually selects one project and one direction and then finds some partners to work it out. Founders of companies he invested in call him "boss" and he is the largest shareholder in many companies.
- His investments are large in amount, generally RMB2–10 million.
- For more than half of the projects, he invests in them right from the beginning; he usually selects projects together with entrepreneurs and participates in their operations.
- Basically he only invests in the projects of former employees of Tencent and those recommended by friends and those he knows.

JI Qi	Founder and Chairman of Hanting and Co-founder of Ctrip.

- His investment in a project will not exceed US$1 million and he usually holds shares of 10%–20%.
- He is rarely engaged in a company's operations after investment.

HE Boquan	Chairman of Invest Today (2003 to date); Founder of former Robust.

- His investment is based on customers and he mainly focuses on service industry.

CAI Wensheng	Chairman of CNZZ and Meitu; Founder of 265.com

- He has accurate and quick judgment of innovation trend and even faster actions.

LV Tanping	In 1988, he and Liu Chuanzhi jointly founded Legend Computer Ltd. (Hong Kong); in 1997, he set up APTG Ventures; in 2000, he established Authosis Ventures; in 2005, he together with several partners jointly set up a new VC fund — Startup Capital Ventures.

- Projects he invested can be divided into two types: one for economic returns and the other to offer help in which economic returns are not the major consideration.
- He is inclined to invest in TMT (technology, media and telecommunications) industries.
- He is against valuation adjustment mechanism and claims that no investment should be made without trust.

(*Continued*)

Appendix I (*Continued*)

Name	Background	Personal Style
BAO Fan	Founder and CEO of China Renaissance (2004 to date).	• His investment usually ranges from RMB 500,000 to several million. • He gives support to startups but does not involve much in the operations of such companies.
YANG Xiangyang	Founder and Chairman of Yuanzheng Ventures (1994 to date).	• He has some unique views about healthcare industry. • His investment is not targeted at certain medicine and drugs but the whole market. • He believes healthcare reform is sure to come. • He believes that it is the new dawn of R&D of new drugs.
Alvin Liu	Founder and CEO of A8 Music (2000 to date).	• He mainly invests in industries he is familiar with or those with enough resources and he often holds shares of no more than 30% in companies.
Kevin Day	Comsenz CEO (2001 to date).	• He often finds projects through recommendations of friends and holds shares of no more than 20% in companies. • He focuses on consumption-based Internet and game-related projects.
ZHOU Hongyi	Chairman of Qihoo 360 (2006 to date).	Real angel investors share three common characteristics: • Investors should be entrepreneurs themselves with the experience in founding enterprises. This enables them to have a deep understanding of the operation, especially the overall development, of enterprises, and gain experience and learn from lessons.

	• Angel investors have to invest in a specific industry in which they have profound understanding rather than shooting in the dark. • Angel investors should have a good knowledge of the rules of capital operation.
YANG Ning	Partner and Founder of LeBox (2011 to date); former president of Kongzhong; CEO of Sun Wukong.
	• Devoted to investment in telecommunication, Internet and media industries.
MAI Gang	Founder and Producer of Ventures Lab (2005 to date).
	• He has preference for smart, hard-working and persistent teams with foresight and plans and the capacity of self-denial. • Investment amount: RMB500,000–5,000,000.
WANG Lijie	Partner of PreAngel (2011 to date); Founder of Mobile 2.0.
	• Investment amount: RMB100,000–1,000,000. • Early involvement with supports in addition to funds for enterprises.
LI Zhu	Partner of Innovation Angel Funds (2013 to date); CEO of Beijing UUsee Interactive Technology Co., Ltd.
	• Tend not to be that rational and usually decide to invest after several meetings with entrepreneurs and finding them nice. • Investment amount: RMB3–5 million.
TONG Weiliang	Founder of Wutongshu Capital (2013 to date); active angel investor.
	• Very good at strategic planning, business development and marketing integration with nearly 20 years' experience in TMT industry. • Good-tempered and willing to share risks with startups in the early period; a lover of culture and arts when he was young.

(*Continued*)

Appendix I (*Continued*)

Name	Background	Personal Style
ZHOU Zhe	Former Senior Manager of Google.	• Provide technical support. • Not involved in company management.
WANG Tong	Original Founder and Managing Partner of Beiruan Angel (2013 to date).	• Help and grow with entrepreneurs and provide more than funds. • Learn from entrepreneurs and keep innovating.
WANG Xiao	Partner of Unity Ventures (2011 to date); former original Senior Manager of Baidu.	• Prefer technical or product-type projects. • Investment amount: less than RMB2 million; joint investment in case projects need more than RMB2 million. • Shareholding percentage: 10%–25%.

Source: Compiled by Zhao Changhai (doctoral candidate, Renmin University of China) based on data from the Internet, research reports and literatures.

Appendix II: Interview Summary

Category	Information of Interviewees	Interview Summary
Angel investors (Individual/ Group/ Organization)	**Mr. Tang Tao**, one of ten "Prominent Angel Investors" named by *The Founder*; his new book *Angel Investment* has been endorsed by over 50 angel investors including Xu Xiaoping and Lei Jun. (San Francisco, US; April 17, 2013).	• The fundamental characteristic of angel investment is high risk, which requires people engaged in angel investment to have a rational understanding of and certain tolerability to it. • For entrepreneurs, they themselves are their biggest and earliest investors. • Angel investors in China are mainly defined "commercial angel investors". No matter for relatives, friends, acquaintance or strangers, angel investment operation should be standardized.
	Mr. Cao Haitao, General Manager and Director of BGCapital, former Deputy Director of Beijing Equity Investment Fund Association Office and former Auditor of KPMG. (Beijing, China; May 27, 2013).	• Before starting new businesses, university students should try to establish a good concept of internship and entrepreneurship values. • Investment in enterprises is in essence investment in "people". In addition to interpersonal skills, leaders of enterprises should be honest, kind, charitable and grateful and know how to maintain proper relationships with subordinates and employees.

(*Continued*)

Appendix II (*Continued*)

Category	Information of Interviewees	Interview Summary
	Mr. Liao Wenjian, Chairman of Blue Source Investment Group and concurrently Executive Chairman of Hong Kong China Educational Fund, Vice President of China Equity Investment Research Center and Lecturer for SMEs Listing Alliance of the Chinese Ministry of Industry and Information Technology. (Ningbo, China; June 17, 2013).	• Projects attracting interests from angel investors are usually at seed stage or startup stage with high risks; therefore, high requirements are imposed on angel investment organizations in terms of insights into and decisions on macro policy orientation, industry development prospect, profit forecast, quality of project teams. • Angel investment is essentially different from PE and VC; hence, transformation in concepts is required for practitioners of angel investment.
	Mr. Pan Jiancheng, Chairman of Pivot PE and concurrently Director General of Xin'anjiang Forum, Lecturer of EMBA Investment Training Class of Shanghai Jiaotong University, Chief Researcher of Xi'an Institute of Optics And Fine Mechanics of Chinese Academy of Sciences and Trainer of Business Model of China MBA Entrepreneurship Finals. (Beijing, China; June 17, 2013).	• Angel investment is about the investment stage rather than the size of investment amount, as we know some high-tech projects may require an initial fund of dozens of millions. • Institutionalization is a possible trend of angel investment since the entire market in China would have great moral hazards and many factors beyond control without marketization. For angel investment, resources integration, great efforts in training and guiding, following closely with industrial economy, mobilization of various resources to help investees are required. The investment industry is itself a financial service industry and will be nothing without the real economy.

Mr. Zhang Jun, Partner of Preangel Fund. (Shanghai, China; June 27, 2013).

- Angel investment transactions sometimes lack formal binding agreements and some projects are subject to informal investment agreements based on mutual trust. However, it cannot serve as a common practice. A formal investment agreement helps to bind behaviors of entrepreneurs and reduce risks for investors.
- Angel investment is not only a business for pursuing economic returns. Angel investors are sometimes enterprising and hope to contribute to growth of a great company. However, it is hard to tell a great company right from the beginning. Therefore, persistent support for projects is required rather than exiting in haste.

Prof. Feng Guanping, Chairman of Leaguer Angel Partnership and concurrently Chairman of Shenzhen Enterprise Merger & Acquisition Promotion Association; former President of Research Institute of Tsinghua University in Shenzhen. (Shenzhen, China; July 8, 2013).

- Angel investment in China has just started with only a few investors. Why? Firstly, the number of successful entrepreneurs is small. They mainly focus on their businesses and some of their companies have gone public, requiring more time and effort from them. Therefore, they can find no time for angel investment. Secondly, it is believed that angel investment has poor returns and quick success is the prevailing mindset in China for a long time. There are many overnight millionaires in China and one of their features is earning big bucks in a short time.
- Government should also focus on angel investment although its experience is limited.
- We need to learn from successful experience or lessons from the failures of angel investment in China.

(Continued)

Appendix II (*Continued*)

Category	Information of Interviewees	Interview Summary
	Mr. **Liu Hao**, Partner and Deputy General Manager of Green Pine Capital Partners (Shenzhen, China; July 8, 2013).	• An angel investor should have the following characteristics: recognition, professionalism, good state of mind and service awareness. • Study of angel investment requires entrepreneurial education with young people and trainings with angel investors. This is of great practical significance for the popularization of the knowledge in angel investment and innovation & entrepreneurship and for establishing a culture of innovation & entrepreneurship and angel investment.
	Mr. **Yu Bo**, Partner of Inno Valley with years' experience in Internet, games and media industries and rich experience in product R & D, content operation and marketing (Shenzhen, China; July 10, 2013).	• Many angel investors in China were fake ones who always reviewed projects but never made investment. • Incubating services provided by investment institutions are mainly for finding quality projects and improving conversion rate.
	Mr. **Lu Enze**, current Partner of Edwards Wildman Palmer and concurrently Honorary Legal Advisor and Member of HKBAN (Hong Kong, China; July 11, 2013).	• Investment culture of angle investment market in China needs further development and improvement. • Entrepreneurs usually lack specialized knowledge in corporate governance and finance. Angel investors with relevant resources may involve deeply into projects on the premise of not affecting daily decision making of startups; otherwise, initiatives of entrepreneurs will be compromised.

Dr. Dominic Chan, current Founder of Dark Horse Investment and D & S Consulting and concurrently Honorary Project Director of Center for Entrepreneurial Studies of Chinese University of Hong Kong; former Senior Manager of international companies including McKinsey and EF. (Hong Kong, China; July 15, 2013).

- Since angel investment is still a vague concept, different investors define angel investment in different ways. Therefore, it will be challenging.
- Angel investment group pattern requires a more efficient and rigorous management system.
- Angle investment research institutes, angel investment agencies and incubators need to pay attention to the training of entrepreneurs' operation and project valuation capabilities and should collect proper fees for those training sessions to increase the survival rate of their projects.

Mr. Li Jun, current Founding Partner of iCamp. Graduated from Peking University and majored in semiconductor, Mr. Li Jun took part in founding five well-known enterprises in the semiconductor industry in America and Japan, including SPLX and CDNS. He also participated in the early stage investment and incubation of over 10 startups in America, Japan and China. Besides, he is a member of Silicon Valley Angel. (Silicon Valley, US; March 20, 2014).

- Silicon Valley has two kinds of incubations: 1. product-based incubators, such as Y Combinator; 2. market-based incubators, such as 500 Startups. Instead of incubation, it is about helping enterprises to grow fast and incubators gradually evolve to accelerators in this process.
- Immaturity of investment projects in China is down to its immature legal, regulatory and entrepreneurial environment.

(Continued)

Appendix II (*Continued*)

Category	Information of Interviewees	Interview Summary
	Mr. James Connor, Senior Member of Sand Hill Angels with nearly thirty years' experience as an angel investor. (Silicon Valley, US; March 20, 2014).	• Angel investment is different from VC in the ways it deals with invested enterprises. VC tends to control invested enterprises, while angel investment tends to cooperate with them. • Angel investment is like gambling, both with a high risk and the possibility of losing all. However, angel investment is a positive boost to social climate. It is better to invest in entrepreneurs and industries you are interested in and consider promising rather than losing money in Las Vegas.
	Mr. John Glynn, Partner and Manager of the century-old Glynn Capital Management in America; teaching entrepreneurship courses in Stanford Graduate School of Business, University of Cambridge and University of Virginia's Darden School of Business. (Silicon Valley, US; March 21, 2014).	• Quality of entrepreneurs can be measured bytheir passion, confidence, spirit of adventure, no fear for failure and excellent business capability. • There are many angel investors and venture capitalists in the Silicon Valley and their network of relationships helps to locate great projects.
	Mr. Sherman Ting, current Member of the Board of Directors of Sand Hill Angels with 25 years' technical, management and entrepreneurial experience in hi-tech field and a very active angel investor. (Silicon Valley, US; March 21, 2014).	• There are more and more micro VCs with capital of US$10–35 million in the Silicon Valley devoted to investment in small startups. Some of them evolve from large VC funds and are willing to spend more time in entrepreneurs and others are platform funds brought by Google and Facebook.

Interviewee	Viewpoints
Mr. Allan W. May, Partner and Chairman of the Board of Life Science Angels, a non-profit angel investment club in America. (Silicon Valley, US; March 21, 2014).	• The social network is an important source of projects for angel investors. • All startups in the life science industry are bound to get into trouble. As angel investors, we need to try every means to help them out, not only for economic benefits, but also for the benefits of future generations brought by such companies.
Mr. John May, current Partner of New Vantage Group, Honorary Chairman of ACA and Co-Chairman of WBAA. (Washington DC, US; March 28, 2014).	• He lays emphasis on "human" factors in startups, namely passions, professionalism and patience. • Compared with individual investment, angel investment funds invest in more projects. Meanwhile, VC is not in the opposite toangel investment and sometimes they can be in cooperative relationship.
Ms. Susan Preston, General Partner of CalCEF. She focuses on projects in clean technology. She is a world-renowned expert in angel financing and investment and non-profit organization management. (Washington DC, US; March 28, 2014).	• She supports development of angel investment fund markets and underlines the importance of standardized operation. • Crowd funding platforms help to create healthy angel investment competition environment.

(Continued)

Appendix II (*Continued*)

Category	Information of Interviewees	Interview Summary
Angel investment organization/ association	**Ms. Dai Shuang**, current Director of Government Procurement Executive Office of Zhongguancun and Executive Vice Secretary-General of Beijing Association for Science and Technology and Zhongguancun Entrepreneurs Angle Investment Union. (Beijing, China; May 20, 2013).	• The government needs to introduce public policies to address urgent and common problems in the processes of angel investment. Startups are still eager for funds even after obtaining angel investment. The most urgent problem now is that most products from startups after entering the market will have an impulse-type financing demand. The government should pay attention to financing and marketing problems of invested projects, create conditions and continuously give support to them.
	Mr. Yang Debin, current Chairman of Hong Kong Business Angel Network (Hong Kong, China; July 15, 2013).	• The government may guide angel investment institutions towards more standardized operation via some investment guiding plans to further enhance development potential of angel investment.

Source: Interviews by the authors of the book during April 2013 and June 2014, some of which have been published in *China Venture Capital and Securities Herald.*

Appendix III: List of Selected Angel Investment Organizations and Agencies in China

Organizations/Agencies	Types	State of Development (Founding Time and Current Status)
China Young Angel Investor Leader Association	Angel Group	• Founded in January 2013, China Young Angel Investor Leader Association aims to encourage more people to get involved in angel investment and provide better assistance for angel investors. • In 2014, Shanghai Branch, Guangdong Branch and Zhejiang Branch were established. • Main activities: angel investment salons, VC salons and VC Face-to-Face salons.
Zhongguancun Hundred Angel Investors' Meeting	Angel Group	• As a secondary branch of Zhongguancun Private Equity & Venture Capital Association, it aims to train angel investors and create a project information communication platform to introduce top talents, financial resources and technological resource nationwide and even worldwide to settle in Zhongguancun, in order to provide great angel investment projects for member organizations.
China Business Angel Association (CBAA)	Business Angel Network	• Prepared at an early stage and legally registered in Hong Kong, CBAA is an angel investment association for the Greater China Region. • Officially founded in June 2013, CBAA is the only member of World Business Angels Association an international authoritative angel investment organization, in China. It is affiliated with the China Association of Technology Entrepreneurs under the Ministry of Science and Technology.

(Continued)

Appendix III   *(Continued)*

Organizations/Agencies	Types	State of Development (Founding Time and Current Status)
Angel Camp	Angel Group	• It was founded in 2014. • It is a non-profit platform for angel investing training.
Angel's Home	Angel Group	• It was founded in 2015. • It provides angel investing training, seminar, co-investment opportunities and post-investment service for business angels and potential angels.
Zhongguancun Angel Capital Association (Zangels)	Business Angel Network	• Established in July 2013, the association has enrolled hundreds of organization members and individual members since then. • It focuses on serving for active angels and angel groups based in Z-park, and it aims to create an open platform and organization for sharing domestic angel investment resources and services.
Canton Angel Investment Association	Association	• Founded in 2012, Canton Angel Investment Association is a non-profit, professional angel investment industry organization legally incorporated with legal personality. • It advocates transparent angel investment, promote rational innovation and entrepreneurship, and create an early stage financing platform to secure win-win situation for projects and funds.
Grassroots Angel Investor Club	Angel Group	• Initiated and founded on June 17, 2012 in Shenzhen, Grassroots Angel Investor Club is devoted to serving grassroots angel investors in China by providing project selection, incubation, training and financing and investment services.
South China Angel Investor Club	Business Angel Network	• It was jointly founded by South China University of Technology and Guangzhou Venture Capital Promotion Association in 2006.

Shenzhen Angel Investor Club	Business Angel Network	• Founded in 2007, it is a non-profit social organization voluntarily organized by individuals and institutions engaged in angel investment in Shenzhen and surrounding cities and affiliated with Shenzhen Financial Advisor Association. • It prepares regular internal angel investment references and holds "angel investment lunches" and "angel investment project roadshows" from time to time.
Shanghai Angel Investment Club	Business Angel Network	• Founded in 2008, it is affiliated with Shanghai Technology Entrepreneurship Foundation for Graduates. • It aims to gather angel investors nationwide, increase professional standards of angel investment and further improve social entrepreneurial financing and investment environment. Shanghai Angel Investment Club welcomes people of all circles who have passions for angel investment.
Tianfu Angel Investment Club	Business Angel Network	• As the first angel investment club in Sichuan founded in 2011, Tianfu Angel Investment Club focuses on excellent Internet projects. • It advocates transparent angel investment, promote rational innovation and entrepreneurship and create an early stage financing platform with an aim to secure win–win situation for projects and funds. It mainly serves entrepreneurs and teams in western China.
Henan Club of Angel Investor	Business Angel Network	• It was jointly initiated and founded by Henan Youth Federation, Henan Young Entrepreneurs Foundation, Henan Investment Guarantee Industry Alliance, Henan Businessmen Federation and Henan Youth Entrepreneurship and Employment Association (the Articles of Association were adopted in January 2011). • It provides professional angel investment training, exchange and sharing of experience, projects coaching and investment and financing.

(Continued)

Appendix III (Continued)

Organizations/Agencies	Types	State of Development (Founding Time and Current Status)
China Optics Valley Angel Investment Club	Business Angel Network	• Founded in April 2014, China Optics Valley Angel Investment Club was planned by Donghu Hi-Tech Zone and conducts business at Optics Valley Startup Café. • It aims to establish a platform to connect angel investors with projects in the early stage, arrange meetings between VC funds with entrepreneurial teams in the Optics Valley, promote the combination of technology and finance and help startups solve the problem of insufficient funds with broader financing channels to achieve the goal of "gathering global resources and make Optics Valley known in the world".
Nanjing Golden Angel Venture Capital Club	Business Angel Network	• Founded in 2011, Golden Angel was initiated by Nanjing Committee of Science and Technology and admitted 23 members when founded. It aims to create an early stage investment and financing public platform for technology business incubators in Nanjing, especially for entrepreneurs in Zijin Technology Incubation Special Park, technology projects and businessmen in Nanjing.
Dalian Jinshi Angel Investment Club	Business Angel Network	• Founded in November 2005, it is a network investment service platform mainly for angel investors and technological entrepreneurs. • It provides such services as e-magazines, e-books, investment funds, project financing and resources integration for mutual growth.
AngelVest	Angel Group	• Founded in 2007, it is a subordinate body of Asia America Multi-technology Association Shanghai Branch. • It is devoted to helping Chinese entrepreneurs obtain angel investment or early stage investment from well-recognized and trustworthy angel investors and providing necessary professional knowledge and social network for business operation.

Shaanxi Angel Investment Club	Business Angel Network	• It brings a large number of angel investors and projects together in a scientific and reasonable manner in order to help young entrepreneurs in starting new business and investors in selecting projects.
Chuangxiang Angel Investment Club	Business Angel Network	• It was jointly initiated and founded by www.angelcn.net and Mingshan (Shanghai) Investment Management Co., Ltd. in 2010.
		• Consisting of individual angel investors and angel investment organizations, it aims to locate projects at their early stage suitable for investment by its members and provide angel investment and project services. It also organizes regular entrepreneurship and investment salons.
Zhongguancun Entrepreneurs Angel Investment Union	Angel Group	• In 2008, 50 entrepreneurs in Zhongguancun, including Liu Chuanzhi, DuanYongji, Feng Jun, Lei Jun and Wang Wenjing, initiated such a union in Beijing.
China Business Angels Network (CBAN)	Business Angel Network	• CBAN was jointly initiated and founded by China Center for Financial Research, Chinese Center for Entrepreneurial Studies and EMBA Center of Tsinghua University in 2009 with a membership system and admitted 100 members when founded.
Keiretsu Forum (K4) Beijing Branch	Business Angel Network	• K4 is devoted to helping SMEs to achieve long-term development and bridge funds and projects as well as domestic and foreign markets.

(Continued)

Appendix III (*Continued*)

Organizations/Agencies	Types	State of Development (Founding Time and Current Status)
Jiangsu Business Angels Association	Business Angel Network	• It was jointly initiated by 20 influential VC organizations and angel investors inside or outside Jiangsu Province, including Govtor Capital, Jiangsu Provincial High & New Technology Innovation Center and China–Singapore Suzhou Industrial Park Ventures Co., Ltd. in 2013.
		• It aims to build an interactive platform for the development of angel investment, promote efficient capital and technology connection between investment institutions and technological entrepreneurs and create good social environment by promoting the idea of angel investment, cultivate angel investors and arousing passions in scientific and technical personnel for entrepreneurship.
Fudan High & New Technology Industry Base Angel Investment Association	Business Angel Network	• It was jointly initiated by China Angel Investment Summit and Fudan High & New Technology Industry Base.
		• It aims to connect angel investors with entrepreneurs and help implement governmental policies for small and micro businesses.
Shanghai Super Angel Association (SSAA)	Business Angel Network	• Founded in 2013, it is a public and open angel investment organization gathering together dozens of influential entrepreneur service institutions and investment organizations. It is devoted to integrating investment experience and business resources of angel investors and helping entrepreneurs and incubators to thrive.
		• It builds together with the industrial park, café, media and entrepreneurs services active and efficient exchange and cultivation platform for projects at early stage with regular lectures, project roadshows and field trips.

AngelCrunch	Online Platform	• Set up in 2011, it aims to connect entrepreneurs with angel investors quickly using the Internet's advantage of efficiency and transparency. • In October 2013, it united many top investors to publish the "Chinese Angel Investment Crowd funding Rules". • In June 2014, it announced its pullout from 100X Accelerator.
VC.CN	Online Platform	• Set up in June 2011, it is the first company invested by Tianshihui and Innovation Works jointly, which is an investment platform to serve early projects. • Offline events: "120 Seconds Challenge", "Secret Matchmaking Meeting", "Angel Banquet". • In 2014, it launched the Dynamic Fund 2.0, providing free matchmaking service and updating its domain name to vc.cn.
ZhenFund	Early Stage Fund	• In 2006, ZhenFund 1.0 was set up — created by Xu Xiaoping which aims to encourage the youth to do entrepreneurship and innovation. • In 2012, ZhenFund 2.0 was set up — created by Xu Xiaoping and Sequoia Capital China, with a capital scale of US$300 billion; and planned to invest 100 early phase entrepreneurial enterprises within three years, in areas including e-commerce, mobile Internet, games, education training, consumer goods and medical treatment. • The main cases include more than 100 enterprises, such as JUMEI.com, Yongche.com, coolban.com, chuangyepu.com, 51TALK, and so on.

(*Continued*)

Appendix III (*Continued*)

Organizations/Agencies	Types	State of Development (Founding Time and Current Status)
Shunwei Fund	Early Stage Fund	• In 2011, the Fund was set up by famous investor Lei Jun, with a first phase financing amount of US\$225 billion. • The main cases include koudai.com, hahapinche.com, leiphone.com, and so on.
Legend Star	Super Angel	• Set up in 2008, it raised a fund amounting to RMB400 million. With a professional; investment and business advisory team and abundant business and community resources, it provided the high-tech start-ups with high value-added financial support and comprehensive incubator services. • The main cases include idreamsky.com, mCloud.com, Face++, vhall.com, zhiguoguo.com, and so on.
Taishan Invest AG	Early Stage Fund	• Set up in 2008, it is an angel investment fund providing financing for enterprises in the "angel phase" and the "early stage". • The main cases include more than 20 projects, such as ushi.com, lashou.com, xishiwang.com, jiapin.com.
Qingsong Angel Investment	Early Stage Fund	• It was set up in June 2012 by Liu Xiaosong and others jointly. This fund was aimed at the Internet and mobile Internet projects in the early phase (especially in angel investment phase). • The major cases include RSSdiO, Papa Sanguo, Beiwo music, and so on.
Yingnuo Angel Fund	Early Stage Fund	• Set up in 2013, it focuses on the relevant angel investment fund of Internet and mobile Internet, especially on mobile games, online education, O2O, Internet finance, mobile health, and so on. • The major cases include Juwan Games, Dazhongkahui, Paomianba.com, and so on.

LeBox Capital	Early Stage Fund	• Set up in 2012, it is an angel fund focusing on individuals or groups that have growth potential and are a very early stage.
		• It mainly focuses on the TMT industry and the rapidly growing service industry, and investment for each project does not exceed RMB5 million and shareholding stands between 15% and 30%, without any additional investment.
		• The major cases include Powerful technique, 365 Health Guardian, Wukong Games, and so on.
PreAngel	Early Stage Fund	• PreAngel is an early angel investment fund, including PreAngel fund, PA Leili fund, PA Jianrui fund, PA Huiyi fund, and so on.
		• The major cases include Tomoon.cn, JDguanjia.com, Aunt Kitchen, and so on.
China Renaissance K2 Ventures	Early Stage Fund	• This fund was created by Bao Fan, the founder of China Renaissance Partners, and Chen Keyi. It is an early angel fund that focuses on Internet, mobile Internet and technology projects, with a capital of RMB1,000 million.
		• The major cases include Jumei.com, centaur.cn, Xiyou Menstrual Assistant, and so on.
STEP Angle Fund	Government Fund	• The STEP focuses on angel investment, devoting itself to helping the startups to better utilize capital, gain resources, experience and grow.
		• The major cases include Explosion of The Three Kingdoms, Job Resume, and so on.

Source: Compiled by Zhao Changhai (doctoral candidate, Renmin University of China) based on data from the Internet, research reports, and surveys.

Appendix IV: List of Selected Policies for Promoting Angel Investment in China

Provinces/Cities	Type	Notes
Chengdu Hi-Tech Industrial Development Zone Venture Angel Investing Fund (2012)	Direct investment	• The Admistration of Chengdu Hi-Tech Industrial Development Zone provided RMB80 million to the Fund, and it is allowed to invest in equities directly. • The investment amount depends on different stages of the invested companies, which usually do not exceed RMB2 million, and the Fund cannot be the majority shareholder after the investment.
Ningbo Angel Guiding Fund (2012)	Co-investment fund	• The total amount of the Guiding Fund is RMB200 million, and RMB40 million is planned to be invested per year in five years by specific financial funds. • The Fund will only co-invest in innovative start-ups that have already secured angel investing. • The investment usually does not exceed RMB2 million for each project, with the upper limit standing at RMB5 million. For those projects that need more than RMB1 million investment, the total investment amount cannot exceed 60% of Fund.
Taxation support to the development of angel investing in Jiangsu Province (2012)	Tax incentives	• According to relevant policies, for those angel investing funds that invest in non-listed small- and medium-sized high-tech enterprises for more than two years, 70% of the investment made can offset the taxable income of the invested enterprises; if the taxable income does not reach the 70% threshold, it can be carried forward in the subsequent tax year. • The angel investment institutions partnering with and investing in early stage technology-based SMEs will be exempted from income tax.

- The dividends and profits from the investment can be directly assigned to the partners and the partners are subject to the enterprise income tax and personal income tax after they gain the profits.
- In accordance with the relevant provisions of the tax law, the transfer of shares shall be exempted from business tax.

Jiangsu Angel Guiding Fund (2013)	Risk compensation	<ul><li>The guiding fund provides a certain risk sharing and loss compensation for the investment made by angels to hi-tech small and micro enterprises in the seed period or early stage.</li><li>The amount of the risk reserve should s not exceed 30% of the first round actual investment made by provincial-level angels and should not be more than RMB3 million, and for the angel investment institutions in cities, counties (including city-level counties), and national high-tech zones, the matching amount will be 20%.</li><li>If angel investment institutions have not incurred losses within three years after the investment, then they should fully refund the guiding fund and local matching fund; if loss occurs, they can claim 50% of the loss for the first round investment from the given risk reserve as compensation, of which 30% comes from the provincial angel guiding fund, and 20% will be borne by the local matching funds, and the rest of reserve needs to be returned after the compensation.</li></ul>

(*Continued*)

Appendix IV (*Continued*)

Provinces/Cities	Type	Notes
Shanghai Angel Guiding Investment (2015)	Stage investment as LP (Limited Partner) and FoF (Fund of Fund)	• The Angel Guiding Fund can invest in angel investing institutions by stages and set up FoF for angel investing, and generally the upper limit of investment is RMB5 million to 30 million, which should be no more than 50% of the total investing amount by angel investing institutions. • The Angel Guiding Fund does not participate in the daily operation of angel institutions, but has the rights of supervision.
Shanghai Risk Compensation System for Angel Investing (2015)	Risk compensation	• Angel investors can claim financial compensation up to a certain proportion for the loss of their investment in seed stage, innovative science and technology enterprises. • For investment losses to seed science and technology enterprise project, the compensation amount shall be no more than 60% of total loss. • For investment losses to the start-up period of science and technology projects, the amount shall be no more than 30% of total loss. • And the loss compensation amount cannot exceed **RMB300 million** for each project, and the loss compensation amount does not exceed **RMB600 million** per investment institution.

Source: Compiled by authors based on official document from the local governments.

Afterword

Dr. Wang Jiani and I have been working together in investigating and researching on Chinese angel investment for many years. Our hard work finally produced this book. We are utterly pleased.

My research interests in angel investment started in the summer of 2001. One evening that summer, I had coffee with a Harvard Business School student. While chatting, he mentioned, among other things, about a book on angel investment he and his professor were writing. That was the first time I have ever heard of the concept of angel investing. I was curious at the flexibility and creativity of the new type of investment. I have deep respect for those angel investors who take the risk to help young start-ups at the very early stage.

This conversation changed my research agenda. I started to lead a group of my graduate students to do some research on international angel investments. At that time, angel investment was still a pretty novel concept. But the students who did the research with me learned a lot. Now almost of all of them became active venture capitalists and/or angel investors.

From that time on, I have been hoping from the bottom of my heart that I could find some young researchers or students who are interested in doing the similar research in Chinese angel investment. During the past 10 years or so, I have had a few students who were originally interested in doing angel research but eventually switched from researchers to practitioners. I do not blame them. On the one hand, it makes a lot of economic sense being a practitioner than being a researcher — one can make a lot of more money. On the other hand, it is very hard to do research on angel investment in China, as there is no base data and researchers have to start from scratch. Moreover, it is also difficult to collect firsthand information and it will probably remain so for some time to come.

However, my hope is nevertheless becoming reality: my research agenda somehow crosses paths with that of Dr. Wang Jiani's. She is different from others. I am very impressed and pleased by her persistence and determination to seek her own research interests without weighing too much on short-term economic gains. The first output by our collaboration is the publication of this book.

My fate has been very kind to me. For one, I appreciate Mr. Peter Chow and his Chief Group in Hong Kong. They have been consistently and selflessly supporting my research. I would not have been able to focus on my research, and this book would not have been published without the help from Mr. Chow and his Chief Group colleagues.

Manhong Mannie Liu

Index

Printed in the United States
By Bookmasters